NATURE RESERVES

D1384962

NATURE RESERVES

Island Theory and

Conservation Practice

Craig L. Shafer

Smithsonian Institution Press   Washington and London

Edited by Norman Rudnick

Library of Congress Cataloging-in-Publication Data
Shafer, Craig, L.
Nature reserves : island theory and conservation practice
/ by Craig L. Shafer.
p.   cm.
Includes bibliographical references.
ISBN 0–87474–805–4 cloth; 0-87474-384-2 paper
1. Natural areas—Management.
2. National parks and reserves—Management.
3. Island ecology.
4. Nature conservation—Management.
I. Title.
QH75.S474   1990
333.95—dc20   90–9602

British Library Cataloging-in-Publication Data is available

Manufactured in the United States of America

97   96   95   94   93   92   5   4   3   2

Contents

Preface

As of September 1989, the 4,025 national parks and equivalent reserves in the world had a total area of 4,621,717 km² and were located in 139 countries (IUCN, pers. com.). All are 10 km² or larger in the United Nation's site management categories I–V as described in IUCN (1985). Nature reserve management for many of these sites is increasingly challenged by activities outside the site boundaries, and the challenge is likely to escalate as time goes on. The overall context of individual nature reserves, in relation to one another and to their man-modified landscapes and their people, needs more careful concern. By present knowledge and thinking, nature reserves are the best overall tool we have to preserve examples of natural landscape and their biotic communities for future generations.

What follows is a discussion of the theoretical aspects of nature reserve size, isolation, and design, as well as planning and management implications. My goal is to clarify and integrate much of the scientific and other related literature, and thus make it useful to the people who have the responsibility to act. Since I hope to reach beyond the scientists who contribute to this literature, I have tried to present information in a fashion that makes it accessible to readers unfamiliar with the key ideas and conclusions of the cited authors. I have therefore relied on many one-sentence summaries.

My assumption in writing this book is that many biologically trained nature reserve planners, managers, and natural resource specialists, as well as researchers, may be confused by the complexity of the literature on the theory of island biogeography, frustrated by its volume, and perhaps misinformed owing to the scientific controversy surrounding its interpretation for conservation application. It is no longer wise for planners and managers simply to rely on any one scientist's translation of this literature into conservation guidance, however well intended, since controversial aspects, differing viewpoints, and the inadequacy of empirical support are not often brought to their attention. I have tried to include conflicting interpretations on as many points as possible, but satisfactory resolution of many of the arguments is beyond the scope of this work. Indeed, some of the questions are unanswerable until more data are generated.

I have also referred to more than just the technical modeling literature of academia but brought in aspects of the real world of nature reserve management, mostly ignored up to now in such papers. This demands mention of much secondary or planning types of literature. Chapters 15 and 16, on paleobiogeography and the future of the evolutionary process, may seem remote from our present conservation crises but are included to compare our current dilemma with past earth events and processes.

Although the focus of this review is on natural science, I hope it also illustrates how the social sciences (e.g., sociology and economics) and even the law must be brought to bear on the conservation problem. I also hope it draws more attention to matters beyond continuing academic debates on well-trodden issues like empirical support for the equilibrium theory of island biogeography. I hope it encourages more synthesis and translation of the scientific literature for a technically trained managerial audience, but not so simplistically as to evade complex issues and debate. I hope it encourages more and better guidance, which often comes with the luxury of hindsight in assessing earlier innovative theories or solutions, than may be provided here. Simple answers are not easy to give for multidimensional problems, but a survey of the facts already at our disposal can shed light and reduce confusion.

Writing this book has been a humbling experience. Denning (1987) states that the "production of scientific information is exceeding anyone's ability to assimilate and use it." I have begun to share his view, but this review is nevertheless an attempt at such assimilation. It began many years ago, and grew with what seems to be an exponentially expanding literature.

While well-intended conservation guidance that is insufficiently supported by good data may help some conservation efforts in the long run, it also has some potential for actual harm. This, of course, begs the question of what is sufficient data. Yet, unless biologists provide their best advice even if imperfect, decisions may be based on no scientific contribution at all. I hope this work advances the guidance and conclusions that have survived the critical tests of evidence and controversy. I do not believe we are yet ready to write, with confidence, a well-supported "how to" handbook about nature reserve size, numbers, and other design issues, however badly we need such a guide. We perhaps know in a very fuzzy way what is required to maintain biological diversity.

The conservation guidance I have advanced, and the well-supported guidance proposed by others I have highlighted, will undoubtedly be impugned by many who have contributed to this disputatious literature. However, I believe an attempt to identify clearly what we do know is a necessary first step. It may be depressing to recognize how little of some rather elaborate theory is unequivocally supported, but perhaps being mildly depressed is preferable to being misinformed. Too often in this literature, general theory is confused with empirically documented facts by scientists, nature reserve planners, and managers alike. Conservation guidelines based on insufficient empirical data are made necessary today by the enormous management problems we face, but such guidelines should be clearly identified as stopgap measures, and work should begin in earnest to provide the solid information and analysis still lacking. Since we cannot afford the time needed to acquire such information in full measure, synthesizing what we already know is imperative.

I hope this review is used by all those hardy individuals carrying the heavy responsibility of on-ground management and planning of national parks and nature reserves—those beset heroes and heroines who have to devote more time to "stemming the tide" than to studying the tide tables. We are becoming aware that the conservation task is not over when a national park or nature reserve is established. Since early reserves were often established when their relationship to their surroundings was not fully appreciated, in many cases we are just now beginning to confront the conservation task in earnest.

I

Introduction

A   The Problem: Fragmentation with Insularization

Instead of an essentially continuous forest cover . . . the landscape now presents the aspect of a savanna, with isolated trees, small clumps or clusters of trees, or small groves scattered in a matrix of artificial grassland of grains and pasture grasses.

(CURTIS 1956)

The late plant ecologist John Curtis in the mid-1950s recognized that landscape alteration in this country was leaving isolated remnants of natural communities. The condition of natural landscape both here and abroad has steadily gone downhill.

We suddenly are faced with the stunning realization that continuing fragmentation of the landscape has left the world at the doorstep of the 1990s with mere patches of natural habitat. The fragmentation process has been documented over a long period in fine resolution in only a few locations. Examples include Green County, Wisconsin, between 1831 and 1950 (Fig. 1) and the secondary heathland in the Poole Basin mostly in the county of Dorset, England, between 1759 and 1978 (Fig. 2). Marsh (1874) bemoaned the loss of forest in many parts of the world and might be appalled at present conditions more than 100 years later.

Population pressures and their associated land uses already have crowded out large chunks of natural habitat in this country; Figure 3 represents land-

scape fragmentation on a much grosser scale than Figures 1 and 2. Insularization of some national parks and reserves in this country and in other parts of the world could be turned into semi-isolated "habitat islands" in a sea of man-dominated or man-altered landscape. The cartoon illustration in Figure 4 resembling an actual aerial photograph (e.g., see Fig. 45 in Chapter XII) of a small nature reserve suggests that the cartoon is becoming a reality. The LANDSAT imagery of large U.S. national parks in Figures 5 and 6 also illustrates dramatic land-use changes outside park boundaries. The impact of insularization on the fauna confined to these reserves or habitat islands may be predicted theoretically. Theory says that a) potential sources of immigrants will be eliminated, b) immigration will be reduced by conversion of the natural landscape between habitat patches or reserves, and c) vital resources outside reserve boundaries will be lost (Wilcox 1980; Wilcox and Murphy 1985). Data show, for instance, that bird species seem to be disappearing from small woodlots (see Section VIB). One purpose of this review is to examine the data and to pose questions as to why this is happening and what should concern us.

The issue here is pertinent to the future of some animals residing in the multitude of small nature reserve systems—in both the United States and oth-

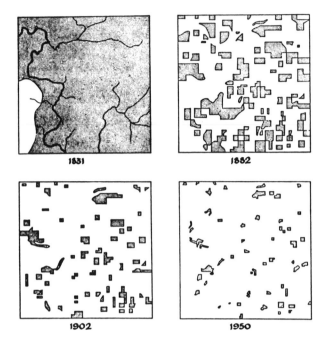

Figure 1. The fragmentation of forest in Cadiz Township (94.93 km²) Green County, Wisconsin, into habitat "islands" during the period of European settlement. The almost continuous expanse of forest in 1831 was fragmented into 55 small forest islands by 1950. There were 111 forest islands by 1978 averaging 0.09 km² in size (Sharpe et al. 1987). (From Curtis 1956; reprinted by permission of The University of Chicago Press.© 1956.)

(World Bank 1984). Not only very wise but heroic strategies will be needed to save tropical forests, and likely other biomes as well. Gómez-Pompa et al. (1972) implied that insularization due to logging might lead to rapid loss of the many rare species typical of tropical forests, and therefore its hazards should not be forgotten during our present preoccupation with the threat and rate of tropical deforestation (Fig. 8). The overall biological diversity crisis we are facing will not be outlined here and has been eloquently stated by others (e.g., Wilson 1985a). The island dilemma is just one aspect of the overall problem.

Therefore, an awareness that some terrestrial national parks and other reserves are becoming "insular," as landscape alterations outside their boundaries continue, is essential if land-management agencies or organizations are to acknowledge and deal with the implications. We will examine whether any present or future guidance is derivable from the sciences of ecology, biogeography, evolutionary biology, genetics, and even paleontology.

This review does not encompass all aspects of nature reserve design but primarily those relating to habitat fragmentation and insularization. It focuses more on animals than on plants because animals are more mobile and more likely to be affected by landscape alteration, and because there is simply much more literature about animals. It also deals more with large reserves for large mammals than small reserves for small mammals, birds, reptiles, amphibians, or insects. Biological diversity conservation certainly has much to do with small creatures, but larger ones are more amenable to the illustration of ideas.

The ideas that follow are interrelated and the order of presentation was chosen to make interrelationships clear to the reader. Because some readers may not want to peruse every part from start to finish, summary sections are provided. Cross-references are made throughout the text. Allusions to the United States situation, for example, in U.S. national parks, will be made to illustrate points.

er countries—as well as in the generally larger national parks and wilderness areas. Figure 7 depicts logging activity outside park boundaries that may, if it worsens, threaten the unhampered movement of large mammals into and out of the park.

The current destruction rate of tropical forests is alarming and now widely appreciated. At this rate, Wilson (1988) pointed out, all tropical forests will be clear-cut or seriously disturbed by A.D. 2135; he also noted that the World Bank predicts the human population will plateau at 11 billion people by A.D. 2150

B   The Concern: Theory vs. Data

Within the remnant forest stands, a number of changes of possible importance may take place. The small size and increased isolation of the stands tend to prevent the easy exchange of members from one stand to another. Various accidental happenings in any given stand over a period of years may eliminate one or more species from the community.

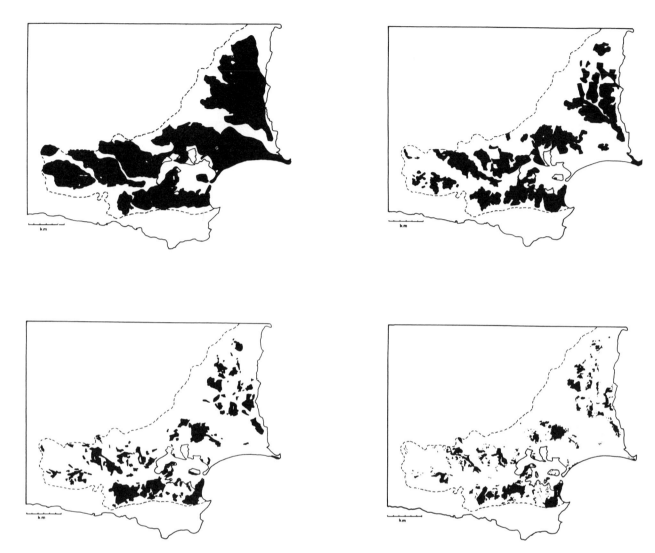

Figure 2. During the period 1759–1978, the area of heathland in the Poole Basin, mostly in the county of Dorset, England, was reduced from about 40,000 ha to about 6,000 ha, or an 86 percent loss. In 1759, the heathland consisted of ten large blocks separated only by rivers (top left). By 1934, fragmentation and insularization was well underway (top right). Moore (1962) showed that in 1960 the heathland had fragmented into more than 100 pieces with an area of 4 ha or more (bottom left). Webb and Haskins (1980) showed that by 1978 the heathland had fragmented into 160 pieces with an area of 4 ha or more (bottom right). The remaining fragments in 1978 consist of 608 pieces less than 4 ha, and 476 of these are less than 1 ha. There are 14 sites larger than 100 ha, and three of these are nature reserves. Chapman et al. (1989) reviewed these 1978 data and the comparability of the definition of heathland in 1759 and 1978, and concluded Webb and Haskins (1980) exaggerated the loss of heathland, but not markedly: 80 percent loss instead of 86 percent, and 18 areas of heathland exceeding 100 ha instead of 14. (From Webb and Haskins 1980; reprinted by permission of Elsevier Applied Science Publishers Ltd., England.)

Figure 3. Night satellite image mosaic of the United States on October 18 and 21 and December 16, 1985. Our large natural area parks and reserves are presumably located somewhere between the areas of heavy urbanization, indicated here by lights. More of the lights should coalesce in the future as urbanization expands and eliminates more natural landscape. (This image was produced from U.S. Air Force Defense Meteorological Satellite Program film transparencies archived for the National Oceanic and Atmospheric Administration/National Environmental Satellite, Data, and Information Service at the University of Colorado Cooperative Institute for Research in Environmental Sciences/National Snow and Ice Data Center, after Jenkins 1978.)

Such a local catastrophe under natural conditions would be quickly healed by migration of new individuals from adjacent unaffected areas. . . .

In the isolated stands, however, opportunities for inward migration are small or nonexistent. As a result, the stands gradually lose some of their species, and those remaining achieve unusual positions of relative abundance.

(CURTIS 1956)

This statement by John Curtis indicates his early recognition that size and isolation of habitat patches could influence the viability of their biota. Both of

Curtis's statements were highlighted in Burgess and Sharpe (1981a), presumably to illustrate the antiquity of this awareness with regard to the U.S. Eastern Deciduous Forest.

It should be obvious that the perceived potential effects of forest fragmentation described by Curtis are closely related to those of progressive nature reserve isolation. Curtis's prediction is still widely accepted, and understandably so. A loss of species due to area reduction is now a widely accepted prediction for both habitat islands and nature reserves, for example, by Wilson (1988 and in Lewin 1986).

Figure 4. National parks and reserves are becoming isolated from surrounding natural habitat by encroaching civilization. When compared with the pattern of small nature reserves in the United States, in some instances this cartoon is not that far from reality. (Miller and Harris 1979.)

We will look at such predictions in some detail as well as at other possibly important factors.

A popular perception holds that habitat loss or fragmentation is the leading cause of species extinctions today (e.g., Norton 1986). Wilcox (1980) more precisely divided fragmentation into two components, habitat loss and insularization, both able to contribute to a reduction in the number of species. Habitat loss can 1) exclude some species, particularly if rare or with patchy distributions, and 2) increase the likelihood of extinction of remaining species because of reduced population sizes. Insularization can 3) decrease or eliminate colonization of reserves from outside areas, and 4) remove resources outside reserve boundaries that species in the reserve depend on for survival. Some of these processes are depicted in Figure 9. All four effects of habitat fragmentation could influence the biota of a habitat island or nature reserve.

The effects are difficult to separate in practice. That the habitat loss component (1 and 2) of habitat fragmentation has a negative effect on species, or could eliminate species, is not questioned (see Wilcox and Murphy 1985). We will look closely at the empirical, not the theoretical, basis for the insularization component (3 and 4) of habitat fragmentation for habitat islands and nature reserves. In fact, this review focuses more on insularization of habitat and nature reserves than on the process and effects of fragmentation per se (e.g., see Wilcove et al. 1986). We will scrutinize issues of this kind with an eye to differentiating between good theory and its empirical support. Soulé (1987b) stated:

Administrators, policy makers, and managers have a right to ask for the bottom line. . . . And biologists have the right and sometimes the obligation not to give an oversimplified, misleading answer to such a question. . . . Nevertheless, I think that scientists owe it to the rest of society to provide rules of thumb, even when they know that sometimes the rules will be misunderstood and misused.

I agree with Soulé, but we should still strive to prevent misunderstanding and misuse. Nature reserve planners and managers need to know more about the foundation and adequacy of the guidance they are provided.

Figure 5. LANDSAT image of March 9, 1979, illustrates land-use patterns on the Florida Peninsula that cause insularization of Everglades National Park and Big Cypress National Preserve on the north and east sides. The developed land along the eastern edge of the peninsula consists of Miami to the south and West Palm Beach to the north. In a sense, Big Cypress National Preserve (dotted line) serves as a partial buffer zone for Everglades National Park (solid line). (Image printed by U.S. Geological Survey Earth Resources Observation Satellite Data Center.)

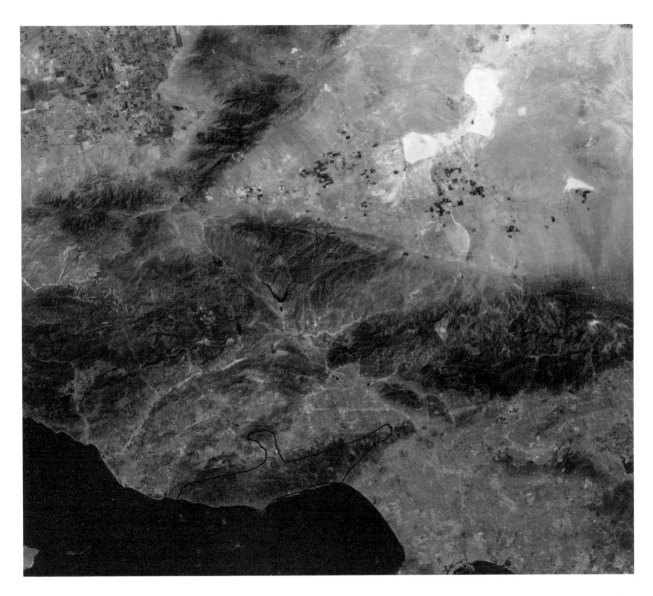

Figure 6. LANDSAT image of June 8, 1979, illustrates land-use patterns that surround the Santa Monica Mountains National Recreation Area, Los Angeles and Ventura Counties, California. Metropolitan Los Angeles can be seen in the lower right corner. The angular (V) Point Dume juts out into the Pacific Ocean to the left of Los Angeles. The Recreation Area was not established until 1978. This mountain tract therefore was close to urban expansion at the lower elevations to the east before it was given status as a National Recreation Area. Note the potential difficulty a large mammal might have in moving from the northern edge of the Recreation Area down and through the valley to the next mountain range to the north and northeast. A potential connecting corridor to the north may still exist near the "thumb," but many other options have likely been completely eliminated by development. (Image printed by the U.S. Geological Survey Earth Resources Observation Satellite Data Center.)

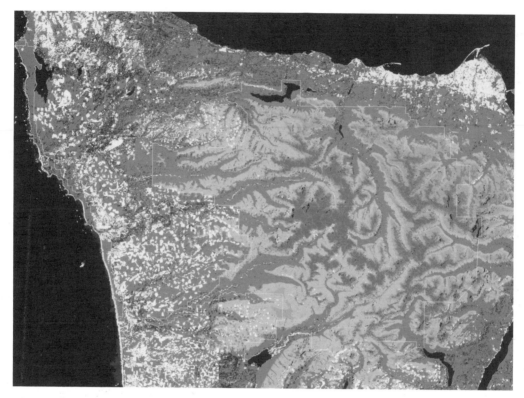

Figure 7. LANDSAT image illustrates land-use patterns on the Olympic Peninsula, Washington, on June 2, 1978. The white patches outside the park boundary represent mostly clearcutting, some agricultural fields, and a few scattered towns. Note the white, blocky clearcuts scattered all around Olympic National Park, most abundant on the west and south sides. Some clearcuts occur right on the boundary. (Satellite data was classified to show clearcuts by National Aeronautics and Space Administration Earth Resources Laboratory and National Park Service Denver Service Center, Division of Geographic Information Systems.)

C   *The Need: Guidance for Nature Reserve System Design*

The problem facing us is simply that much of the world's terrestrial biota will soon be confined to nature reserves and national parks. Most countries will or should have some form of nature reserve system. Also, many of these reserves are likely to be separated from each other by a landscape more disturbed than the reserves themselves.

Many nature reserves are established as opportunities permit, without much thought for the guidance that science and other fields can provide. This is understandable. Such opportunities are rare and should be grasped as they occur. But the old opportunistic hit-or-miss approach is no longer adequate. Suddenly too much is at stake: no less crucial a human concern than the long-term welfare of much of

the world's terrestrial biota. We must, therefore, approach the "island dilemma" in as systematic a way as we can. We need first to distinguish what is factual and what is useful that can guide us. May (1984) stated, "Plans for the establishment and management of conservation areas and refuges in many different parts of the world rest on guesstimates and principles that are not yet—and may never be—established on an unarguable factual foundation."

This review attempts to identify whatever factual basis does exist. But we also need to understand what we do not know much about. We need to identify the problems. We need to organize our thinking and identify what we are facing now and can expect

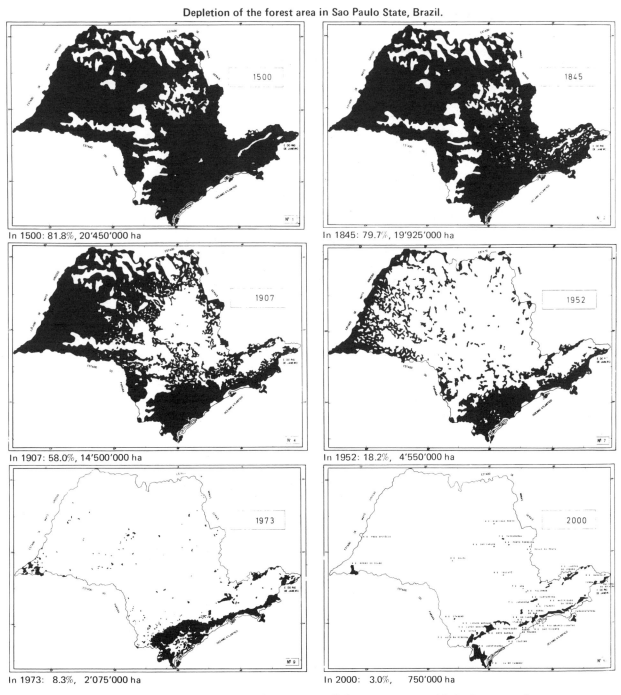

Depletion of the forest area in Sao Paulo State, Brazil.

In 1500: 81.8%, 20'450'000 ha

In 1845: 79.7%, 19'925'000 ha

In 1907: 58.0%, 14'500'000 ha

In 1952: 18.2%, 4'550'000 ha

In 1973: 8.3%, 2'075'000 ha

In 2000: 3.0%, 750'000 ha

Figure 8. Reduction of tropical forest in São Paulo State, Brazil, from year 1500 with 81.8 percent forest coverage to year 1973 with 8.3 percent forest coverage. By the year 2000, only 3 percent forest coverage is projected. São Paulo State is about the size of the Federal Republic of Germany or the state of Oregon. (From Oedekoven 1980; reprinted by permission of Elsevier Science Publishers Ltd.)

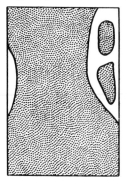
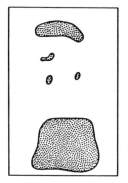

Original equilibrium situation   Situation at time when protec-   Final equilibrium situation
                                  tive measures go into force

Figure 9. Fragmentation includes both habitat loss and insularization, which typically proceed together. This process of insularization, as Wilcox (1980) suggested, could theoretically have a distinct effect on a nature reserve's biota. Although the figure refers to an equilibrium, there is much controversy as to whether an equilibrium number of species exists for real or habitat islands. (From Diamond 1975b; reprinted by permission of Elsevier Applied Science Publishers Ltd., England.)

in the future. Wilcox (1980) indicated that of all the biological approaches to conservation, the continuing study of natural area isolates is our present most pressing need, and that this field of study must be considerably developed before long-range conservation strategies can be well defined. I certainly agree.

Particularly, we need to understand that time is running out on available options. Raven (1980) predicted that most opportunities to set aside reserves in the tropics, where most of this planet's species reside, would be precluded by 1990. This projection may have been too pessimistic, but Soulé (Frankel and Soulé 1981) was probably right that the end of this century will see the termination of most of our options for reserve size, design, and organization.

Harrison et al. (1982) and Miller (1988) allow us to calculate that the number of protected areas in the world has increased from 500 in 1960 to over 3,500, from a total of 120 million ha to 425 million ha. This accomplishment justifies great pride, but we cannot afford to be complacent. Tropical forests cover only 7 percent of the earth's surface but harbor more than half the world's species (Wilson 1988). Additionally, setting aside a national park does not mean the attainment of preservation and the end of our worries. We need to set aside many more reserves in as enlightened a fashion as possible and to carefully scrutinize the capability of those already established to provide protection in perpetuity.

II

The Theory of Island Biogeography

A Some Basic Concepts

The topic of nature reserve size and the related question of progressive reserve insularity have received much attention in scientific literature. Since the theory of island biogeography has dominated considerations of conservation application, a brief description of its most relevant concepts is appropriate.

The theory of island biogeography should be distinguished from other attempts to understand biotic abundance and dispersal on islands, which date back to the nineteenth century. Darwin (1859) and Wallace (1869, 1880) were among early naturalists who wrote books about islands, as described in Browne (1983), and Carlquist (1974), Lack (1976), Williamson (1981), and others continued the work.

1 HISTORICAL PERSPECTIVE

Darlington (1957) found that the number of reptile species in the West Indies doubles when habitat area increases by a factor of ten. This finding stimulated further work by others. MacArthur and Wilson (1963) described their "equilibrium theory of insular zoogeography," which they said was independently suggested by Preston (1962).

Preston thought of equilibrium in several ways:

1) generally as a result of immigration onto oceanic islands or between continents; 2) more specifically as a hypothetical canonical log-normal species abundance distribution (Section IIC6) and its relationship to "samples" and "isolates" (Section IIB1); and 3) as a balance between extinction and evolution (Section XVA). MacArthur and Wilson (1963, 1967) defined it as that state in which the mortality rate of individuals in a population equals their birth rates, or the rate of species extinctions of a biota equals the rate of immigration of new species. Preston (1960, 1962) also provided much about the species-area relationship that MacArthur and Wilson adopted.

It was MacArthur and Wilson (1963), however, who explicitly proposed an equilibrium model characterized by a balance between extinction and immigration. They subsequently produced their landmark monograph, "The Theory of Island Biogeography" (MacArthur and Wilson 1967). In the 1963 and 1967 works they set forth many new ideas in what was one of the first attempts to quantify the field of biogeography. Simberloff (1972) saw the field up to that time as largely descriptive, and the quantitative equilibrium model for islands approximately coincided in time with other quantitative approaches such as delimiting biotic provinces. He also noted that the theory of island biogeography motivated a focusing

11

of studies on the extinction process in terms of local short-term ecological events rather than global evolutionary events in geological time. The MacArthur and Wilson work also caused scientists to attempt to apply the theory of island biogeography and, in so doing, to study a factor, largely neglected before, that theoretically may contribute to species extinctions—habitat/reserve size and isolation.

2   PREDICTIONS OF THE THEORY OF ISLAND BIOGEOGRAPHY

Three long-perceived patterns found on islands were instrumental in causing MacArthur and Wilson to develop their theory of island biogeography: species-areas relationships (larger islands usually have more species), isolation effects (remote islands usually have fewer species), and species turnover (when islands are colonized, the new colonists seem to replace species that become extinct). In other words, species number will usually be larger on larger islands (the area effect) and smaller on islands more distant from continental land masses (the distance effect). Naturalists were aware of these size and distance effects for at least fifty years before MacArthur and Wilson's papers (Simberloff 1974a). In fact, Wallace (1869) recognized that island size and isolation influenced the number of bird species (Simberloff 1983b), and Johann Forster, a naturalist with Captain Cooke's second voyage around the world, discussed the species-area affect on islands in 1778 (Browne 1983). The turnover effect also was known before the 1963 and 1967 papers but was not studied intensively until later.

The central idea of the MacArthur and Wilson theory was that an "equilibrium" number (a stationary probability distribution) of species (plants or animals) on an island is achieved over time because two principal opposing processes come into approximate balance. Equilibrium between increases in species number owing to immigration from the nearest continental land mass and decreases in species number caused by local extinctions on the island result in "turnover" (Fig. 10), the extinction of species and their replacement by other species. Schoener (1983) maintained that lower organisms have a greater turnover rate than higher organisms. The theory of island biogeography therefore predicts that immigration rates will vary with distance from the mainland, and extinction rates will vary primarily with area and secondarily with distance, as illustrated in

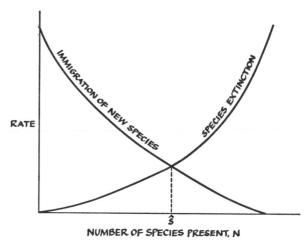

Figure 10. Equilibrium model of a biota on a single island. The equilibrium species number is reached at the intersection of the curve depicting rate of immigration of new species and the curve depicting extinction of species on the island. Use of the term immigration means colonization, specifically, the arrival of new species not already on the island that survive and persist there. The equilibrium is dynamic, resulting from constant turnover of species. MacArthur and Wilson (1967) admitted they knew little about the precise shape of extinction and immigration lines but portrayed them as monotonic downarching curves. Providing that the curves were monotonic, the authors maintained, their precise shape was not essential to the basic theory. However, MacArthur (1972) later justified their originally proposed shape theoretically. (From MacArthur and Wilson, *The Theory of Island Biogeography.* ©1967 Princeton University Press. Figure 7 reprinted with permission of Princeton University Press.)

the more elaborate model (Fig. 11). MacArthur and Wilson (1963, 1967) also predicted that 1) reduction of the pool of immigrants will reduce the number of species on islands, and 2) all other conditions being equal, a species is more likely to die out on an island with a higher extinction rate. Other predictions of MacArthur and Wilson (1963), more clearly expressed by Rey (1981), include: 3) The number of species at equilibrium increases with area faster on islands more distant from the mainland. 4) The number of species at equilibrium increases with distance faster on smaller islands. 5) The turnover rate should be greater on less remote islands. 6) The effect of area on immigration should increase regardless of distance from the mainland. Williamson (1981) sorted predictions of the theory of island biogeography into three primary sets: on equilibrium, on turnover, and on species-area curves

(Section IIC). Studies listed in Table 1 address various combinations of these predictions.

MacArthur and Wilson (1967) made many other predictions. The idea that immigration and extinction rates could be in balance can also be developed as a formal model of the standard birth and death process type in probability theory, related to stochastic population lifetimes (Sections IVA–C). Stepping-stone colonization predicts that an outer island with a stepping-stone island between it and the source area or mainland will have a higher rate of immigration, and that clustering of islands raises each island's immigration rate. It was implied that the difference between biotas of the mainland and those of land-bridge or oceanic islands, reflected by differing species-area curves and their z-values

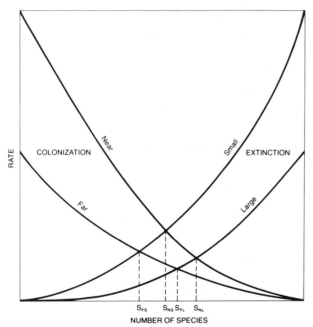

Figure 11. The MacArthur and Wilson equilibrium model in more complex form suggests additionally that colonization rates on islands will decrease with distance from the mainland and that extinction rates on islands will be greater on small islands. Changes in either of these rates will alter the point of intersection of the curves, and hence the equilibrium point. The decrease in number of species on islands with distance is weak for birds and angiosperms, and almost absent for pteridophytes (Williamson 1981). The increase in extinction rate on small islands is consistent with the stochastic theory that small populations will go extinct faster by chance; supportive evidence (e.g., Diamond 1984b) was widely cited. (From Wilcox 1980; reprinted by permission of Sinauer Associates, Inc.)

(Sections IIB1,C5), is a function of their history of separation and the difficulties of dispersing over the water barrier. The compression hypothesis states that competing species should decrease the number of habitats they occupy instead of the kinds of foods they eat within a habitat. The radiation zone is a zone near the outer limits of the distribution of a taxon where immigration from other archipelagos is so uncommon that speciation and radiation occur readily within the archipelago. The taxon cycle predicts the cyclical evolution of species on island archipelagos: species arise, widely disperse because of their inability to live in marginal habitats, move to more central, species-rich habitats when they lose their ability to disperse, and then move back again (Wilson 1961; Ricklefs and Cox 1972). Staging area is a habitat or locality from which, due to structure or location, propagules have a high probability of crossing barriers or moving outward for long periods.

All of these concepts of the theory of island biogeography relate to the topics that follow about nature reserves. Pielou (1979), Williamson (1981), and Brown and Gibson (1983) thoroughly discuss the complexities of the theory. For additional definitions of terms used by MacArthur and Wilson (1963, 1967) or by others in this review, consult the glossary.

The central ideas of the theory were in part an attempt to explain why faunas on remote oceanic islands were depauperate due to problems of dispersal. MacArthur and Wilson indicated that the same effect could be predicted from a nonequilibrial hypothesis that the distant islands have not yet filled up because of a lower immigration rate and not from a balance between extinction and immigration. Subsequent workers (e.g., Heaney and Patterson 1986) have distinguished between equilibrial and nonequilibrial approaches to studying islands.

Explanations that have nothing to do with dispersal have been proposed to explain depauperate biotas on distant islands. Lack (1969, 1970, 1976) suggested that the general ecological poverty on distant islands fosters fewer species of land birds with broader niches. The birds form a stable community that excludes the arrival of new species with similar ecological requirements, and is not based primarily on dispersal abilities. Hence, once a population is established, it becomes entrenched. Abbott (1980) described still other theories on island bird distributions.

TABLE 1

A representative list of studies that focus on (1) equilibrium, (2) the species-area equation $S = cA^z$, (3) turnover, or (4) combinations of the above. For a thorough review of those addressing $S = cA^z$, see Connor and McCoy (1979). Most of the literature on the species-area relationship and turnover for birds on real islands is not listed because of its size, but see Gilbert (1980) and Abbott (1980). Much of the literature dealing primarily with plant population dynamics has been excluded.

Description of Research	Citation
small mammals and birds isolated on mountains in the Great Basin	J. H. Brown (1971, 1978); Johnson (1975); Behle (1978)
birds in alpine grasslands on mountains in the northern Andes	Vuilleumier (1970)
arthropods in caves	Culver (1970, 1971); Culver et al. (1973); Vuilleumier (1973)
marine invertebrates on benthic artificial discs or panels	Schoener (1974a,b); Schoener et al. (1978); Schoener and Schoener (1981); Goren (1979)
marine invertebrates on rocks	Osman (1978)
polycheate worms in the intertidal zone	Dauer and Simon (1975)
sessile marine invertebrates on coral heads	Abele and Patton (1976)
fresh-water mussels in rivers	Sepkoski and Rex (1974)
fresh-water snails in lakes and ponds	Lassen (1975); Aho (1978)
fresh-water protozoans on plastic floats	Cairns et al. (1969); Cairns and Ruthven (1970); Henebry and Cairns (1980)
diatoms settling on glass slides	Patrick (1967)
dispersal of small aquatic organisms into bottles of sterilized water on land	Maguire (1963)
small aquatic organisms in artificial freshwater ponds	Hubbard (1973)
fish in lakes	Barbour and Brown (1974); Magnuson (1976)
insects on host plants	reviewed by Strong (1979)
fish in reefs	Smith (1979); Talbot et al. (1978); Molles (1978)
flies on dead snails	Beaver (1977)
flies in laboratory vials	Wallace (1974)
flies on real islands	Jaenike (1978)
flies and beetles in city parks	Faeth and Kane (1978)
mice on islands in the Gulf of Maine	Crowell (1973)

(continued)

Table 1 (*Continued*)

Description of Research	Citation
rodents on the Virginia barrier islands	Dueser and Brown (1980)
molluscs, fish, and zooplankton in central New York lakes	Browne (1981)
arthropods on mangrove islands in southern Florida	Simberloff and Wilson (1969, 1970); Simberloff (1969); Wilson and Simberloff (1969)
arthropods on *Spartina* islands in northwest Florida	Rey (1981); Strong and Rey (1982)
ants on islands	Wilson and Taylor (1967); Goldstein (1975)
arthropods on the Seychelles Islands	Muhlenberg et al. (1977a,b)
spiders on Bahamian islands	Toft and Schoener (1983)
plants, lizards, and invertebrates on a Puerto Rican cay	Heatwole and Levins (1973)
general biogeography of islands off Puerto Rico	summarized in Heatwole et al. (1981)
mammals on islands	Grant (1970); Ahlen (1983); Lomolino (1982)
grasshoppers and their relatives in the Channel Islands	Weissmann and Rentz (1976)
land snails on the Aegean Islands	Heller (1976)
land snails in the Pacific	Solem (1973)
reptiles on islands of Eastern Papua–New Guinea and in the West Indies	Heatwole (1975); Williams (1969)
certain insects and land molluscs in the Solomon Islands	Greenslade (1968, 1969); Peake (1969)
mites on mice	Dritschilo et al. (1975)
man in the Solomon Islands	Terrell (1977)

Species-area curves (Section IIC), the probability of extinction as a function of population size (Chapter IV), turnover, the island-distance effect, and the island-area effect, as well as a certain notion of equilibrium, were known before. What MacArthur and Wilson did was to integrate these and other ideas into an impressive holistic theory.

3 CRITIQUES OF EQUILIBRIUM/TURNOVER CONCEPT

Attempts were made to verify or disprove the MacArthur and Wilson theory of island biogeography or to pursue studies directly related to it (Table 1). Simberloff (1974a) was the first to review the literature on the theory. F. S. Gilbert (1980) published a highly critical review. Schoener (1976), Diamond (1972–86), and Brown (1986) wrote more favorable reviews.

How well all this work documented the equilibrium aspect of the theory has been a matter of considerable controversy. Williamson (1981) found no correspondence between model and data, in the sense of a causal relationship between immigration and extinction. He thought the data supported the concept of turnover of species at equilibrium but considered this a "numerical reflection of a variety of ecological processes." F. S. Gilbert (1980) judged that the literature he reviewed validated no aspect of the equilibrium theory but thought that Simberloff and Wilson (1969, 1970) had unequivocally demonstrated an "equilibrium turnover" for arthropods on Florida mangrove islands. Simberloff (1969) and Wilson and Simberloff (1969) also described the Florida mangrove work. However, Gilbert did not point out that Simberloff (1976b) later largely discounted his own earlier findings. Simberloff concluded that the data demonstrated mostly a "pseudoturnover" caused by movement of transient arthropods from island to island, and not a true equilibrium turnover due to an immigration-extinction equilibrium. In contrast, Rey (1981, 1984) found the results of a similar study of arthropods on *Spartina* islands generally consistent with predictions and assumptions of the theory: larger areas and populations had lower extinction rates; but greater isolation did not lead to a lower immigration rate and smaller species number, as predicted.

MacArthur and Wilson (1967) pointed out that a species-area curve is not proof of an equilibrium. Connor and McCoy (1979) stated that the power function species-area model $S = cA^z$ (Section IIC) has been incorrectly interpreted as evidence of an equilibrium, and vice versa. F. S. Gilbert (1980) agreed that the widely held assumption—that demonstration of a species-area relationship proved an equilibrium—was incorrect: it unjustifiably assigned specific causes to general correlative data. Simberloff (1972, 1976b) and Connor and McCoy (1979) observed that even though the power-function model may be consistent with the concept of an equilibrium, alternative explanations are not thereby excluded.

The equilibrium aspect of the theory probably remains just a "hypothesis" as Simberloff (1976b) observed, but he did suggest that a short-term constancy of species numbers and some turnover often appeared, but may be due to transient movement. F. S. Gilbert (1980) felt that none of the continental and few of the insular situations conclusively demonstrated the predictions of the equilibrium model. Simberloff (1983a) proposed a statistical way to evaluate objective criteria for an equilibrium, by means of a "runs" test. Simberloff (1983b) questioned whether any observation could ever falsify the equilibrium prediction of the theory of island biogeography, even with statistics. Some still think that islands are at equilibrium for mammals (Lomolino 1986; Hanski 1986; Crowell 1986; Lawlor 1986).

The large literature dealing with birds will not be discussed at length here. Much of it addresses the species-area relationship and turnover on real islands (e.g., Lynch and Johnson 1974; F. S. Gilbert 1980; Abbott, 1980). The literature is muddled because much of the reported observations of "immigrations" and "extinctions" could be accounted for by the transient movement of birds, as MacArthur and Wilson (1967) warned. Carrying the argument to an extreme, Smith (1975) pointed out that robins in an apple tree could be regarded as becoming extinct many times in a day when they fly elsewhere. Questions of census intervals, human influences, the breeding status of species (breeding transients?), and "successional turnover" further contribute to making the literature subject to debate, some of which Lynch and Johnson (1974) described.

For examples of studies reportedly demonstrating turnover on real islands, see Jones and Diamond (1976) for the California Channel Islands, Diamond and May (1977) for the Farnes Islands of Great Britain, Diamond (1980b) for other British islands, and Vaisanen and Jarvinen (1977) for the Krunnit Islands of Finland. For examples of apparent turnover on mainland tracts, see Whitcomb et al. (1976) and Kendeigh (1982) for Illinois woodlands, Lynch and Whitcomb (1978) for eastern North American woodlands, and Jarvinen (1979) for northern European woodlands. Most of these studies suggested that about 1–30 percent of the bird population turned over every year. The Kendeigh (1982) report on a 50-year study of species composition in William Trelease Woods and in other tracts in east-central Illinois for shorter periods revealed that turnover was higher in more isolated stands. Similarly, Whitcomb et al. (1977) reported high bird species turnover in eastern deciduous forest fragments, but McCoy (1982) found no such extinctions in the data and attributed the observations to transient movement and other causes. Abbott (1983) discussed our lack of understanding of what ultimately causes turnover. Any lack of turnover observed in such studies does not invalidate the equilibrium theory if it is the result of low or zero extinction rates. We point out that viewpoints differ on turnover but will not try to resolve the issue.

Simberloff (1980b) indicated that MacArthur and Wilson's dynamic equilibrium theory could explain, at least in part, the number of bird species on islands, though turnover rates are much lower than initially perceived. However, Simberloff (1983a,b) found reports equivocal as to the existence of an equilibrium (for birds or other organisms), and even less supportive of the notion that it is dynamic with substantial turnover. Simberloff (1983d) used a simple colonization model to demonstrate, by computer simulation for one- and two-island systems, that the trajectories of avifaunal species richness through time do not show the predicted regulatory tendencies if species interactions caused species number to change in the direction of an equilibrium. Some papers in Heaney and Patterson (1986) suggested that some large island systems may approach but never attain equilibrium because geological conditions change or become manifest at the same rate.

4   CRITIQUES OF THE OVERALL THEORY OF ISLAND BIOGEOGRAPHY

MacArthur and Wilson (1967) admitted that their proposed theory was crude without enough documentation and hoped it could account for 85 percent of the variation in some phenomena, but others quickly suggested it was even cruder than that (e.g., Sauer 1969). Pielou (1979) listed eight chief objections to the "simple qualitative version of the theory" based on its assumptions and concluded that the model, and most models, suffer from the drawback of being difficult to disprove. Brown (1981) claimed that the theory's qualitative predictions can indeed be tested rigorously and described it as "one of the few models of community ecology that have been repeatedly and unequivocally falsified." Brown and Gibson (1983) listed six major problems with the theory, derived from a review of the literature, and Brown (1986), while admitting the model's lack of verification, applauded its stimulation of work and thought. Williamson (1981) compiled a good summary of the theory's strengths and weaknesses. Case and Cody (1983) thought it extremely unlikely that the equilibrium theory alone can account for the distribution and dynamics of all the different organisms studied on the islands in the Sea of Cortéz. Levins (1966) said "all models leave out a lot and are in that sense false, incomplete, inadequate." Simberloff (1983a) stated:

And the more realistically a model describes a given community, the less likely it is to describe realistically any other community, making a test of the model as an hypothesis

increasingly difficult if not impossible. The model then ceases to be a generalized abstraction of elements common to all communities, but rather becomes just an increasingly elaborate narrative description.

It appears that the passage of time has borne out the statement by MacArthur and Wilson (1967) in the preface of their monograph: "We do not seriously believe that the particular formulations advanced in the chapters to follow will fit for very long the exacting results of future empirical investigations."

5   NULL MODELS

Strong (1982) made the following brief assessment of the theory of island biogeography:

The theory has been inspirational, motivating a tremendous amount of work with island species and ecological biogeography, but it deals with different species as if they were virtually identical, and with processes such as extinction and colonization as if they were deterministic. Thus the theory cannot hope to describe more than a ghost of the heterogeneous and stochastic real world.

Strong's statement requires clarification since some elements of the theory of island biogeography are both stochastic and deterministic (Brown 1986). MacArthur and Wilson (1967) presumed that increasing colonization of islands by new species increases competition and lowers the species' populations, making extinction more likely. On later examination this was found not completely consistent with the data (MacArthur et al. 1972). Simberloff (1978d) examined a number of colonization models, ranging from completely stochastic and noninteractive through deterministic and governed by interspecific competition, and complained that statistical tests are often ignored so the purely stochastic model cannot be convincingly rejected. Strong's (1982) use of the term stochasticity probably reflects his view that colonization and extinction could conceivably be governed by chance events, uninfluenced by dispersal ability or competitive interactions. This is possible, though unlikely. Strong really indicated the need for null hypotheses. Grant and Abbott (1980) agreed that stochastic models are useful tools for testing hypotheses, but thought their usefulness minimal until they are made more realistic. Strong et al. (1979), Strong (1980, 1983), and Simberloff (1980a, 1983c) presented arguments concerning null hypotheses, stochastic models, and competition theory. Simberloff and Strong claimed that more hypothesis testing should use null hypotheses, which should rely on a stochastic model. For instance, the random placement/passive sampling hypothesis for species-area studies (Section IIC2) should be tested and refuted before other hypotheses can be accepted (Simberloff 1976a; Connor and McCoy 1979; McGuinness 1984a). Colwell and Winkler (1984) examined biases inherent in null models and argued that the development of a good, unbiased null hypothesis is most difficult.

B   Some Conservation Applications

1   ISOLATES AND SAMPLES

Preston (1962) was one of the first to allude to conservation implications of ideas incorporated into the equilibrium island theory. He proposed that the isolation or approximate isolation of a natural habitat should cause the number of species that can reside there to fall to some lower level because of the relationship between "isolates" and "samples" (Fig. 12). Preston (1960, 1962) viewed isolates as complete "ensembles" of individuals making up a community—containing a nontruncated canonical lognormal distribution (Figs. 13 and 14)—as on an island. Samples, he said, are subsets of species making up a community, like a nature reserve within a continent. He thought that enlargement of the sample (reserve) to the size of a continent might make the two indistinguishable. This concept was adopted by MacArthur and Wilson (1967). Preston also noted that species-area regression lines are flatter for samples on continents than on isolated islands of the same size as the sample. That is, the samples contain more species per unit area than islands do, reflecting a certain fixed range of z values (Section IIC5). This point was later questioned (Connor and McCoy 1979; F. S. Gilbert 1980). Preston proposed an explanation: isolates (islands) have fewer species than land-locked samples because they are not subject to invasion by immigrants from adjacent land. An alternative explanation might be that samples can sustain smaller-size populations than isolates because they are readily sustained by immigrants, thus allowing a larger number of species each represented by fewer individuals.

Preston went on to question whether it was possible to preserve a total replica of a region's fauna in a small area like a nature reserve. His recommendation was to connect small areas by means of "corridors." MacArthur and Wilson (1967), contrary to what is often portrayed as their position, only implied that the principles of the theory of island biogeography could be applied to "natural" continental habitat islands. Such islands as caves, gallery forests, tide pools, taiga as it grades into tundra, and man-made continental habitat islands (e.g., forest fragments formed by deliberate landscape alteration) might, they suggested, demonstrate the theory, but they went no further than this in terms of conservation application. MacArthur (1972) suggested that mammals might be lost from landbridge islands with time, which agreed with Diamond's (1972) findings for tropical birds (Section IIB2).

2   RELAXATION ON ISLANDS— EARLY PAPERS

Diamond (1972) suggested that relaxation,[1] a local extinction due to insufficient island area, should be taken into account when establishing tropical forest reserves. He reported documentation for relaxation on islands obtained while studying tropical forest birds on New Guinea land-bridge islands and others in the Southwest Pacific. His method was to interpret species-area regressions.

Willis (1974) documented the loss of bird species on Barro Colorado Island, Panama, a hilltop isolated by artificial flooding, and concluded that the loss demonstrated what he called an "island effect" (i.e., area effect) but indicated other factors were inevitably involved. The island was then undergoing secondary succession, so he felt that some fraction of the observed extinctions may have been due to habitat change. He recognized the conservation

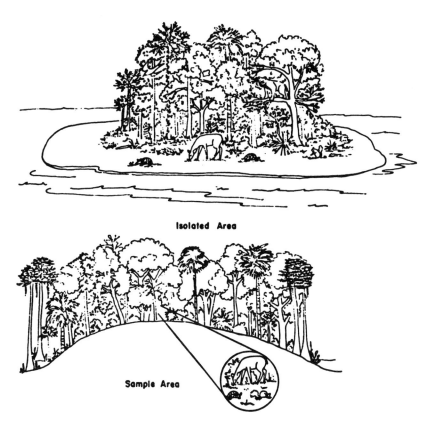

Isolated Area

Sample Area

Figure 12. A graphic demonstration of the distinction between insular and sample communities. It was perceived by Sir Joseph Hooker in 1866 that real islands typically contain fewer species than a "sample" of equal size on the mainland (Williamson 1981). Since Preston (1962) maintained that insular communities are self-contained while sample communities interact with surrounding species, some have subsequently argued that national parks and other reserves might be regarded as sample communities when their boundaries were first established and they were adjoined by "buffer zones" of natural habitat (e.g., Miller and Harris 1977, 1979). It has been claimed that transformation of the sample into a "habitat island" by encroachment might result in species loss with time, because the tract adjusts to isolation, caused by reduced or eliminated emigration (e.g., Miller and Harris 1977, 1979; Wilcox 1980). (From Miller 1978; reprinted by permission of the Foundation for Environmental Conservation and of the Founding Editor of their Journal, *Environmental Conservation*.)

implications of an area effect and, like Preston, recommended that tropical forest reserves be connected by "corridors."

Terborgh (1974), applying the data of Willis (1974), used a mathematical model derived from Diamond's New Guinea land-bridge island relaxation data to predict extinctions at Barro Colorado Island, Panama. The island is not a remnant forest surrounded by development but a hilltop surrounded by an artificially created lake. He warned that the two situations, real and habitat islands, were analogous but not equivalent. Many conservation-minded scientists were excited about the Terborgh (1974, 1975) papers, cornerstones to all subsequent applications of the theory of island biogeography, because they explicitly applied concepts that emerged from theoretical ecology/biogeography to the prediction of possible faunal species extinctions in continental parks, reserves, and other protected areas. The method again was interpretation of species-area regressions. Chapters VI and VII will elaborate on habitat size and species loss.

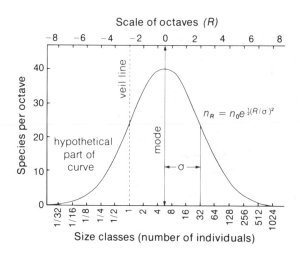

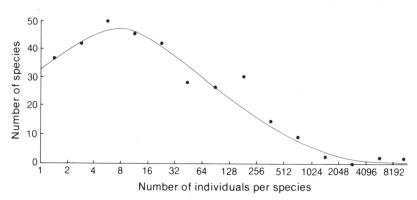

Figure 13. Preston (1948) proposed the log-normal distribution of species abundances in the upper figure. The *x*-axis is logarithmic (log₂). Each class of abundance (e.g., 1–2 individuals, 2–4 individuals, 4–8 individuals, etc.) he called "octaves" because each is twice as large as the previous class. That part of the curve left of the "veil line" represents species with less than one individual in the sample. One standard deviation (σ) on both sides of the mode takes in two-thirds of all the species. The equation n_R describes the normal curve. The important point is that it requires a doubling of the area sampled to shift the curve one octave to the right. Thus a very large area must be sampled to completely "unveil" this theoretical curve. Using Preston's (1948) data, the lower figure illustrates the relative abundance of species of moths attracted to light traps near Orono, Maine. Note its similarity to the theoretical curve in the upper figure. (From *Ecology 2/E*. By Robert E. Ricklefs. ©1979 by Chiron Press. Reprinted with permission by W. H. Freeman and Company.)

3   DISSENTING VIEWS

As further attempts were made to document both the basic and applied aspects of the theory of island biogeography, the literature mushroomed. Some scientists became aware that some of the new information lent itself to application by conservation planners and managers to the designing and/or management of wildlife reserves. A surprisingly wide array of attempts have been made to apply the theory to conservation of different habitats, for example, by Davis and Glick (1978) who reasonably

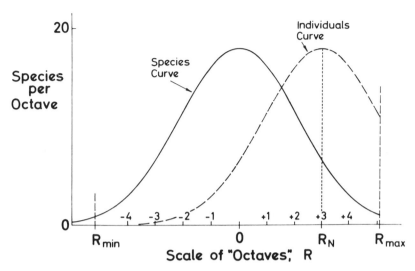

Figure 14. The solid curve is a log-normal species-abundance distribution. The dashed curve is the corresponding log-normal distribution for the total number of individuals. The x-axis is plotted in Preston's octaves (i.e., $\log_2$). The boundary at R_{max} represents the approximate position of the last, most abundant species; R_N is the octave where total numbers are maximum. Preston's "canonical hypothesis" is that R_{max} and R_N coincide. (From May 1975b; reprinted by permission of the publishers from *Ecology and Evolution of Communities*. Martin L. Cody and Jared M. Diamond eds., Cambridge, Mass.: The Belknap Press of Harvard University, ©1975 by the President and Fellows of Harvard College.)

suggested extending the island theory concepts to habitat islands in cities, and then wondered whether it might be pertinent to comparisons of entire cities with one another (Figs. 15, 16). Some of the attention the theory of island biogeography has received, especially its equilibrium concept, may be related to what Reed (1983) described as "its intuitive simplicity being one of its more beguiling aspects."

Some scientists argued that much of the theory of island biogeography as applied to real islands, in spite of the continuing flood of papers, remained unsupported by good data, making any extrapolations to continental habitat islands premature (Simberloff and Abele 1976a; Simberloff 1976b). This argument was later buttressed by other authors (Abele and Connor 1979; F. S. Gilbert 1980).

C   Species and Area

1   BRIEF HISTORY OF THE SPECIES-AREA RELATIONSHIP

One attempt to express the species-area relationship was made by Jaccard (1908). The relationship between quadrat size and number of plant species was demonstrated by Arrhenius (1921, 1923) and Gleason (1922, 1925). A conflict arose as to whether

Arrhenius's log species-log area plots (power function) or Gleason's species-log area plots (exponential function) (Fig. 17) gave more consistently straight-line relationships (terminology from Connor and McCoy 1979). Willis (1922) showed the relationship between number of species per genus and area for both plants and animals.

The increase in species with increasing area was

Figure 15. LANDSAT satellite image map at 1:100,000-scale of Washington, D.C., and vicinity taken on November 2, 1982. The arrow is to the right of Washington, D.C. Note the fragmented natural landscape in all directions. Habitat fragments occur both in the city and in surrounding suburban and rural areas. The arrow also identifies the location of Figure 16. (Image courtesy U.S. Geological Survey Earth Resources Observation Satellite Data Center.)

Figure 16. The 43-acre Belt Woods represents one of the few remaining old-growth upland hardwood forests on the Atlantic Coastal Plain. It is located within 15 miles of downtown Washington, D.C., near Lanham, Maryland. (The 1:40,000 scale photo was taken 4-10-88 by the U.S. Department of Agriculture Agricultural Stabilization and Conservation Service.)

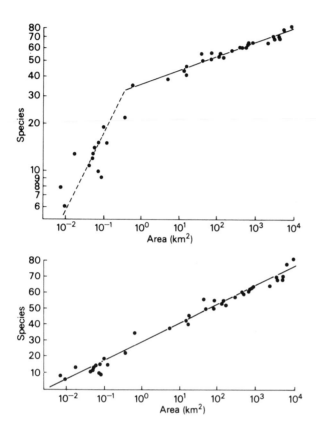

Figure 17. Species-area plots for birds in the Solomon Islands, using data from Diamond and Mayr (1976). In the lower graph, the log species-log area plot (Arrhenius plot, or power function) is linearized, while the upper graph, with a species-log area plot (Gleason plot, or exponential function), is not. As Williamson (1981) indicated, log species-log area plots more frequently linearize the data from a diverse group of organisms. However, Preston (1962) claimed that species-log area plots and log species-log area plots can both give approximately straight line plots using the same data over an abscissa range of one order of magnitude. (From *Island Populations* by Mark Williamson, published by Oxford University Press 1981; modified from Diamond and Mayr 1970, reprinted by permission of the author.)

described as one of community ecology's few genuine laws (Schoener 1976). Strong (1979) stated that the log species-log area relationship (power function) is to ecological biogeography as allometric relationships are to morphology, recognizing that both are governed by the same type of equation. Gould (1979) pointed out that the power function had been used in studying allometric growth (scaling of brain size) since 1891. For other uses of the power function, see Connor and McCoy (1979). Simberloff (1974a, 1978b) indicated an awareness that the basic species-area relationship (species number increases with area) had been known since 1835, and Connor and McCoy (1979) said that Watson (1835) had implied that the relationship was logarithmic. Therefore the basic idea of the species-area curve predated the 1963 theory of island biogeography by at least 128 years, and the species-area and species-distance relationships were noted for islands at least 212 years ago (Section IIA2).

2 SPECIES-AREA HYPOTHESES

Numerous hypotheses exist to explain the species-area effect. One, proposed by Williams (1943), is called the "area-habitat diversity" hypothesis: Species numbers should increase with area because larger areas usually contain more habitats. Another is MacArthur and Wilson's (1963, 1967) "area per se" hypothesis in their theory of island biogeography, actually described by Preston (1960, 1962): Species numbers should increase with area because population increases and species interactions presumably diminish with increasing area, thus decreasing the probability of extinction of individual populations. Arrhenius (1921, 1923), Preston (1960, 1962), MacArthur and Wilson (1963, 1967), and Simberloff (1978 b,c) all pointed out or alluded to one more, the "passive sampling" hypothesis: Any site contains only a portion of a larger community arrayed according to its species-abundance distribution. Thus, the number of individuals within any site is a function of site size, and a smaller site is expected to have fewer individuals because it represents a smaller sample. The terminology used in describing the above three hypotheses follows Connor and McCoy (1979).

However, Simberloff (1978b,c) sometimes portrayed the third hypothesis in a slightly different way: each continental tract or island community may act as a giant "net," sweeping out fragments from some larger community, presumably in proportion to the size of the sample. For islands at least, his "disperser intercept" idea was essentially a part of the passive sampling hypothesis. The disperser intercept idea can be stated more precisely: the probability that an individual can colonize a site or island is proportional to the island's area, providing that individuals colonize independently of one another.

Coleman (1981) introduced the term "random

placement" as a hypothesis, and McGuinness (1984a) considered it the same as the passive sampling hypothesis. In contrast to Boecklen and Simberloff (1986), for simplicity I will recognize only three hypotheses: "area per se," "area-habitat diversity," and "passive sampling."

The passive sampling hypothesis indicated that the species-area relationship could be strictly a passive sampling phenomenon: larger areas receive larger samples with more species. McGuinness (1984b) incidentally found some support for the passive sampling, or random placement, hypothesis, finding it a good model for species-area curves at more than half the intertidal marine communities sampled. It is a null hypothesis (Section IIA5) for biological explanations such as the area-habitat diversity hypothesis or the area per se hypothesis; the hypotheses were not necessarily mutually exclusive (Connor and McCoy 1979; F. S. Gilbert 1980). Sugihara (1980, 1981) did not accept Simberloff's (1972, 1976b) and Connor and McCoy's (1979) point that the species-area relationship might be explained by just the passive sampling hypothesis. He thought that the species-area constant and canonical log-normal abundance pattern reflected a genuine regularity in species abundances, which he proposed was due to a hierarchically structured communal niche. Connor et al. (1983) disputed this point.

3 AREA-HABITAT DIVERSITY

The Problem. Area-habitat diversity, which is one aspect of the species-area relationship, is here singled out for further treatment because of its rather direct relationship to nature reserves. Specifically, MacArthur and Wilson's theory of island biogeography used the area per se hypothesis and did not (could not) take environmental heterogeneity into account. The authors indicated that area alone cannot be assumed to be a precise predictor of species diversity, although they thought it likely that area accounted most heavily for species richness on islands. Western and Ssemakula (1981), and many other authors, subsequently pointed out making predictions about species number based on area per se is difficult because habitat heterogeneity also can increase with area. However, Simberloff (1976a) provided evidence, based on a census of arthropods on Florida mangrove islands, that the effect of area can be independent of the effect of habitat. Abele

and Patton (1976) thought their data suggest that area alone affected the number of decapod crustaceans on coral heads.

Review of Pertinent Studies. Power (1972) and Johnson (1975) found area a poor predictor of bird species number, but habitat diversity a good one. Watson (1964) concluded that habitat diversity is more significant than area in determining the number of birds on the Aegean Islands. Hamilton et al. (1963) found that in addition to area, island relief and isolation are correlates of species number in the Galapagos. Hamilton et al. (1964), using multiple regression to determine the effect of island area, elevation, and isolation on the number of bird species, found that area accounted for 93 percent in the West Indies and 72 percent in the East Indies. Hamilton and Armstrong (1965), also using multiple regression, found area the most significant predictor of bird species number on islands in the Gulf of Guinea, but Hamilton and Rubinoff (1967) found no area effect for finches in the Galapagos. Johnson et al. (1968) reported that area was the best predictor of plant species number on island and mainland plots, and Johnson and Raven (1973) found that area consistently exhibited the highest correlation with number of plant species in the Galapagos. Johnson and Simberloff (1974), using multiple regression, found area, latitude, and distance from Britain significant predictors of plant species number in the British Isles. Harner and Harper (1976) found area highly correlated with plant species number in thirty pinyon-juniper sites in Utah and New Mexico, environmental heterogeneity slightly less so, and the two together accounted for 98 percent of the variation. Lawlor (1983) reported that numbers of plant species and distance from the mainland were the best correlates of mammal species numbers on the oceanic islands but not on the land-bridge islands in the Sea of Cortéz. Bekele (1980) found that the number of Kuchler vegetation types correlated well with the numbers of large mammals in fourteen western U.S. national parks. Newmark (1986) determined that vegetative cover was a poor predictor of mammal species numbers in the same parks. None of the above studies deals directly with habitat diversity but all attempt to approach it by identifying measures assumed to be correlated with it.

Simberloff (1974a) and Connor and Simberloff (1978) reviewed work that used simple and multiple regression and used multiple regression and other methods themselves to ascertain the roles of area and other factors in influencing numbers of species on oceanic and habitat islands. They concluded that some previous generalizations about the determinants of species numbers based on multiple regression and correlation are suspect, for example, in the Galapagos Islands. Buckley (1982) proposed a method to get around the problem of within-island habitat heterogeneity. Singling out the roles of area and habitat in regard to species numbers is a future challenge. Attempts to separate area from habitat diversity in studies of nature reserves have not fully succeeded (e.g., Bennett 1987).

4 THE SPECIES-AREA EQUATION

Miller and Harris (1977, 1979) argued that the equilibrium aspect of the theory of island biogeography (balance between immigration and extinction) had not been documented on real or habitat islands, but that such documentation was not necessary since the information can be derived from the species-area curve (Fig. 18), which can be plotted on arithmetic or logarithmic axes. The species-area curve, typically illustrated with species numbers and areas logarithmically transformed as in Figures 17 (lower), 18 (upper), 19, 20, and 21, is another prediction of the theory of island biogeography and is expressed below:

Equation 1 $\qquad S = cA^z$

where S is the number of species, A represents area, and z and c are fitted constants, derived by log-log regression. Constant c, the intercept, reportedly varies widely among taxa, biogeographic region, island isolation, and taxon population density. Many (e.g., Stenseth 1979) thought it reasonable to use a power function (Equation 1) to describe the species-area relationship.

The species-area equation (Equation 1) was expressed by Preston (1960, 1962) although it was implied in an earlier mathematical description by Arrhenius (1921). Figure 19 illustrates the species-area curve with intercept $c = 3.3$ and the slope of the regression line $z = 0.301$.

Equation 1 is usually approximated by a double logarithmic transformation, Equation 2 below, which represents the regression equation:

Equation 2 $\qquad \log S = \log c + z \log A$

Gleason (1922) proposed an exponential function, Equation 3:

Equation 3 $\qquad S = \log c + z \log A$

which reflects a species-log area plot (see Fig. 17 [upper]).

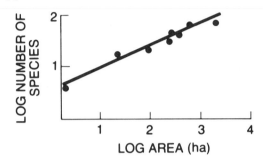

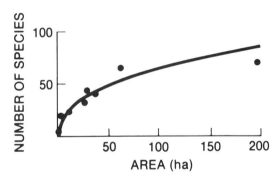

Figure 18. The species-area curve plotted for the number of breeding bird species in different size plots of North America. The graph directly above is plotted on arithmetic axes, while the uppermost graph is plotted on logarithmic axes using log-transformed data (i.e., a log species-log area plot). Preston's (1960) data ranged from a 0.5-acre plot in Pennsylvania with 3 species, to all of the United States and Canada (4.6 billion acres) harboring 625 species. The straight-line relationship in finer resolution actually falls off at the very ends of the plot (see Figure 20). Numerous taxa of vertebrates, invertebrates, and plants display straight lines in log species/log area plots. May (1975b) indicated that the slope of the log species-log area plots, if relative abundance is log-normal, should range between a z value of 0.16 and 0.39, and most plots seem to. The perceived small range for the slope z has inspired much faith in its application and interpretation. However, slope, intercept, and scatter can vary widely (Williamson 1981). The straight-line relationship is predicted as a result of the log-normal species abundance distribution for large areas or samples from large areas, but a straight-line relationship is also predicted as a result of the logarithmic-series distribution for small areas or samples from small areas (Williamson 1981). (From Wilcox 1980; reprinted by permission of Sinauer Associates, Inc.)

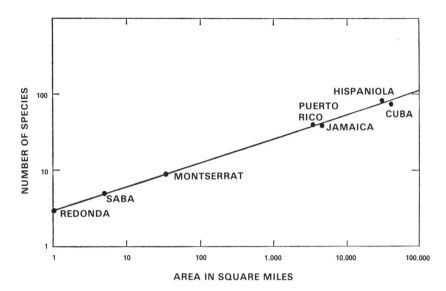

Figure 19. The species-area curve for herpetofauna (amphibians plus reptiles) on islands in the West Indies on a log species-log area plot using data provided by Darlington (1957). (From MacArthur and Wilson, *The Theory of Island Biogeography.* ©1967 Princeton University Press. Figure 2 reprinted with permission of Princeton University Press).

5   THE SPECIES-AREA EQUATION PARAMETERS (*c* AND *z*)

Preston (1962) made a unique interpretation of the species-area equation by noticing that *z* usually falls between 0.20 and 0.35 for isolates and between 0.12 and 0.17 for samples. He thought the difference in *z* values between isolates and samples (Fig. 12) related to the inability of samples to enclose entire ensembles of species, that is, an isolate gave a fair approximation of a "complete" log-normal distribution curve while a sample gave a truncated one. Preston (1962), and later MacArthur and Wilson (1967), explained that isolates generally have fewer species than samples, that is, larger *z* values (steeper slopes of the regression line), so the log species-log area plot ascends more rapidly (Fig. 21). Lawlor (1986) compared the world's oceanic with land-bridge islands and concluded that Preston's (1962) expectation for *z* values held for bats, in accordance with the equilibrium model, but not for terrestrial mammals. He hypothesized that this was due to a historical legacy of low immigration rates and to fragmentation of once continuous continental faunas to form relictual populations.

Connor and McCoy (1979) thought that consis-tent *z* values in the power function $S = cA^z$ fitted by linear regression may be a statistical artifact: The transformation turns any monotonic function into a straight line and so does not reflect a log-normal distribution. They were skeptical that any biological significance could be attached to the power function parameters *c* and *z* and proposed that perhaps only deviations from a certain range of *z* values possess biological significance. They felt that the power function was regarded as a paradigm and suggested that fitting it to species-area data was based on widespread but unwarranted confidence that species demonstrate a log-normal relative abundance distribution.

Wright (1981) claimed to show that iterative, non-linear regression is free of a statistical artifact and still yields *z* values in the predicted range. Sugihara (1980, 1981) purported to demonstrate that the *z* values are not due to statistical artifact and have a biological basis.

F. S. Gilbert (1980) thought that *z* values for samples are very often, but not always, lower than for isolates, but the scatter of points using regressions is nearly always greater. He concluded that explanations for the differences are only speculation. To Williamson (1981) the expected *z* value difference

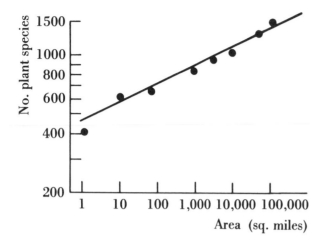

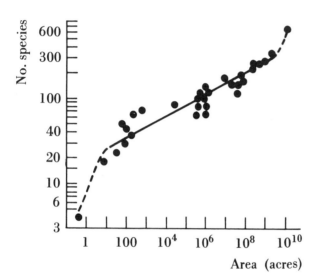

Figure 20. Using the data of Williams (1964), the upper graph illustrates the species-area relationship for flowering plants in England. The smallest plot is 1 square mile in Surrey, and the largest includes all of England. Using the data of Preston (1960), the lower graph illustrates the same species-area relationship for North American birds given in Figure 18. Note that both graphs are plotted on logarithmic axes and show a straight-line relationship except at the extremes of the plot in the lower one. (Figures from *Ecology: The Experimental Analysis of Distribution and Abundance*, by Charles J. Krebs. ©1978 by Charles J. Krebs. Reprinted by permission of Harper & Row Publishers, Inc.)

between isolates and samples, if it existed at all, appeared only weakly indicated, but he concluded that samples contain more species per unit area than do islands. Martin (1981) analyzed data for land birds on archipelagos and found that the species-area slope can change with area (i.e., small areas have

higher slopes than large areas). This effect, together with the interaction of source pool size, isolation, latitude, and environmental heterogeneity, can cloud real biological patterns. Connor et al. (1983) continued to stress that many slopes between 0.2 and 0.4 are expected to be independent of any biological basis.

May (1984) concurred with Sugihara's (1980, 1981) analysis indicating that Connor and McCoy's null hypothesis can be rejected: the variance in z values of the null model is significantly more than observed in nature. Wright (1988) added to the uncertainty with his conclusion that species abundance distributions (Section IIC6) do not determine species-area relationships for islands.

If we assume the constants c and z have a biological basis, the problem becomes one of defining them in a way that gives the equation predictive power. R. I. Miller (1976, 1978) pointed out that z values have been derived from insular communities and not from "equilibrated" reserves (i.e., reserves

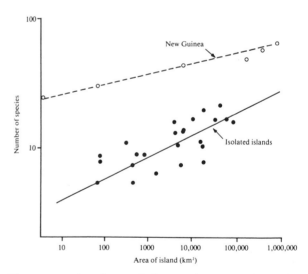

Figure 21. The slope of the species-area relationship here is steeper (higher z value), and its position lower relative to the y axis, for "isolates" (isolated islands) than for "samples" (tracts within a large island or continent). The data are for pomerine ants on the Moluccan and Melanesian islands (lower) and for sites of increasing area on New Guinea (upper). Although it has been widely accepted that isolates and samples typically reflect such z-value differences, this general rule has been questioned (Connor and McCoy 1979; F. S. Gilbert 1980). In fact, they questioned the biological significance of the regression slope, as have others (e.g., Haila 1983; Abbott 1983). (From Wilson 1961; reprinted by permission of The University of Chicago Press. ©1961.)

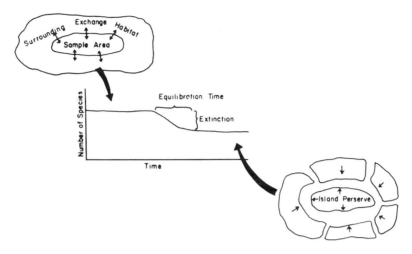

Figure 22. Miller (1978) introduced the term equilibration time, that required for a reserve to lose species until its species number reaches a level that can be sustained over time by the smaller reserve. Note that the theoretical concept of samples and isolates appears to underlie this concept of equilibration. (From Miller 1978; reprinted by permission of The Foundation for Environmental Conservation and of the Founding Editor of their Journal, *Environmental Conservation*.)

whose number of species has dropped to a level sustainable over time in accordance with area constraints) because such reserves do not exist (Fig. 22). He also indicated that c varies with vegetational diversity, environmental heterogeneity, species diversity of the taxon, and degree of isolation, and that both c and z have a mutual dependence on isolation. MacArthur and Wilson (1967) concluded that they could not develop any theory that would allow precise predictions of c. Disagreement continues as to all the factors that influence c, and its theoretical basis remains elusive (Haas 1975; Gould 1979).

6 RELATIVE ABUNDANCE

Preston (1960, 1962) linked two independent ecological generalizations—the species-area curve and the species-abundance curve. He demonstrated that the species-area relationship can be derived from the canonical log-normal species-abundance curve.[2] He maintained that if relative abundance corresponded to a log-normal distribution, it was possible to estimate the approximate total number of species in a community, including rare ones not yet encountered. Preston (1962) indicated that a canonical log-normal distribution (Figs. 13, 14) should give a straight line on a log area-log species

plot with a z value of 0.263, and that this accounted for the observed distribution of z. Theory suggests that the form of the species-area relationship (e.g., power function or exponential function) is determined by its species-abundance distribution. Therefore, what is known about relative abundance distributions should influence our confidence in the form of the species-area relationship.

May (1975b) thought the log-normal pattern of relative abundance is roughly accurate for large or heterogeneous assemblages of species, and that small samples taken from a large and homogeneous area will obey a logarithmic series (log-series). A log-series distribution reasonably fits some kinds of samples and seems to produce a better fit in some situations, for example, the case of parasites and their hosts (Williams 1964), but has not been widely applied since its introduction. In the log-series, the most abundant classes of species have the fewest individuals. In the log-normal pattern, the most abundant classes of species have a medium number of individuals, while species with very few or very many individuals are rare (Fig. 23). The closeness of fit of the two distributions (Fig. 24) is often great in small samples, making it difficult to distinguish the log-series from the righthand part of the log-normal (Williams 1964; Pielou 1977; Taylor 1978).

The log-series distribution can be traced to Fisher

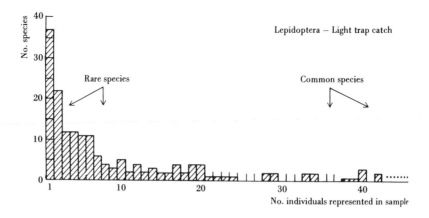

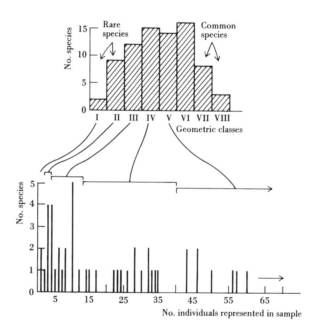

Figure 23. Fisher, Corbet, and Williams (1943) found that the data they plotted gave a "hollow curve" best fitted by the log-series distribution. Williams (1964) depicted such a hollow curve for *Lepidoptera* caught in light traps at Rothamsted, England, in 1935 (top). Individuals numbering 6,814 were caught, including 197 species. Thirty-seven species were represented by one specimen each, and one common species had 1,799 individuals. Six common species represented 50 percent of the total individuals caught. However, Bliss (1965) analyzed the data for the years 1933 to 1936 and found that the log-normal distribution provided a somewhat better fit than the log-series distribution.

Preston (1948) found that the data he plotted conformed to a log-normal distribution. Using the data of Williams (1964), depicted are the abundances of nesting-bird species in Quaker Run Valley, New York (bottom). The lower part of the figure above uses an arithmetic *x* axis, and the upper part uses a logarithmic ($\log_3$) *x* axis. Preston used a ($\log_2$) *x* axis.

(Figures from *Ecology: The Experimental Analysis of Distribution and Abundance*, by Charles J. Krebs. ©1978 by Charles J. Krebs. Reprinted by permission of Harper & Row Publishers, Inc.)

et al. (1943), the log-normal distribution (Fig. 13) to Preston (1948), who suggested it might describe relative abundance better than the log-series. Williams (1953) concurred with Preston (1948) that, at least for larger samples, the relative abundance of species is nearer to log-normal than to log-series. Brian (1953) described species abundance as a negative binomial distribution. Preston (1962) advanced the canonical log-normal distribution, and MacArthur and Wilson (1967) incorporated it in their theory of island biogeography.

Why species abundance corresponds frequently to log-normal, sometimes to log-series, and occasionally to even other distributions is still a mystery (Pielou 1975). May (1975b) concluded that the characteristics of the canonical log-normal distribution are simply mathematical properties of the family of log-normal curves, a conclusion also reached by Ugland and Gray (1982) but challenged by Sugihara (1980). May (1975b) suggested that the log-normal distribution may be a statistical phenomenon with no biological explanation, a reflection of the Central Limit Theorem, an idea implied earlier by MacArthur (1960). But others would legitimately argue that it is more. Sugihara (1980, 1981) thought the canonical log-normal pattern was real. May (1975b) believed that a log-series distribution reflects features of community biology, while Haga (1981) indicated that its existence demonstrates an environmental disturbance. The MacArthur and Wilson equilibrium model has been viewed as an attempt to provide a biological explanation for the log-normal distribution (F. S. Gilbert 1980).

The evidence, I think, suggests more strongly that these distributions do have a biological basis than that they do not. One important and practical aspect of these distributions was pointed out by Hooper (1971): If one accepts "species abundance curves" as an accurate description of biotic communities—few species can have many individuals but many more species can have few individuals (Fig. 23)—then some species in reserves should be so rare that they have a high probability of random extinction, all other factors being equal.

7 CRITIQUES OF SPECIES-AREA EQUATION APPLICATION

McCoy (1983) thought a simple extrapolation of the species-area relationship to be inappropriate in many situations, and minimum reserve size likely to

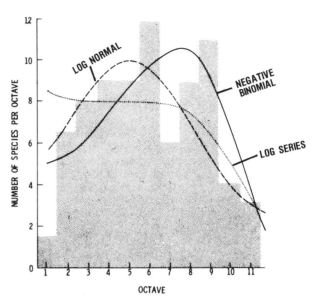

Figure 24. Three theoretical species-abundance curves for a population of breeding birds and the empirical histogram (stippled) to which the curves were fitted, based on Saunders (1936) data given in Brian (1953). (Figure from *Mathematical Ecology*, by E.C. Pielou. ©1977 by E.C. Pielou. Reprinted by permission of John Wiley & Sons; redrawn from Brian (1953), reprinted by permission of Blackwell Scientific Publications Ltd.)

be overestimated. Reed (1983) believed that species-area relationships have a role to play in reserve design but that overemphasis on this single relationship is unrealistic and biologically dubious. Woolhouse (1983) suggested that the species-area equation may be unreliable for designing reserves because a) its parameters may be affected by differences in sampling methods, and b) when data do not conform to Preston's assumptions for the theoretical canonical log species-log area slope of 0.263, there is no point in comparing real slopes with the theoretical value. Boecklen and Gotelli (1984) concluded that extrapolations from species-area regressions are biologically and statistically unreliable and the performance of a reserve based on such extrapolations is extremely uncertain. Zimmerman and Bierregaard (1986) considered the calculation of reserve sizes on the sole basis of species-area data to be no more than uninspired guessing. McGuinness (1984b) reviewed the concept and concluded that more intensive studies involving null hypotheses and manipulative experiments will be needed before the processes generating species-area curves can be understood.

The species-area relationship has been used by some to make minimum reserve size projections (e.g., Kitchener et al. 1980a, 1980b, 1982) and East African reserve "collapse" projections (Soulé et al. 1979). The problems are described in Sections

VIID,F. Picton (1979), Temple (1981), and Goeden (1979) are among those who have made blind-faith conservation applications of species-area regressions; Samson (1980) did the same for the general species-area relationship.

D   An Overview: The Theory's Influence

Some scientists, perhaps overly conscious of the urgent need for guidelines usable by conservation planners and managers as the world faces the current onslaught of natural habitat alteration, have made whatever suggestions appear supportable (e.g., Diamond 1975b; Wilson and Willis 1975; Diamond and May 1976). Others have held that some of these efforts at providing guidelines, however well intended, have outstripped the supporting data (Simberloff and Abele 1976a,b; Abele and Connor 1979; F. S. Gilbert 1980), thereby sparking considerable controversy over both basic and applied aspects of the theory.

Simberloff (1972, 1974a) felt the theory of island biogeography was well supported on oceanic islands, reported successful application of the model to habitat islands, and suggested that many isolated habitat islands are at equilibrium. However, he subsequently became the theory's leading critic, noting a lack of empirical evidence and thereby casting doubt on its conservation application. Simberloff and Abele (1976b) stated that any conservation applications were "based on limited and insufficiently validated theory" and that the paradigm status held by the equilibrium aspect of the theory was unjustifiable.

These claims and counterclaims have no doubt confused some conservation planners and managers, as well as some scientists. There is no unanimity as to just what they can believe in the wake of an evergrowing scientific literature on the basic and applied aspects of the equilibrium island theory since 1963, but recognition of its impugnment is

growing. The mid-1970s saw a growing belief, which has been shaken, that the theory of island biogeography could tell us about the rate of extinction in reserves, the number of species that might survive in a reserve to a certain time, and the number of species expected in a reserve of a certain size. Confusion was compounded by incorrect scientific reporting in the most respected journals (Kolata, 1974):

The realization that national parks can be treated as islands has enabled researchers to predict the rate that species in national parks will become extinct, to predict the number of species that will eventually survive, to describe the type of species most likely to survive, and to specify park designs that will minimize extinctions.

It was further compounded by introductory texts treating the theory of island biogeography as accepted without controversy: Gorman (1979) embraced it as valid for real islands, for habitat islands, and for applications to nature reserves.

Harris (1984) took a much more cautious approach. He was not certain whether island biogeography theory or generalities based on real islands can be applied to habitat islands; nevertheless he proceeded to develop a management strategy on the assumption that they are applicable while pointing out that the overall strategy seems robust enough to be useful even if the theory should prove to be invalid. Sections XIIA,M and Chapter XIII provide more perspective on the theory of island biogeography.

Notes

[1] Relaxation is a drop in species' numbers with time to new levels, presumably because the habitat becomes "oversaturated" with species. The original concept was an "experiment of nature," without human interference, and was portrayed as

taking thousands of years. The concept of "fragmentation" of a land mass into smaller islands by rising ocean waters was later incorporated into this idea.

[2]The canonical log-normal distribution is a special form of log-normal distribution where the "individual's curve" terminates at its crest (i.e., the abundance class with the largest number of individuals correlates with the most abundant species in a particular community). Preston (1980) offered various hypotheses to explain the existence of noncanonical distributions he subsequently discovered.

III

Diversity and Reserve Design: The Basics

A   Introduction

Chapter II dealt with the MacArthur and Wilson (1963, 1962) theory of island biogeography and a few areas of potential conservation application, but we must beware of the danger of not seeing the forest for the trees. Therefore, we will attempt to indicate succinctly in the following sections B through E the elements in the theory and its applications that are best known and most relevant for nature reserves. In Sections F through G we will consider some subjects not addressed by MacArthur and Wilson but useful for an understanding of later sections.

B   Species Number—Area

Studies of real islands usually do find more species on larger islands regardless of which species-area hypothesis one uses to explain it. Studies of mainlands also demonstrate that the numbers of species increase with the size of the tract up to a point and increase less rapidly thereafter. Whether the numbers ever completely level off is controversial. We would expect species in habitat islands to become more numerous with increasing tract size due to area alone, though not all evidence conforms to this expectation (Dunn and Loehle 1988). Therefore, larger nature reserves should contain more species.

C   Species Number—Distance

The decrease in species numbers with increasing distance in real islands is not as well documented as some assume. Documentation is weak for birds and angiosperms and almost absent for pteridophytes (Williamson 1981). The nature reserves analogue—that species on a habitat island will decrease with increasing distance from a source habitat—has even less support. However, barriers to dispersal are known (Section IXB2). For example, the movement of pikas is significantly inhibited by a distance of 1,000 feet between talus outcrops (Smith 1974), and Brown's (1978) data illustrated that isolation on montane islands affects birds less than mammals (cited by Harris 1984). However, some studies of birds in small habitat islands (e.g., Opdam, van Dorp, and ter Braak 1984) found area and isolation effects consistent with MacArthur and Wilson's (1963, 1967) prediction.

D Relative Abundance—Area

Why the relative abundance of species in a community often corresponds to certain probability distributions remains unknown. Such distributions probably have a biological basis, though this is controversial. What the distributions indicate is that few species have many individuals and many species have only a few individuals. Therefore, rare species should not be uncommon in random samples of the landscape. Other factors being equal, we should expect to find rare species in samples like nature reserves.

E Species Composition—Area

Species extinctions have occurred on islands. The taxon cycle is an attempt to explain longer-term changes in whole biotas, presumably due to "natural extinctions." The documentation of selective extinctions on land-bridge islands after isolation is under debate, but some limited fossil evidence does add support (Sections VID). Some data for habitat islands do suggest selective species extinctions. Some evidence for island turnover suggests that local extinctions are more likely on smaller islands. Many extinctions on islands are certainly due to human influence. We therefore expect that extinctions in nature reserves could be selective and a function of reserve size.

F Genetic Variability—Area

Genetic variation is presumed to be more likely in larger areas because larger tracts typically contain more species. Also, larger areas should have more intraspecific genetic variation due to more heterogeneous habitats, more peripheral populations, or more subdivided populations, but evidence to verify this is modest (Section IXA2).

G Species Number—Edges

Boundaries (edges) between very different vegetation types, for example, the abrupt interface of a woodlot with a cornfield, have long been known for their tendency to contain more species than the central part of a vegetation type. The concept of ecotone also applies to the natural transition area between any two vegetation types or ecosystems. The edge contains animal species from both adjoining vegetation types as well as species that thrive best at the edge itself. Edges may be natural or created.

Sometimes, as in the field of game management, edges are created specifically to maximize species number (Leopold 1933b). Game species often are adapted to edges, as are nongame species in agricultural and urban areas. The "island" model applies here, since real islands have edges just as do habitat islands. Therefore, increases in species number in habitat islands and nature reserves could be related not just to larger area but to edges, whether on the perimeter or between two interior zones of the nature reserve. Harris (1988) described

edge history in game management. Noss's (1983) review indicated possible detrimental effects of the concept as a management principle. Yahner (1988) also foresaw such negative effects, including changing distribution and dispersal and increasing nest predation and parasitism. He also feared reductions in size and possible isolation of patches and corridors, so caution should be used when prescribing for general wildlife benefits. Of particular importance is that edges can increase the local but not the regional species number (Murphy 1989).

IV

Minimum Populations

A Introduction

Although incorporated into MacArthur and Wilson's (1963, 1967) work, the probability that extinction rate decreases as the ratio of the death rate to the birth rate decreases and as population size increases was recognized much earlier. In fact, Feller (1939) modeled the impact of change in individual births and deaths on population extinction. Such works were precursors to the concept of minimum viable population sizes as in Shaffer (1981) (Section IVB).

Simberloff (1978a) indicated where food or habitat is absent, the cause of an extinction is obvious and deterministic; when other environmental influences come into play, the cause of extinction is not always clear. He said, however, that we can make probabilistic (stochastic) predictions greatly influenced by population size. Although uses of the term "minimum viable population size" vary, here we will consider that it takes into account all factors impinging on a population.

B Minimum Viable Population Size

Such factors as reproductive and survival success, predation, disease, and natural catastrophes are all determinants of minimum viable population size. When a population dips below this level, local extinctions from various causes become more probable. Conservation efforts would be aided immeasurably if we knew this level for certain faunal species in parks and thus were able to precisely relate population size to probability of extinction.

Shaffer (1981) attempted a tentative definition of this concept: a minimum viable population for any given species in any given habitat is the smallest isolated population having a 99 percent chance of remaining extant for 100 years despite the foreseeable effects of demographic stochasticity (population structure and breeding success), environmental stochasticity (predation, competition, and disease), genetic stochasticity (loss of genetic variation due to genetic drift, inbreeding, and the founder effect), and natural catastrophes (fire, drought, and flooding). Hooper (1971) recognized early that there is no such thing as minimum viable population size unless a probability of extinction is accepted and a time period is defined. Soulé (1983) suggested a fifth component of minimum viable population size, in addition to the four proposed by Shaffer (1981): dysfunction of social behavior that could impact animal aggregations.

C Demographic Stochasticity

May (1973) used the term "demographic stochasticity" but in a different context from the one intended here. Since animal numbers are integers, the population variable is not continuous. We define demographic stochasticity as sampling variation in population variables, such as sex ratio and age distribution, that can produce fluctuations in population size. Sampling variation in these population variables can theoretically cause extinction in a small population.

MacArthur and Wilson (1967) extended the concept of stochastic fluctuations in population size and probability of extinction to colonization, constructing models relating per capita birth rate b, per capita death rate d, carrying capacity (maximum population) K achievable on an island, probability of propagule survival, and average population lifetime. Equation 4 expresses one of the relationships incorporated in the model, making use of the intrinsic population growth rate $r = b - d$.

$$\text{Equation 4} \qquad K = r/b$$

A larger K means a greater chance that a propagule producing young will survive to generate population growth. Figure 25 presents graphs based on the model, showing how lifetimes vary with K for two values of birth rate b and varying death rates d.

Equation 4 is one simple example of demographic stochasticity.

Most extinctions should occur during initial population growth, that is, when the population is small, and not after the population has reached carrying capacity. MacArthur and Wilson (1967) pointed out, on the basis of the theory of stochastic processes, that extinction rates could be expected to be high in populations below some critical size. When a population does reach some critical value, theoretically the probability of extinction during a specific time period approaches zero (Richter-Dyn and Goel 1972). The wider the oscillations below critical population levels, the greater the probability of extinction (Levins 1970).

Shaffer and Samson (1985) questioned the general applicability of these analytical models to conservation strategies because they ignore environmental perturbations, genetics, and population sex and age distribution. Wilcox and Murphy (1985) said that the conclusion of Richter-Dyn and Goel (1972)—expected survival of a population is independent of population size when it exceeds about 20 individuals—is meaningless from a practical viewpoint because of environmental variation. Goodman (1987a) and Burgman et al. (1988) provide much more detail on demographic stochasticity.

D Environmental Stochasticity

The term environmental stochasticity will be taken to include variations attributable to competition, predation, disease, and natural disasters. May (1973) and Roughgarden (1975) use it somewhat differently to indicate random temporal changes in population variables based on some probability distribution. Leigh (1981) used mathematical models to demonstrate an intuitive trait of large populations, that the greater the impact of environmental

variation, the slower the increase in population lifetime with increase in equilibrium size. In other words, environmental variation is the major cause of the population oscillations that lead to extinction. Mertz (1971) used demographic considerations to illustrate the vulnerability of the California condor, a species with a low reproductive rate, when facing predation or catastrophic environmental change. Harper (1981) observed that the relationship be-

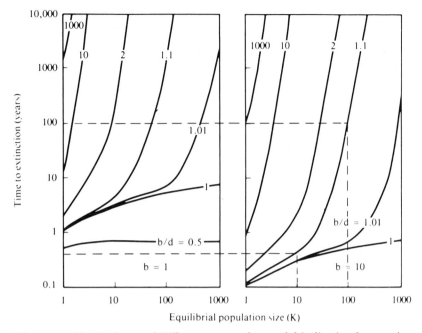

Figure 25. MacArthur and Wilson proposed a model indicating how extinction probability varies with equilibrial population size or carrying capacity (*K*), per capita birth rate (*b*), and per capita death rate (*d*). The projected time to extinction increases with increasing carrying capacity, birth rate, and the ratio of birth rate to death rate (*b/d*). In this very rough theoretical model, with a per capita birth rate *b* of 10 (right graph) and using a birth rate/death rate (*b/d*) ratio of 1.01, note the effect of equilibrial population size *K* on projected time to extinction (follow dashed lines to *y*-axis of left graph). A *K* of 10 gives a projected time to extinction of under 1 year, while a *K* of 100 gives a projected time to extinction of approximately 100 years. Shaffer and Samson (1985), however, pointed out the problems of relying on such simple analytical models. (Reproduced by permission from Brown, James H., and Gibson, Arthur C.: *Biogeography*, St. Louis, 1983, The C.V. Mosby Co.; after MacArthur and Wilson, *The Theory of Island Biogeography*. ©1967 Princeton University Press. Figure 27b reprinted with permission of Princeton University Press.)

tween population size and random events may not be that simple; it may depend on an organism's specific biological properties. Although we can accept the concept of demographic stochasticity in theory,

Simberloff (1976b) reminded us of the impossibility of separating stochastic effects from secular environmental changes.

E   Genetic Considerations

1 THE VALUE OF HETEROZYGOSITY

Genetic variation in a population is determined by the number of polymorphic loci (having more than one allele), the number and form of such alleles at the polymorphic loci, and the degree of hetero-

zygosity per individual. Our focus here is on heterozygosity.

Allendorf and Leary (1986) found a generally positive relationship between heterozygosity and phenotype that is presumed to affect fitness in natural animal populations. Ledig (1986) thought that the evidence for plants suggests a relationship between fitness and heterozygosity. Falconer (1981) documented such a relationship for domestic animals. Evidence for *Drosophila* indicates that the evolutionary rate of a population adapting to a new environment correlates with the population's genetic variability (Ayala 1968) and that heterozygosity increased fitness (Sved and Ayala 1970).

We can therefore infer that a loss of genetic variation in wild animal or plant populations is likely to reduce fitness. However, Fuerst and Maruyama (1986) claimed that management for adequate heterozygosity alone may be misguided and should also consider loss of alleles.

2 BOTTLENECKS

A bottleneck is a dramatic reduction in population size that can be caused by an environmental perturbation, a demographic accident, or a natural colonization event. How small can populations become before they suffer from either loss of heterozygosity (due to inbreeding) or loss of alleles (due to genetic drift)? The question has no precise answers, but it is generally agreed that severe reductions in population can result in a loss of alleles, with possible negative effects on survival, and a less significant loss in heterozygosity. This translates into a potential overall loss in fitness.

For example, one mathematical model predicts that a shrinking population can pass through a bottleneck with only a small loss in average heterozygosity (Fig. 26) if the bottleneck is followed by rapid population growth, but will still experience a substantial drop in the average number of alleles (Nei et al. 1975). This model-based prediction was supported by Allendorf (1986) who maintained that population bottlenecks of short duration probably have little influence on heterozygosity but severely reduce the number of alleles in the population.

Fuerst and Maruyama (1986) demonstrated that allelic variation can be lost more rapidly than genic variation (heterozygosity), indicating a difference between the distributions of allele frequency and interlocus heterozygosity. Allelic variation can be restored only by new mutations.

O'Brien et al. (1983) found 55 South African cheetahs genetically monomorphic at each of 17 allozyme loci (dramatically lower than for cats and mammals in general), which they attributed to a possible population bottleneck. O'Brien et al.

(1985) and O'Brien and Evermann (1988) suggested the cheetahs' lack of genetic variation, due to bottlenecks and inbreeding, may have fostered disease. Cohn (1986) described some of the cheetah data for a general audience. Allendorf and Leary (1986) thought that the animals' low heterozygosity was manifested by negative phenotypic effects. O'Brien et al. (1986) suggested that the cheetah is in genetic peril. Wildt et al. (1987) found a direct correlation between genetic variability and two physiological traits—incidence of abnormal sperm and circulating testosterone—suggesting that reproductive function may be impaired when lion populations contract due to inbreeding.

Numerous examples demonstrate that a population can dwindle to a very small size but somehow recover, for example, the Mauritius kestrel (Temple 1986). Soulé (1987b) pointed out that making it through a bottleneck does not imply an acceptable situation, though it certainly is more desirable than going extinct. He cautioned against confusing bottleneck, the lowest population size ever recorded, with minimum viable population (MVP), the upper limit of a regime.

Exceptional cases remain: A northern elephant seal population possessed no genetic variation at 24 loci, perhaps because of a population bottleneck caused by hunters in the late 19th century, but appeared to be thriving (Bonnell and Selander 1974). Hermaphroditic snails with little heterozygosity seemed well adapted to their environments (Selander and Kaufman 1973). Some plants had surprisingly little genetic variation (Ledig 1986). Selander (1976) gives other examples of bottlenecked populations with very reduced or no genic variability, and O'Brien et al. (1983) give examples of other mammals.

3 INBREEDING STUDIES

Large outcrossing populations reduced to a small number of individuals may suffer lowered fecundity and viability, called inbreeding depression, and may become sterile after a few generations of sibling matings (Fig. 27). Inbreeding is deleterious primarily because more individuals become homozygous for harmful recessive alleles, which can become expressed (Wright 1977; Falconer 1981). Correlations have been found between inbreeding and survival/fecundity in zoos (Ralls et al. 1979, 1980; Ralls and Ballou 1982a,b; Ballou and Ralls

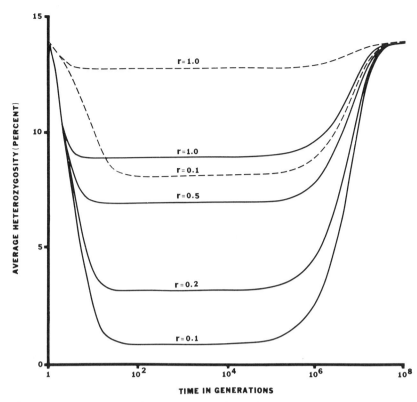

Figure 26. The results of applying a mathematical model showing changes in average heterozygosity per locus when a population of *Drosophila* passes through a bottleneck. The solid lines indicate the case where bottleneck size No=2, and the dashed lines indicate the case where No=10. Population growth is logistic, and r = intrinsic rate of growth. The initial and final heterozygosity is 0.138. Generations are given on a logarithmic scale.

Note that the reduction in average heterozygosity per locus due to a bottleneck depends on bottleneck size and on the rate of population growth after passing through the bottleneck. Loss of alleles reportedly depends mostly on bottleneck size. Note also that once average heterozygosity is reduced, it takes a long time to regain the original level. (From Nei et al. 1975; reprinted by permission of the Society for the Study of Evolution.)

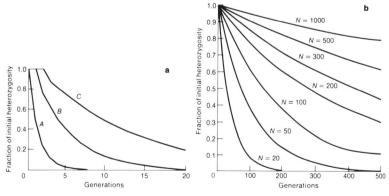

Figure 27. Decrease in heterozygosity due to (a) inbreeding and (b) population size. In the left figure systems of mating include self-fertilization (curve A), sib mating (curve B), and double first-cousin mating (curve C). In the right figure N is the population size. (Left figure from *An Introduction to Population Genetics Theory*, by James F. Crow and Motoo Kimura. ©1970 by James F. Crow and Motoo Kimura. Reprinted by permission of Harper & Row Publishers, Inc. Right figure reprinted with permission of Macmillan Publishing Company from *Genetics*, 3rd edition, by Monroe W. Strickberger. © 1985 by Monroe W. Strickberger. Redrawn figures from Futuyma 1979 with permission of Sinauer Associates, Inc.)

1982; Senner 1980). Ralls and Ballou (1983) cited overwhelming evidence for the deleterious effects of inbreeding in small captive populations, but admitted that conclusive proof may be impossible. Although matings among close relatives in natural populations of birds and mammals are known to be rare, necessary demographic data are lacking to estimate the influence of inbreeding depression in the wild (Ralls et al. 1986). Data allowing calculation of Wright's inbreeding coefficient F in wild populations are extremely meager (e.g., Bulmer 1973; Greenwood et al. 1978). Hence any conclusions are mostly inferred from studies of captive populations. Ralls et al. (1988) estimated the cost of inbreeding in natural populations of mammals using the pedigrees of captive populations. The deleterious consequences of inbreeding in human populations seems accepted (e.g., Stern 1973), and Charlesworth and Charlesworth (1987) concluded that both theory and existing empirical data suggest that inbreeding often affects the growth and survival of progeny.

4   EFFECTIVE POPULATION SIZE

Genetic influences may affect minimum viable population size, on the assumption that genetic variation can become limiting in response to environmental fluctuations or changes. Not all scholars agree (Berry 1971, 1983), but the assumption is here regarded as valid in most cases.

Effective population size N_e is an "ideal" number of individuals whose decrease in genetic variation due to genetic drift equals that of the actual population being studied. Theoretically the "ideal" population reproduces sexually by random mating but with no generation overlap, no migration, no selection, and no mutation. In other words, reproductive heterogeneity reduces N_e, so effective population size is often lower than for the census population N.

N_e is not easy and may even be impossible to calculate in nature (Futuyma 1979) because of difficulties in obtaining the necessary population data, including dispersal distances, effective sex ratio, mating frequency across generations, and variance in reproductive success (Futuyma 1986). Probably all natural populations are "nonideal" and have nonrandom mating (nonpanmictic), overlapping generations, usually unequal numbers of mating males and females, often large population fluctuations, and a nonrandom distribution of offspring in

a statistical (Poisson) sense. For more detail about effective population size, see Kimura and Crow 1963, Kimura and Ohta 1971, Hartl 1981, Futuyma 1986, and Crow and Denniston 1988. One problem causing confusion in the numerous articles attempting to calculate the N_e of wild populations is that the authors do not all use the same formulas (Harris and Allendorf 1989).

Wright's (1931) formula:

$$\text{Equation 5} \qquad \Delta F = 1/2N_e$$

expressed the drop ΔF in heterozygosity per generation in two allele systems. It must make many assumptions that are unrealistic in nature, as previously indicated: no mutation, no natural selection, no immigration, no genetic drift, and others that are assumptions of the Hardy-Weinberg Law of population genetics. Wilcox (1986) thought the ratio of effective to actual population size N_e/N for most natural populations to be 0.25, the ratio Harris and Allendorf (1989) estimated for the grizzly bear.

Small populations can of course be created by dramatic environmental change or natural colonization, either resulting in only a sample of the parent population. Mayr (1942) labeled the genetic context of natural colonizations the "founder principle": propagules starting a new population contain fewer genes than the mother population. Then followed the concept of the "founder effect": genetic alterations in a colonizing population due to chance deviations in the proportions of the genes in propagules from the source population. Mayr (1963) and Templeton (1980) invoked these ideas as a speciation mechanism. Population founding from small inbred samples entails risks but is not always inherently harmful since examples of foundings by single individuals are commonplace in nature (Carson 1983). See Section IXD3.

Franklin (1980) proposed that the drop of a population of some species to 50 individuals may threaten their short-term fitness, in terms of persistence of vigor, fecundity, viability, fertility, and the disease resistance desired by animal breeders. He indicated that other individuals of the species must be introduced immediately to permit gene flow and to limit the potentially harmful effects of inbreeding (for typically outcrossing species) and genetic drift. Franklin further suggested that 500 individuals are needed for long-term fitness in a population to prevent the eventual erosion of genetic variation. But this guideline was derived from Lande's (1976) work on bristle number in *Drosophila,* which Franklin admits is rather inadequate. No one is yet certain of these values.

As Franklin (1980) explained, the recommendation of at least 50 individuals to ensure short-term fitness is based on calculations by animal breeders using Equation 5, showing that fewer than 50 induces a more than 1 percent loss of heterozygosity instead of the 2–3 percent animal breeders usually tolerate. The recommendation of 500 individuals, he said, is based on the assumption that the loss of genetic variation at this size will be balanced by gain through mutation. Seal (1985) maintained that the minimum effective population size to retain genetic diversity of vertebrates in captivity is 250–500.

Bolger et al. (1987) tried to calculate effective population size for the Yellowstone grizzly bear population, assuming Franklin's (1980) 1 percent-effective population size of 50 rule. Taking into account non-Poisson family size distribution and breeding sex ratio, they concluded that the rule is violated when the population drops below 220 individuals. Harris and Allendorf (1989) also found that the calculated N_e for grizzly bears varied widely

when they used the same data in different published formulas. Because data for the formulas are difficult to obtain in the field, they suggested that simulations might yield estimates of the otherwise elusive numbers.

The rough guideline of 50 individuals, based on the work of animal breeders, was recommended for maintenance of short-term fitness to park and other reserve managers, who were told they should begin trying to maximize N_e in small populations in nature reserves, for example, when cropping herds. A population of 500 was suggested for long-term conservation regimes. Both 50 and 500 values are now suspect.

Instead of universal specific numbers such as 50 and 500 for effective population size, Soulé (1985) and Soulé et al. (1986) proposed as a guideline that the captive population should retain 90 percent of the original source (wild) population's genetic variation over 200 years. The number is arbitrary, but the authors intuitively think it distinguishes between a potentially damaging and a tolerable loss of heterozygosity.

V

Extinction Vulnerability

A *Extinction Proneness*

The particular "life-history tactic" developed by a species should evolve to minimize its probability of extinction (Stearns 1976). Although this is a reasonable expectation, the environment is changing too fast for natural selection to keep pace. Soulé (Frankel and Soulé 1981) said that the local extinction question, relevant to most nature reserves in the world because of their modest size, is really: Which species, how many, and how soon? How many and how soon will be addressed under faunal collapse in Section VIID1; which will be discussed here.

Few data decisively shed light on the question of which species are at greatest risk. Factors suggested as correlating with extinction-prone species include large body size, high trophic level, specialized habitat requirements, slow reproduction, limited dispersal ability, and combinations of such factors, for example, in "*K*-selected" species.

Terborgh and Winter (1980) suggested that rarity, like that of many tropical bird species, is the best single overall indicator of vulnerability to extinction. This is widely accepted as sound but has not escaped challenge by conflicting data (Karr 1982a,b). Terborgh and Winter reasonably suggested that rare species will be the first to go extinct in reserves.

Soulé (Frankel and Soulé 1981) predicted that species like birds and mammals, with large body sizes and high trophic demands, will be the first to go locally extinct in reserves. Wilcox (1980) thought, on the basis of some land-bridge island findings (e.g., Case 1975), that poikilothermal vertebrates will persist longer than birds and mammals, and Wright (1981) concurred.

The above correlates of extinction proneness can serve as useful tentative guidance. These and others continue to be proposed, for example, by Bennett (1987) in Section VIIB. Rarity and the prediction that many large homeothermal vertebrates should require a larger home range to meet their energy needs (McNab 1963) are the most solid of the suggested correlates. More work is necessary before "extinction-prone species" (terminology Terborgh 1974) can be more confidently identified.

B   Extinction Linkage

Soulé (Frankel and Soulé 1981) warned that faunal collapse will precipitate chain reactions leading to the loss of other taxa (particularly in the tropics), since some species extinctions may be "linked." His prediction of a chain reaction arose from a demonstration by Paine (1966) of how the loss of a predator in a marine intertidal environment reduced overall community diversity from 15 to 8 invertebrate species. Paine theorized that removal of the predator opened the way to severe competition among certain dominant prey species, causing the disappearance of some. Paine (1969) used the name "keystone" to describe a species that played a key role in determining the presence or absence of many other species in a community. Hence at least some evidence, including some of Paine's later work (e.g., Paine 1974, 1980) indicates that certain faunal extinctions may be "linked." Harper (1969) cites less convincing evidence for a drop in plant species diversity, possibly due to the removal of rabbits.

Terborgh and Winter (1980) asserted that we know next to nothing about the consequences of losing top predators in terrestrial environments and predicted a rush of extinctions following the loss of any key species. Raven (1976) predicted that the loss of one tropical plant species could bring about the demise of 10 to 30 animal species. According to Erwin (1983), since hundreds of insect species may be restricted to one host canopy tree species in tropical forests, we might infer that the loss of a host tree could precipitate mass insect extinctions.

L. E. Gilbert (1980) elaborated on Futuyma's (1973) prediction of linked extinctions in describing "mobile links" and "keystone mutualists" in the Neotropics, emphasizing the complexity of animal, plant, and insect interactions. Mobile links are animals needed by some plants for dispersal and reproduction. Keystone mutualists are plants that support mobile links. Howe (1984) suggested management methods for tropical reserves to reduce extinctions when "pivotal" plant species are rare or confined to special habitats.

Therefore Soulé's prediction that large mammal extinctions, for whatever reason, could result in the extinction of many more species warrants further consideration. Such interactions are presently very dimly understood. The theory has also been introduced to explain the large mammal extinctions during the Pleistocene (Owen-Smith 1987).

C   Differential Extinctions

The degree to which extinction is selective remains controversial. Diamond (1984b) reviewed a wide range of evidence, some of it questionable (Boecklen and Simberloff 1986). Some fossil evidence from mammals in Pleistocene relict communities supports the occurrence of selective extinctions (Hope 1973; Heaney 1984; Patterson 1984; Grayson 1987; see Sections VIIC,E).

An elaborate theory based on the expectation and interpretation of differential extinction is frequently encountered (see Soulé et al. 1988), but good evidence is weak. However, the principle seems intuitively logical and should be considered in nature reserve design.

VI

Habitat Size and Species Loss

A Introduction

There is a widespread belief that isolation or inadequate size of habitat may lead to loss of species (see Section XIIIA). Here we will examine some of the most pertinent real data. Concerns surrounding such findings will be largely postponed until Chapter VII.

B Forest Habitat Fragmentation

1 U.S. FOREST BIRDS

Lynch and Whitcomb (1978) documented a decline of bird species in isolated or semi-isolated forest patches over short time periods for a number of sites in some states in the Eastern Deciduous Forest. They indicated that species disappear faster in smaller forest tracts and Neotropical migrants that usually reside in the forest interior disappear fastest. Robbins (1979) called such species "area-sensitive."

Whitcomb et al. (1981) found that bird species composition depended on isolation as well as size in the forest patches they studied, as did Butcher et al. (1981) in another site. Whitcomb et al. (1981) identified 15 species that were restricted to forest interiors but seemed to be absent from forest tracts smaller than 0.7 km². Eleven of the 15 were Neotropical migrants. Whitcomb (1977) and Whitcomb et al. (1977), on the basis of four Maryland forest plot censuses, concluded that forest fragments of at least 0.14 km² will permit most forest interior bird species to breed if the tract is subsidized by a nearby larger forest fragment. Lynch (1987) summarized the eastern North American forest fragmentation studies on birds.

2 BRAZILIAN FOREST BIRDS

Willis (1979) studied birds in three forest tracts on the São Paulo plateau in southeastern Brazil on which once unbroken forest is now fragmented into small forest islands. The areas of the tracts he studied

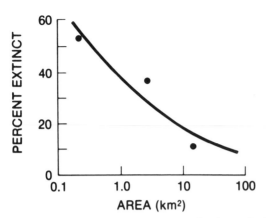

Figure 28. Percentage of apparent extinctions during roughly the last century, based on "presumed" initial bird species composition in three Brazilian forest tracts in the State of São Paulo. It is not known when the forest tracts became isolated from the formerly continuous forest, though it could have been as recently as a few decades ago. Note that all three tracts seem to have lost species, the smallest at the quickest rate. (From Terborgh and Winter 1980, based on data of Willis 1979; reprinted by permission of Sinauer Associates, Inc.)

during 1975–78 were 14.0, 6.2, and 2.5 km² harboring 175, 119, and 76 breeding birds, respectively. Of the original 203 species, when the forest was continuous, he thought the largest tract had lost 28, the medium tract 84, and the smallest 127. The largest tract contained almost all the species of the medium tract, and the medium tract contained almost all the species of the smallest tract. He thought that the three forest plots had lost the bird species in a particular sequence (Fig. 28) and that large-bodied and sedentary species had a higher rate of extinction.

3   ECUADORIAN FOREST BIRDS

Leck (1979) studied a 0.87-km² forest patch known as Río Palenque Field Station, isolated when surrounding forest was cleared for agriculture. It was a national forest, located on the west side of the Ecuadorian Andes and well studied by ornithologists. He noted a loss of 44 bird species of an estimated 170 original total in a period of 6 years, 1973–78.

This study was unusual in documenting such a rapid change in the number of bird species. Nine of the lost species were large-bodied, five were rare; several mammals also were lost. Isolation reportedly has accelerated greatly since 1970, but presumably began before the first biotic inventory.

4   BEYOND AREA PER SE

Some habitat fragmentation studies have not shown area alone to be the primary determinant of bird species abundance. For wooded sites in Great Britain, Helliwell (1976a) concluded that the size of a forest patch and its isolation had no influence on its bird fauna. Lynch and Whigham (1984) found the local abundance of some bird species in Maryland significantly influenced by habitat size and isolation, but a larger number were very dependent on habitat physiognomy and floristics rather than on forest geometry alone. Ambuel and Temple (1983) suggested that forest-edge and farmland bird species exclude certain forest-dwelling, long-distance migrants from small woodlots, and the exclusion is more important to the bird community than are area-dependent changes in habitat or the degree of woodlot isolation. Freemark and Merriam (1986) examined 21 forest fragments with areas from 3 to 7,620 ha in an agricultural landscape near Ottawa, Canada, and found that larger forests were beneficial for forest-interior and resident species, while habitat heterogeneity was more important for edge-related species. They concluded that regional conservation strategies should maximize both size and habitat heterogeneity. Loyn (1987) and Bennett (1987) reported that forest area, habitat diversity, and disturbance were all closely correlated with bird and mammal species number. Kitchener et al. (1980a,b, 1982) also found correlations between abundance and other variables besides area (Section VIIB). However, Opdam, van Dorp, and ter Braak (1984), using multiple regression analysis on data from 36 Netherlands woodlots, most smaller than 50 ha, demonstrated that bird species numbers were significantly affected not only by habitat island size but by the acreage of nearby forest and the distance to an extensive forest tract. Opdam et al. (1985) found that isolation affected only the number of bird species restricted to mature woods in the Netherlands.

C Barro Colorado Island, Panama

The creation of the Panama Canal and Lake Gatun, by damming the Chagras River, changed many former hilltops into islands within the lake. The best studied island is Barro Colorado.

Willis (1974) discovered that 45 of the original 209 breeding forest bird species on Barro Colorado disappeared during 1923–1971. Karr (1982a) said the number missing was 50–60. Since the study of the island did not begin until after flooding, the original number of species may have been greater.

Willis (1974) also indicated that birds inhabiting second-growth forest probably were lost due to forest maturation, and with some contribution by predation and heavy or scarce rainfall. Nevertheless, he felt that the loss was an area effect and documented the consequence of isolating a park or nature reserve from nearby vegetation. Karr (1982a) agreed that the loss of bird species on Barro Colorado was far too complex to be a simple function only of island size.

Willis (1974) pointed out that 32 of the lost bird species were second-growth inhabitants, but 13 had inhabited the mature forest. The implication is that succession cannot explain the disappearance of the 13, and perhaps area and other factors were involved. Morton (1978, 1985) followed up on a suggestion by Willis (1974) and reintroduced extirpated species to try to separate the effects of succession and of area, but the sample was too small to permit confident conclusions.

The reason for the decline of bird species on Barro Colorado Island remains unclear, for example, whether it was an area effect. Willis (1974) said that "possibly the true causes of the decline of the ocellated antbird have not and will never be understood." See also Wilson and Willis (1975), Willis and Eisenmann (1979), and Karr (1982b). Inferred correlates of rarity, like large body size, high trophic level, or high metabolic level, were not consistently observed (Section VA).

D Pleistocene Land-Bridge Islands

Land-bridge island studies were extensions of the theory of island biogeography, invoking equilibrium and the species-area relationship. The effect of habitat size was determined by using observational data, since the required scale and time prohibited performing the proper experiment. Papers describing "relaxation" experiments performed by nature, the reduction of species number to a new level by the flooding of Pleistocene land bridges, include Diamond 1972, 1973, 1975b, 1976b; Terborgh 1974, 1975; Case 1975; Wilcox 1978; Faaborg 1979; Soulé et al. 1979; Terborgh and Winter 1980; Heaney and Patterson 1986. The authors argued that after isolation from continental land masses by rising ocean waters, the islands became "supersaturated" with species, which then gradually diminished (relaxed) toward a lower species number. Relaxation was viewed generally in terms of thousands of years, but could be only hundreds of years or less for extremely small islands. Many tropical birds are capable of flight but refuse to cross water gaps (Diamond 1976b) and so, like nonflying mammals, are suitable subjects for a study of differential extinction.

1 PACIFIC BIRDS

Diamond (1972) noticed that the large New Guinea land-bridge islands have about twice as many lowland bird species as do oceanic islands of equal area and distance from New Guinea but far fewer than do tracts of equal size on the New Guinea mainland (Fig. 29). Also, 134 New Guinea lowland bird species were unable to cross water gaps and resided only on land-bridge islands. Bird species number fell sharply with decreasing island size. Diamond proposed that excess species have gone extinct, due to insufficient island size, since their Pleistocene land bridges were severed by rising ocean waters. Diamond (1973, 1975b, 1976b) also described this study.

Similarly, Diamond and Mayr (1976), Diamond and May (1977), and Diamond (1983) concluded that many islands in the Solomon Archipelago were joined during the Pleistocene into one single island, called Greater Bukida, that was fragmented as sea level rose. They noted that the number of relict bird populations increased greatly with increased island

Species/area relation for New Guinea region

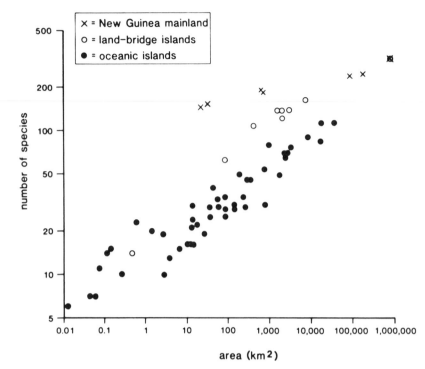

Figure 29. Species-area relationships for bird species on oceanic islands and land-bridge islands in the New Guinea region and for sites of various sizes on the New Guinea mainland. The land-bridge islands have fewer species than equal-sized areas on the New Guinea mainland. Diamond (1972) theorized that the land-bridge islands lost species since the end of the Pleistocene due to insufficient size. Other authors have subsequently adopted this explanation for work that followed. However, Simberloff and Abele (1976b) did not accept this "relaxation" explanation of species loss on land-bridge islands. Boecklen and Simberloff (1986) impugned many such subsequent explanations of land-bridge island relaxation. (From Diamond 1984b; reprinted by permission of The University of Chicago Press. ©1984; modified from Diamond 1972; reprinted by permission of the author.)

size, and no relict population had survived on islands smaller than 5 km². This corroborated the New Guinea islands conclusion that extinction is more probable on small islands, presumably because of small population size.

2   GULF OF CALIFORNIA LIZARDS

Soulé and Sloan (1966) published data on supersaturated lizard faunas on islands in the Gulf of California. Case (1975) added to the data, also not-

ing that relaxation depended on island size and relaxation time was longer for lizards than for mammals.

Wilcox (1978) thought that the land bridges of the Gulf of California islands were truncated 6,000–12,000 years ago. After taking into account fluctuations in species number due to area and latitude, he found that extinction on the islands increased with time since land-bridge truncation. From comparisons with extinctions of lizards and birds on Pleistocene land-bridge islands in the New World, he concluded that birds go extinct ten times faster than lizards on islands of the same size.

3 SUNDA ISLANDS MAMMALS

During the Pleistocene the Sunda Shelf, roughly between Thailand and Australia, was part of the mainland of Asia, and a rising sea level fragmented it into the present array of islands (Fig. 30). The smaller the island, the less its mammalian fauna resemble the fauna on a mainland area of equal size. Soulé et al. (1979) and Wilcox (1980) concluded that more extinctions occurred on smaller than on larger islands. Fossil evidence supported this claim for 10 large mammals, which today persist on the three largest islands: Borneo, Sumatra, and Java. Heaney (1984) largely confirmed their conclusion of area-dependent post-Pleistocene extinction of mammals on these islands. Hope (1973) also studied mammals on land-bridge islands—Tasmania and the Bass Island Straits—with supportive fossil evidence and similar conclusions.

4 OTHER STUDIES

Terborgh (1974, 1975) studied tropical birds on oceanic and land-bridge islands in the Caribbean and also concluded they exhibited differential extinction. Terborgh and Winter's (1980) examination of data on bird faunas from five land-bridge islands around the world found corroboration of their view that relaxation was more pronounced on land-bridge islands than on mainland tracts of similar size. Faaborg (1979) reviewed the literature on avian extinction on Neotropical land-bridge islands and offered conservation guidelines. MacArthur et al. (1972) studied Neotropical birds on islands in Panama. Diamond and Gilpin (1983) studied birds on the Greater Sunda Islands. All concluded that smaller islands lost species faster and had lost more of them than larger islands.

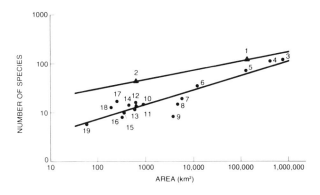

Figure 30. Figure 30 shows the Sunda Islands and the extent of dry land of the Sunda Shelf during the Pleistocene. The dashed line is the 100-fathom contour today and is believed to approximate the coastline of 18,000 years ago. The graph illustrates species-area relations for the land mammals (excluding bats) of the Malaysian mainland (upper curve) and Sunda Islands (lower curve). The upper curve ($S = 15.4A^{0.17}$) is presumed to approximate the species-area relation of the Sunda Shelf prior to fragmentation by the rising sea level at the close of the Pleistocene. The lower curve ($S = 1.8A^{0.30}$ by linear regression) differs, they explain, as a result of fragmentation and collapse of isolated faunas. Key: (1) Malay Peninsula, (2) Krau Game Reserve, Pehang, Western Malaysia, (3) Borneo, (4) Sumatra, (5) Java, (6) Banka, (7) Bali, (8) Billiton, (9) Siberut, (10) S. Pagi, (11) North Pagi, (12) Sipora, (13) Singapore, (14) Tanabala, (15) Tanamasa, (16) Pini, (17) Penang, (18) Tuangku, (19) Bangkaru. (From Wilcox 1980; reprinted by permission of Sinauer Associates, Inc.)

E   Natural Extinctions vs. Human Influences

How much have human activities accelerated extinction rates? Morgan and Woods (1986) estimated a loss of 37 species of nonvolant mammals in the West Indies since humans arrived 4,500 years ago, equivalent to an extinction rate of one species every 122 years. These last extinctions were more likely due to persecution than relaxation. Olson and James (1982) suggested that about 50 percent of the native endemic Hawaiian bird species went extinct while the Polynesians were there. Atkinson (1989) claimed that 90 percent of post-1600 extinctions of birds, reptiles and amphibians and almost half the extinctions of mammals occurred on islands. Brown (1986) cautioned against assuming that any island settled or affected by humans can reflect the natural processes of origination, extinction, or equilibrium. Indeed, this is the core of the problem of trying to apply the equilibrium model to nature reserves. Blondel (1987) argued that insular patterns of mammal communities on Mediterranean islands cannot be explained by island biogeography theory because the present species have been introduced by man in the last 8,000 years. However, Richman et al. (1988) concluded, from a study of the land-bridge faunas of South Australia and Baja, California, that little evidence there indicated large-scale environmental alteration by man since the end of the Pleistocene, and the cause of extinctions is more reasonably explained by natural background extinction rates due to area effects.

F   Pleistocene Mountain Refugia

J. H. Brown (1971, 1978), in studying 17 mountain ranges in the Great Basin (Fig. 31), thought that the montane mammals on these isolated mountain "islands" originated in the Sierra Nevadas to the west and the Rocky Mountains to the east. However, mammalian species number did not correlate with distance between islands, distance from island to mainland, or elevation of high mountain passes, in contrast to what the equilibrium aspect of the theory of island biogeography would predict. He therefore concluded they must be true relicts and not the result of immigration-extinction equilibria.[3] A comparison of species-area regressions between the Great Basin mountain "islands" and areas of "equivalent" size in the Sierra Nevadas or Rocky Mountains suggested species loss from the mountaintops. Smaller mountain islands appeared to have lost more species than larger ones. Grayson (1987) furnished supportive archaeological and paleontological evidence, and Patterson (1984) reached similar conclusions for 28 ranges in the southern Rocky Mountains. The smallest mountains appeared to exhibit preferential extinction of populations of carnivores, large mammals, and habitat specialists.

G   Pleistocene Forest Refugia

Pleistocene refugia theory suggests that forests shrank during periods of local aridity (Fig. 32). Some authors claim that the Pleistocene refugia, including both tropical forest remnants (Prance 1982) and Chapman (1983) and vast expanses of boreal taiga (Hoffmann 1981), also are governed by island biogeography theory principles. But the focus of attention has been on the relationship between speciation rates and the hypothesized shrinkage of forest into forest islands during Pleistocene dry periods, not on the potential loss of species.

Lovejoy (1979) described the use of the Pleistocene refugia theory in selecting reserves, for example, in Amazonia (Wetterburg et al. 1981). The theory is controversial (Raup 1988), as is the use of centers of endemism as a conservation tool for locating reserves in Amazonia (Gentry 1986), but the Pleistocene refugia concept has been reviewed favorably (Simpson and Haffer 1978). The idea has been invoked to explain more than gradual forest shrinkage due to climatic change. For example, King and Saunders (1984) theorized that catastrophic disruption of habitat resulted in floristic insularity, causing the American mastodon extinctions during the Pleistocene.

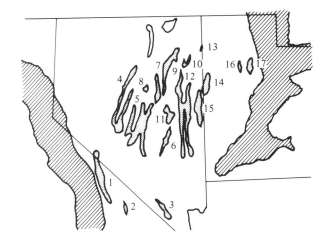

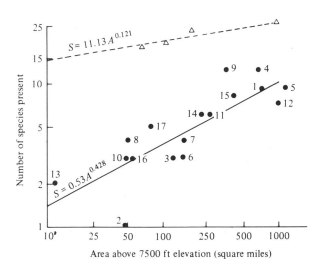

Figure 31. The illustration (top) shows the 17 mountain ranges in the Great Basin (stippled) between the Sierra Nevada (hatched on left) and Rocky Mountains (hatched on right). These mountain ranges, mostly higher than 3,000 m, are Pleistocene islands surrounded by sagebrush desert. It is believed that these desert valleys are complete barriers to dispersing small mammals. The Sierra Nevada and Rocky Mountains are viewed as the source areas, or "mainlands," for Pleistocene relict fauna. In the graph above, the lower plot (dots) illustrates the number of mammal species in the mountain area above 2,300 m for each of the mountain ranges. The upper plot (triangles) illustrates the same data for four sites in the Sierra Nevada. The differences in the slopes and intercepts of the regression lines have been interpreted to mean that the 17 mountain ranges have lost species, presumably due to their isolation and size. (From Brown 1971; reprinted by permission of The University of Chicago Press. ©1971.)

Figure 32. Pleistocene forest refugia in South America, proposed by Prance (1981) because they are now centers of endemism for woody angiosperm families. Additional centers of endemism have been proposed for birds, lizards, and butterflies by other workers. The hypothesis is that during glacial periods the Amazon Basin was grassland or savanna habitat, the tropical rain forest shrank to these isolated patches, and these refugia were centers of speciation. (Reproduced by permission from Brown, James H., and Gibson, Arthur C.: *Biogeography*, St. Louis, 1983, The C.V. Mosby Company. After Prance, Ghillean T. *Vicariance Biogeography: A Critique.* ©1981 Columbia University Press, New York. Used by permission.)

H   *National Parks*

We know of local species extinctions in some national parks since the parks were established. Weisbrod (1979) questioned whether 13 mammalian extinctions in Mount Rainier National Park, Washington, over the last 60 years were a function of reserve size and insularity or the result of regional land management practices. Harris (1984) cited these data in an overall discussion that stressed the importance of area and isolation on extinctions, but area may or may not be causally related.

Miller (1976) thought that Everglades National Park, Florida, (Fig. 5) was already somewhat functionally isolated. Although the factors influencing the species-area equation were hard to define, he noted that a continued decline of certain mammal species in the park was at least consistent with (not necessarily a direct result of) the hypothesis of decline due to progressive isolation. R. I. Miller (1978) indicated that the 4 mammalian extinctions in Mkomazi Game Reserve, Kenya-Tanzania, over the past 25 years, were consistent with the isolation model, though specific causes could be loss of permanent water, cattle grazing, and illicit hunting. In other words, he reasoned that isolation may not directly cause extirpations but produce adverse conditions that do. He calculated that the reserve would be a condition of island equilibrium in 300 years. Seidensticker (1987) attributed the extirpation of tigers from small (under 500 km²) habitat blocks and reserves in Bali and Java to extensive habitat fragmentation and insularization, the loss of important prey species due to disease, and killing by man.

The contribution of inadequate area to the demise or extinction of any animal species, if any, in a U.S. national park is unclear. Newmark (1986, 1987) found a significant correlation between mammalian extinctions in western North American national parks and park size; smaller parks had more extinctions. Although the report of extinctions in these parks is alarming, the culpability of area cannot be conclusively demonstrated. Area may have been directly responsible, had some influence, or conceivably played no part. Unfortunately, a popular interpretation of this research held that almost all western North American national parks are too small to sustain all their mammalian fauna, presumably because of "faunal collapse" claimed to be documented (Bloch 1987). The concept of faunal collapse introduced by Soulé et al. (1979) attributed the loss of large mammals to insufficient area alone (see Section VIID1), with no human interference (i.e., benign neglect). Whether the fauna did collapse in this sense solely because of inadequate area will likely never be known with any certainty.

More research is needed, but the lack or inaccessibility of data and the difficulty in demonstrating causality are frustrating. One problem is the paucity of historical faunal records for U.S. national parks. Data documenting the existence of species in newly established parks are often not available and when they are usually relate only to charismatic large mammals. Reanalysis of the data of Newmark (1986, 1987) revealed that such reported extinctions were highly exaggerated (Quinn et al. in press). For instance, Newmark (1987) listed 37 natural postestablishment extinctions of large mammals in 12 western U.S. parks or park assemblages. Nine of these vanished groups have been acceptably reintroduced, and at least 22 others have been reliably sighted by park staff the past 5–10 years in the parks and adjacent national forests. Quinn et al. (in press) concluded that the updated data show only a weak or nonexistent relationship between park size and extinction rates, and no minimum park size below which mammals rapidly become extinct. They indicated that the data at least do not preclude an important role for small-to-moderate-sized reserves in conserving mammals, nor do they support the land-bridge island comparison.

The best population abundance data for large mammals I am aware of in the U.S. National Park System is for moose and wolves in Isle Royale National Park, Michigan (Mech 1966). Although data gathering started in 1958, statistically reliable information dates to 1969, thus spanning only 21 years. Also, the "present" status of fauna in U.S. parks, needed for comparison, is often imperfectly known.

This is part of the larger need for comprehensive park resource inventories, whose inadequacy was recognized early (Adams 1925), and for better U.S. nationwide (Tangley 1985; Kim and Knutson 1986) and worldwide inventories (Wilson 1985a). The most basic type of biotic monitoring should answer the question: Does the species still exist in the park and/or closely adjacent to its boundaries?

Figure 33. Aerial photograph of two isolated rain forest patches 80 km north of Manaus, Brazil, and part of the Minimum Critical Size of Ecosystems Project. A 10-ha forest patch at the lower left was isolated August 1983. The cleared band around this forest patch is only 100 m on three sides, though other 10-ha patches have wider clearings. A 1-ha forest patch can be seen in the center surrounded by a wider expanse of cleared forest. (Photo by Robert Bierregaard, provided courtesy of Thomas E. Lovejoy.)

I A Brazilian Experiment

The largest "pre-isolation" experiment ever conducted is ongoing in the Amazon Basin near Manaus, Brazil (Lovejoy, pers. com.), under the direction of the U.S. World Wildlife Fund and in cooperation with Brazil's Instituto Nacional de Pesquisas da Amazonia (INPA) and the Brazilian government (Fig. 33). Other similar experiments are needed in biomes outside of tropical forests (Lovejoy 1980). Lovejoy (in Lewin 1984) wanted to see a similar project in every habitat type in the world.

Lovejoy et al. (1983) found that one 10-ha forest patch lost seven species of large mammals. Lovejoy et al. (1984) indicated that the results for birds, based on the isolation of one 1-ha and one 10-ha forest patch, reflected edge rather than area effects. Lovejoy et al. (1986) presented impressive data for both edge and area effects for both birds and mammals. Lovejoy (1987) reported that patches of all sizes (1, 10, 100 ha) lost understory bird species, but thought attention must turn to 100-ha reserves to study area-related effects. Certain results have caused some field researchers (Zimmerman and Bierregaard 1986) to question the predictive ability of island biogeography theory and the associated species-area relationship and to suggest that autecological data of individual species may be more valuable.

As additional information accumulates from this important experimental undertaking, the question remains as to the applicability of the data to biomes outside of tropical forests. Few other experiments are even remotely similar (e.g., Harris 1984). Such experiments demand a great amount of time to monitor possible faunal species changes in large habitat patches, and the urgency created by present landscape destruction does not permit the luxury of time. The urge to design long-term experiments elicits a lukewarm response when our pressing need is for immediate information. We may have to confine our endeavors to small habitat patches and attempt to extrapolate from them, as Lovejoy et al. (1986) sought to do from the smallest of their patches. Ehrlich and Ehrlich (1981) thought that an ideal experiment, even just for butterflies, was clearly impossible in the past, presumably because of the required experimental scale and time. Even had some experiment been designed and begun hundreds of years ago, could it have been maintained undisturbed? Diamond (1986) and Wiens (1986) discussed such experimental design and spatial and temporal scale problems in ecological research.

J Species Gain and Invasion

Lovejoy et al. (1984) observed an influx of species into their forest patches immediately after isolation. This may have been a short-term phenomenon associated with the creation of an edge, and not an area or distance effect. Nevertheless, it raised the question of whether habitat islands could gain species other than by turnover. Mader (1984) found the species/individuals ratio for mice and carabid beetles highest in small isolates, in contrast to island biogeography theory predictions, and thought it was due to the incoming of individuals from surrounding agricultural areas.

A related question is whether a habitat island can be invaded by species to an extent that might alter the original species composition. MacArthur and Wilson (1967) suggested that species on habitat islands face constant pressure by immigration of less well-adapted species from surrounding habitats. Terborgh (1974) concurred that levels of competition may be high within habitat islands because barriers to immigration are less than on true islands, though MacArthur and Wilson (1967) thought that colonization could be harder to establish because of the diversity of competitors. Stamps and Buechner (1985) found a link between intruder pressure and territory size and overlap, population density and growth rate, and reproductive success that also might apply to reserves. Janzen (1983) suggested it might be better in some circumstances to surround a small patch of forest with species-poor vegetation containing noninvasive species (grain fields, cropped pastures, cotton fields, etc.) than to surround it with land undergoing secondary succession and full of plants and animals that will invade the pristine forest or reserve. He thought smaller tracts face more invasion.

Such potential invaders could be "exotics." For an indication of how severe this problem is in both island and continental nature reserves, see Duffey (1988). The question remains as to whether progressive isolation of nature reserves encourages invasion—a possibility suggested by Slatyer (1975). Loope's (in press) estimates of the proportions of alien plants among the vascular flora of selected U.S. national parks ranged from 6–9 percent at Sequoia-Kings Canyon (a continental park) to 64 percent at Hawaii Volcanoes (an island park). His data supported the idea that real islands are suffering more than mainland parks from exotic species, but mainland parks are not yet isolated. Usher (1988) reviewed case studies for 24 nature reserves containing introduced plants and vertebrates and concluded that arid lands and Mediterranean-type reserves showed no relationship between the number of introduced species and reserve size. Loope et al. (1988) suggested that nature reserves on islands, with all their endemic biota, may prove to be less difficult to protect and manage than many fragmented continental reserves. We are still learning which communities are most easily invaded (Mooney and Drake 1986) but already know that exotics can have a devastating impact.

Note

3The author described this study as "non-equilibrium" island biogeography because there presumably was no colonization. Some Pleistocene land-bridge island studies might also be so categorized.

VII

Nature Reserve Size: The Application
of Theory and Data

A Introduction

How big should reserves be? This is a simple and straightforward question that carries great weight. In discussing the minimum area needed to retain natural diversity, Wilson (1984) said that "no process being addressed by modern science is more complicated or, in my opinion, more important."

Most authors preferred large areas, but recommended dimensions vary. Some specific estimates were based on data from terrestrial habitat fragmentation and Pleistocene refugia, estimated minimum viable population sizes or effective population sizes, and autecological needs of individual species. Here we will examine recommendations generated by various approaches and cite critiques or contrasting conclusions. The SLOSS debate will be ignored until Chapter IX.

B Habitat Fragmentation Extrapolations

On the basis of studies of birds in British woodlots, Moore and Hooper (1975) recommended that reserves be 100 ha or larger. Whitcomb (1977), Whitcomb et al. (1977), and Whitcomb et al. (1981) concluded that thousands of contiguous acres may be required to assure the long-term survival of forest-interior bird species. Whitcomb (1987) repeated this recommendation for both birds and mammals of North American forest and grassland biomes. For the tropics, Leck (1979) did not think that rain forest reserves smaller than 25–30 km² would be successful for tropical birds and that areas larger than 100 km² often would be needed. Wilson (1988) crudely summarized these woodland bird studies: When habitat patches range from 1–25 km² (the size of many smaller parks and nature reserves), the extinction rate in the first 100-year period will be 10–50 percent.

Studies of small remnant forest patches began after patches were isolated, for example, in Wisconsin (Bond 1957), Great Britain (Moore and Hooper 1975), and New Jersey (Forman et al. 1976; Galli et al. 1976). This reduces confidence in the results, because initial species composition was typically uncertain. For example, Willis (1979, 1980) inferred species loss from forest fragments by comparing their species compositions with those in tracts of the same size in larger continuous forests.

The exact reasons underlying such observed bird extinctions, if they are true extinctions, remain unclear and relate to the question of proximate versus ultimate causes of extinction (Simberloff 1986c). Influences outside these small forest tracts, and not just area per se, remain suspect. Some proximate factors may generate ultimate forces or causes, but this does not appear to be the original conception of "area-effects." Habitat quality and diversity are factors often not considered. Evidence for area-dependent and distance-dependent extinction rates remain slim (Opdam, Rijsdijk, and Hustings 1985), which is in part a reflection of the experimental difficulty in accounting for so many variables, some intercorrelated. Even if we accept these studies as evidence for a relationship between local extinctions of bird species and habitat island size, they often tell us nothing about the "rate" of loss. Leck (1979) and some other studies may be exceptions, and Lovejoy et al. (1986) and Lovejoy (1987) definitely demonstrated species changes in forest fragments but for very small tracts (1 and 10 ha).

Lynch (1987) concluded that "in attempting to determine the optimal size and spatial arrangement of forest reserves for bird conservation, the absolute geometric scale of potential reserves, the functional 'grain' of the regional habitat mosaic, and the degree of ecological specialization of the bird species to be conserved, and their dispersal must all be considered." Kitchener et al. (1980b) found that mammal species number in 23 nature reserves in the western Australian wheatbelt correlated most highly with reserve area. The correlation increased only slightly when adjacent land was considered, and slightly when adjacent land was considered, and

species did not tend to become fewer with more recent clearing for reserves in regions cleared in 1905, 1920, and 1950. Kitchener et al. (1982) found no correlation of numbers of bird species in the reserves with isolation from adjacent land, either spatially or based on time since clearing, but rather with reserve area and certain habitat variables. Whether bird species had become extinct in this region was difficult to document. Kitchener et al. (1980a) found lizard species number in these reserves related not to adjacent uncleared land, either in space or in time, but to habitat in the reserves. The inclusion of reserve area or other variables did not affect the correlation. Lizard species in the wheatbelt have suffered few extinctions. Kitchener et al. (1980b) then speculated that the primary factor responsible for the many mammal extinctions in the wheatbelt during the last century was changes in the pattern of fires (burning can reduce the intervening matrix to the same seral stage) that diminished the traversibility of distances between habitat patches. The authors indicated that factors other than land clearing, such as browsing and grazing by introduced livestock and rabbits, predation by the exotic feral cat and the fox, disease, and hunting, could have contributed to mammalian extinctions. For more about this study, see Section VIIF.

Bennett (1987) also studied mammals in fragmented forests of Australia. He found mammal species number highly correlated with forest size, habitat diversity, and disturbance due to livestock, but could not distinguish the variance in species number due to area and habitat diversity. Spatial isolation did not significantly influence species numbers, but temporal isolation did. Correlates of survival were small body size, restricted home range, extensive range overlap, stable population structure, dispersal of both large and small individuals and a continuous pattern of reproduction (Chapter V).

C Pleistocene Land-Bridge Island Extrapolations

Terborgh and Winter (1980) thought that land-bridge island studies indicate that extinction rate is inversely proportional to area, so what happens on large land-bridge islands over centuries could happen on small islands, or possibly small continental habitat islands, within decades. We will look at some findings.

Diamond (1972) reported that land-bridge islands 7,770 km² in area have lost 51 percent of their species and 145-km² islands have lost 92 percent. Land-bridge islands smaller than 250 km² in the New Guinea shelf region had about the same number of species as oceanic islands of similar size (Diamond 1975b), the implication being that the land-bridge islands have lost their excess species since their land connections were severed about 10,000 years ago. Diamond then inferred that tropical forest birds on land-bridge islands need a minimum reserve size of 250 km².

Terborgh (1974) calculated in Caribbean studies approximately the same result as Diamond (1975b); land-bridge islands smaller than 250 km² were indistinguishable from oceanic islands of similar size in terms of numbers of bird species. Terborgh (1975) concluded that parks of 2,590 km² will be needed to reduce projected extinction rates for tropical birds to less than 1 percent per century, though he questioned whether this area is sufficient for large predators. Terborgh (1976) later said his data demonstrate that a 250-km² land-bridge island is estimated to lose 4 percent of its tropical bird species in the first century, while a 5,000-km² one will lose only 0.5 percent. Terborgh's (1975) estimate of 2,590 km² for tropical birds, incidentally, provided an official recommended park size guideline (plus a 10-km-wide buffer strip, which doubled the area) for countries in the Amazon-Orinoco region of South America (Wetterburg et al. 1976; Jorge Padua and Bernardes Quintão 1982). It is now uncertain whether the bird extinctions perceived by Terborgh were real (Boecklen and Simberloff 1986). Establishment of the guidelines was nevertheless a positive conservation action despite its now questionable basis.

Simberloff and Abele (1976b) did not accept Terborgh's and Diamond's land-bridge island conclusions for several reasons: they required the assumption that the islands once had the same species complements as areas of comparable size on the mainland; habitat differences were not quantified; and wide variation was possible in determining the best fit of data on species-area plots. Abele and Connor (1979) supported this opposing view and claimed that Diamond's data did not indicate that New Guinea land-bridge islands were supersaturated and Terborgh's data did not indicate that extinction rates vary inversely with land-bridge island size in the Caribbean. Some land-bridge studies (e.g., Wilcox 1978) published subsequent to these critiques have been similarly impugned (Faeth and Connor 1979), questions being raised about whether the extinctions actually occurred.

Biogeographical inferences about island species composition based only on historically known taxa may be incorrect (Olson and James 1982). Although documentation of "prior presence" is weak, direct fossil evidence has been invoked to corroborate several mammal studies from which the inference may be drawn that species loss as a function of island area is selective in Pleistocene relict communities (Hope 1973; Patterson 1984; Grayson 1987), and Diamond (1984b) added supporting evidence from bird studies. Patterson and Atmar (1986) and Patterson (1987) advanced their nested-subset hypothesis, which argued that biotas remaining from Pleistocene land-bridge islands or mountaintops are not random samples but the remains of selective extinction. Diamond (1984b) thought that fossil evidence does not significantly alter conclusions that would be drawn without it by inference from mainland tracts.

Graves and Gotelli (1983) demonstrated that the habitat and mainland geographic range of a species are important factors in determining bird species composition on land-bridge islands. Boecklen and Gotelli (1984) warned against relying solely on area in interpreting species-area regressions derived from land-bridge island studies. Lawlor (1986) pointed out the dangers in using z values and explained that only comparative studies of faunas with the same source pool have much meaning. He showed that species-area curves in different parts of the world vary according to size and taxonomic and ecological composition of the source pool, age of the islands, island location relative to the mainland, and differences in environmental diversity of the islands.

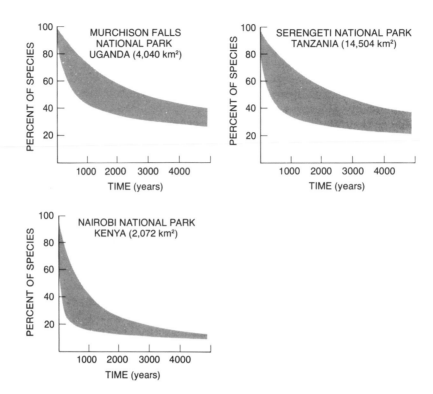

Figure 34. Soulé et al. (1979) faunal collapse trajectories for large mammals in three East African national parks derived in part from data presented in Figure 30. The shaded area indicates the range that bounds the probable trajectory. Such projections have been impugned (Boecklen and Gotelli 1984; Boecklen and Simberloff 1986). (From Wilcox 1980; reproduced by permission of Sinauer Associates, Inc.)

D   *Mammalian Species Number and Reserve Size*

1   MAMMALIAN FAUNAL COLLAPSE PROJECTIONS

Soulé et al. (1979) extrapolated from mammal data on land-bridge islands of the Malay Peninsula (Fig. 30), described in Section VID3, to large mammal faunas existing in East African reserves (Fig. 34). They calculated that after complete "isolation" the "smaller" African reserves will "collapse" and lose 23 percent of their mammal species in 50 years, 65 percent in 500 years, and 88 percent in 5,000 years. They predicted that "larger" reserves will lose 6 percent, 34 percent, and 75 percent, respectively, over the same periods. They thought this will occur even

in the unlikely case of "benign neglect": noninterference by humans. Humans are, of course, tremendously accelerating the extinction process worldwide. The authors did indicate that their "specific" predictions cannot be taken too seriously because habitat diversity and primary productivity differences in reserves are also factors to be considered.

Boecklen and Gotelli (1984) did not accept the predictions of Soulé et al. (1979) and pointed out that the 95 percent simultaneous prediction interval for the small (114 km²) Nairobi National Park spans 10 orders of magnitude! This means that the reserve will lose from 0.5 percent to 99.5 percent of its species in 5,000 years at a 95 percent confidence level. In fact, the faunal collapse models shown in Fig. 34 typically estimate with a 95 percent level of confidence that 0.2 percent–100 percent of the original species will be lost within 5,000 years after insularization (Boecklen and Simberloff 1986). Such predictions have little value but have been cited in discussions aimed to guide managers (e.g., Schonewald-Cox 1983) and in introductory ecology textbooks (Krebs 1985).

African reserves are not yet isolated, but a mixture of both isolation and persecution outside of some reserves seems underway: Lake Manyara National Park, Tanzania; Serengeti National Park, Tanzania; Gombe Stream National Park, Tanzania; Tai National Park, Ivory Coast; Virunga Volcanoes Conservation Area in Zaire, Uganda, and Rwanda; Kibale Forest Corridor Game Reserve, Uganda; Parc National de Niokola-Koba, Senegal; and others. It is reasonable to assume some will be partly or completely isolated in the future. Miller and Harris (1977) indicated that many East African reserves are functionally already islands for large sedentary species. Hence, isolation of some of these reserves is a serious future possibility.

Soulé (Frankel and Soulé 1981), presumably again relying on land-bridge island extrapolations, attempted to clarify the whole issue:

What biogeographers have been discussing is whether roughly 50% of the higher vertebrate species (in reserves) will be extinct in 500 years versus 5000 years.

This statement, intended to indicate that size alone is not the essential question, was made in the context of information presented in Figure 35, though Soulé used IUCN (1975) data. Figure 35 includes updated 1986 data and still illustrates that the vast majority of reserves in the world are very small. Soulé concluded from this that reserves generally appear to be too small, especially in the tropics, to maintain their present faunal species diversity. He thought even those national parks larger than 10,000 km² are much too small to retain viable populations of the largest carnivores.

Western and Ssemakula (1981) disagreed with the specific predictions by Soulé et al. (1979), and their arguments warrant consideration in some detail here. They concluded that the species-area relationship exists for ungulates in East African savan-

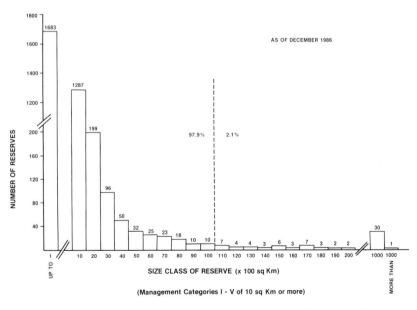

Figure 35. The size distribution of national parks and protected areas included in the 1982 United Nations List of National Parks and Protected Areas (IUCN 1982) and updated through December 1986. The dashed line indicates that 97.9 percent of the reserves are 10,000 km² or smaller. Note also that 84.7 percent are 1,000 km² or smaller. (From International Union for the Conservation of Nature and Natural Resources 1982 with modifications; with permission of IUCN.)

nas, but habitat differences contribute enough to species number to obscure any trend when broader data are pooled. Western and Ssemakula did not regard the species-area relationship by itself as a good principle on which to base the design of savanna reserves for large mammals. They thought careful selection of landscape diversity had far greater value than area alone. They noted that Kenya is half the size of Tanzania and Uganda but contains 13 percent more species, largely due to its greater environmental diversity. They said:

> With a decreasing scale the species-area relationship becomes progressively blurred and within the size range of practical parks or reserves, it is statistically insignificant and therefore of no practical value in designing them. This criticism applies not merely to the East African savannahs. An examination of some classic species-area curves suggests that on a large scale the relationship is obvious, but that within the size range of reserves, the variability is too great to be of practical utility.

On the basis of their analysis, which takes habitat into account, Western and Ssemakula (1981) predicted a single extinction in the Serengeti National Park at "equilibrium," while Soulé et al. (1979) predicted the loss of 50 percent of the park's large mammals in the first 250 years after isolation. In a small park like Nairobi, Western and Ssemakula predicted a 50 percent loss in large mammals at "equilibrium," while Soulé et al. (1979) predicted a 75 percent loss in 250 years. An overall conclusion of Western and Ssemakula was that species in the savanna parks will become extinct mostly due to habitat loss, which correlates with area only in a broad fashion. They also believed that savanna reserves in East Africa will not inevitably become faunal isolates but rather may remain "faunal enclaves," and retain most of their natural features, if integrated human planning is carried out, and erosion (edge effects, disease) is not significant. The authors thought that the designs of reserves in East Africa, given the constraints of the real world, were based on sound ecological principles in most instances, though probably the reserve designers were not aware of this at the time.

East's (1983) results were based on different levels of minimum viable population size (m), intermediate between those of Soulé et al. (1979), for all large mammals, and Western and Ssemakula (1981), for all ungulates. The Soulé et al. (1979) projected losses were similar to or exceeded those based on East's species-area curves for $m = 500$–$1,000$, while

the projections of Western and Ssemakula (1981) were less or equal to those based on East's species-area curves for $m = 25$–50. East warned that his species-area curves should be interpreted with caution but thought that small reserves will over the long term retain less than half the large mammal species found in reserves larger than 10,000 km² in the same region, using $m \geq 100$ (herbivores) and $m \geq 25$ (carnivores). East (1981b) reported that 50 percent of the national parks and game reserves in Africa's savanna zones have areas of at least 7,500 km².

The fact that most of the world's reserves are quite small arouses serious concern, as size should influence the long-term survival of some species confined to parks. However, any specific faunal collapse projections based on area criteria derived from linear regression extrapolations of land-bridge island data are unwarranted and unreliable (Boecklen and Gotelli 1984; Boecklen and Simberloff 1986). Extrapolating to very small sizes from data samples related to larger tracts necessitates broadening the confidence limits enormously (Boecklen and Gotelli 1984).

In theory, isolation by itself will cause mammalian species in reserves to decline, assuming time frames relevant to conservation (Chapter XIVA). Theoretical studies have been misinterpreted as factual evidence that species will decline (e.g., Wood 1983). Wilcox (1984a), after giving earlier faunal collapse projections in Soulé et al. (1979), was uncertain to what extent reserves will collapse. However, what we know about home ranges, population density, migration patterns, problems with small populations, and the fate of dispersing individuals in human-dominated landscapes (e.g., roadkills of Florida panthers) is enough to strongly suggest that many large mammals will not persist in isolated reserves.

2   AREA CORRELATES: SPECIES NUMBER VS. MVP

Bekele (1980) found a significant correlation between numbers of large mammal species and areas of 14 national parks in the western United States, but no appreciable area effect in 12 Ethiopian and 16 Indian reserves. Correlation with habitat diversity was highly significant in reserves on all three continents. Miller and Harris (1977), in contrast, found no relationship between area and number of large resident mammals in East African reserves, and East (1981b) got the same result. Western and Ssemakula (1981) reported significant species-area relationships, with z values in the low range (0.04–0.08), for ungulates in East African reserves when different habitats were separately evaluated. These were lower than Preston's (1962) indication that samples from continental biota have expected z values of 0.12–0.17 (Sections IIB1 and IIC5).

East (1981b) did find presumed minimum viable population sizes correlating with area (i.e., typical insular species-area relationships) for the numbers of large herbivore species having populations of at least 100, 250, and 1,000 in 17 savanna reserves located from Senegal to southern Africa, and for some large carnivores in populations of at least 25 in 7 reserves. East (1981a) continued his investigations of large herbivores and carnivores in both arid and savanna zones of sub-Saharan Africa, which allowed a more thorough look at the area requirements of individual species. East (1983) found significant log S-log A regressions for large herbivores in three mammalian orders occurring in 20 reserves for a minimum viable population size of 25.

Most of East's data argue for large reserves, but East (1981b) did state that a "well-planned and managed" system of small (less than 500 km²) African savanna reserves could maintain almost all resident large mammals. But as East (1981a) pointed out, such management is unlikely in Africa because of the cost; therefore, the best strategy is still maintaining substantial population sizes.

E   Pleistocene Mountain Refugia

J. H. Brown (1971, 1978) inferred an area effect for small Pleistocene mammals isolated on mountaintops in the Great Basin, assuming immigration to have ceased during this time (Section VIF). On the basis of this study, Brown and Gibson (1983) thought that many isolated parks are supersaturated with species, some of which they will lose in the future due to insufficient area. The authors asked: If 1,000 km² of mountaintop cannot stop the extinction of small mammal species in 10,000 years, then what size of reserve is needed to ensure the long-term retention of the grizzly bear, cheetah, African elephant, and others? Brown (1986) thought that reserves smaller than 500 km² will lose more than half their species in a few thousand years.

Although the J. H. Brown study is a classic, the conclusion that species were lost from mountaintops was actually based on a comparison of the regression slopes (z values) of these mountaintops with those of the "mainland" mountains. This approach has received concern (Section IIC5). Unknowns include the actual species composition on the mountaintops before Pleistocene isolation and the degree of subsequent isolation. Grayson's (1987) data alleviated some of these concerns and support J. H. Brown's (1971) explanation. The real problem is that we can never know for certain what did happen during the Pleistocene, but must rely on inference, which is a characteristic problem of paleo-studies.

F   More Species-Area Regressions

In 23 western Australian wheatbelt reserves (Section VIIB), multiple regression found that 72 percent of the overall differences between numbers of mammal species was due to reserve area, 75 percent of the variation in the number of lizard species was due to the number of vegetation associations, and 82 percent of the variation in numbers of bird species was due to a combined effect of reserve area and number of plant species. Proposed optimum reserve sizes for mammals, lizards, and birds were then 400 km², 15 km², and 300–940 km², respectively (Kitchener et al. 1980b, 1980a, 1982). The authors indicated that reserves as small as 30 ha for some mammal and lizard species and 80 ha for birds could still be important. They thought the existing reserve system was adequate for lizards but not for birds or mammals. Since the above analyses relied on linear regression to estimate minimum reserve size, Boecklen and Gotelli (1984) concluded that some of the resulting recommendations may be grossly unreliable. Also, as is common in this literature, z values were interpreted as indicating degree

of isolation. Humphreys and Kitchener (1982) thought that some species (mammals, passerine birds, and lizards) confined solely to reserves have different area requirements than species that also survive outside of reserves. Barnett et al. (1978) also studied some of these reserves.

G   Minimum Critical Size

Lovejoy and Oren (1981) introduced the term "minimum critical size": the area of landscape needed for long-term conservation of all species in a protected zone. They thought that the size needed to retain self-reproducing populations is greater than suggested by species-area curves, which simply indicate a site's species number. The reserve, they thought, should correspond to the asymptote of the species-area curve, the minimum critical size, at which all the species would be retained even if the surrounding landscape were destroyed. Its species-area relationship would be stable over infinite periods.

Lovejoy (in Lewin 1984) defined the concept in less theoretical terms in the context of the Brazilian-U.S. minimum critical size of ecosystems project: It is an area that roughly "will protect the habitat's species/area curve, or something close to it" or will "protect the characteristic species composition of the habitat." However, he recognized that species will be lost no matter where the species-curve is "cut," because some landscape will probably consist of single individuals or extremely small populations incapable of reproduction (Lovejoy 1984).

This approach raises some concerns. Kilburn (1966) said that studies of species-area curves for plants suggested they have no asymptote, hence the number of species in a community has no theoretical limit, and species lists are limited only because

area is. Williamson (1981) also said he had not seen data that convincingly showed that the species-area curve approaches an asymptote. Martin (1981), however, thought species-area curves are asymptotic. If they are not, the precise evaluation of minimum critical size using the species-area curve would be difficult, although the general idea is perhaps useful. Greig-Smith (1969) also criticized the concept of minimal area for a community. Whether a curve is asymptotic also depends on whether one is sampling alpha or beta diversity (i.e., on the definition of "community"). Whittaker (1965) defined the number of species in a community as alpha diversity, the change in species number along an environmental gradient or progression of habitats as approximating beta diversity, and all species within a large geographical area as gamma diversity.

Minimum critical size of an ecosystem, derived from species-area curves, or the minimum area of a community for all its species, derived by any means, still must be calculated. This may come as a surprise. Usher (1986) described "minimum size" of a community as a guess, since an estimate of area requirements exists for so few species, and presumably does not exist for all species in any one community. Diamond (1978) echoed this view when he observed how little we presently know about area requirements for most species.

H   Incidence Functions

"Incidence functions" were suggested by Diamond (1975a, 1978) as a tool to determine minimum reserve area. The incidence function *J* estimates the probability that a habitat island of a given area will

retain a population of a given species. *J* equals the number of habitat islands of a certain size harboring a certain species divided by the total number of habitat islands of that same size (Fig. 36). A *J* value

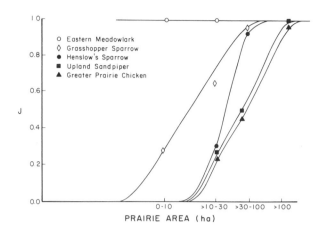

J

- ○ Eastern Meadowlark
- ◇ Grasshopper Sparrow
- ● Henslow's Sparrow
- ■ Upland Sandpiper
- ▲ Greater Prairie Chicken

PRAIRIE AREA (ha)

0-10   >10-30   >30-100   >100

Figure 36. Samson (1983a) plotted data derived from Samson (1980) on breeding populations of six open-prairie bird species during 1978–79 in central and southwest Missouri. The incidence function is the proportion of inhabited prairie of a given area; 0–10 ha, $n = 4$; larger than 10–30 ha, $n = 4$; larger than 30–100 ha, $n = 4$; larger than 100 ha, $n = 2$. (From Samson 1983b; reprinted from the Natural Areas Journal with permission of the Natural Areas Association.)

approaching one indicates a higher probability of species persistence. However, Simberloff and Connor (1981) thought that the validity of incidence functions cannot be assessed until more data are available. As Williamson (1981) indicated, J values tell us nothing about the relative effect of minimum population sizes or habitat heterogeneity on species occurrences. A computer model was developed that simulates the impact of habitat fragmentation on two pools of species having different area needs and dispersal abilities, and the results were used to construct incidence functions that provide some insight (McLellan et al. 1986; Wilcove et al. 1986). Soulé et al. (1988) calculated incidence functions for chaparral-requiring birds in isolated canyons in San Diego, California, which the authors thought to be consistent with the hypothesis that species disappear from isolated habitats in a predictable manner.

I Minimum Dynamic Areas

A naturally patchy distribution of a type of environment powerfully influences the distribution of organisms within it (Wiens 1976). Such biotic distributions are becoming even more patchy as a result of human modification of the landscape, which leaves remnants of once widespread biotic communities (see Figs. 37, 41, 45). Godron and Forman (1983) defined four patch types: environmental resource (heterogeneous spatial distribution of natural resources), spot (disturbance of small areas), introduced (species introduced by people, e.g., pine plantations), and remnant (disturbance surrounding small areas). Thus, real ecosystems today, both natural and disturbed by humans, are often landscape mosaics with different types of patches (Wiens et al. 1985). See Figs. 46, 47.

Forman and Godron (1986) applied terminology from the study of land-bridge islands ("turnover" and "relaxation period") to patches in general. Soulé (1983) argued that patch extinction and species extinction are probably often completely distinct processes, but I think they are related if you consider both natural and man-made patches.

Patch dynamic environments also have a genetic influence: Local fitnesses should decrease as a result of genetic drift over the short term, but over the long term increased variance between populations may increase the rate of adaptive evolution via interdemic selection (Vrijenhoek 1986).

Patch dynamics, a subject related to the theory of island biogeography, refers to the changes in habitat patches caused by patterns of disturbance and succession (Levin 1976; Pickett and Thompson 1978; Pickett and White 1985). The concept of "minimum dynamic areas" (Pickett and Thompson 1978) is theoretically germane to nature reserve management. The hypothesis was that immigration will not contribute significantly to maintaining "equilibrium" in reserves in the future, if indeed there is an equilibrium, because immigration sources outside of reserves will disappear. Therefore we should be more mindful of immigration and extinction of species in the various habitat patches located "within" the reserve. The minimum dynamic area indicates how large a reserve must be to contain enough habitat patches that the likeli-

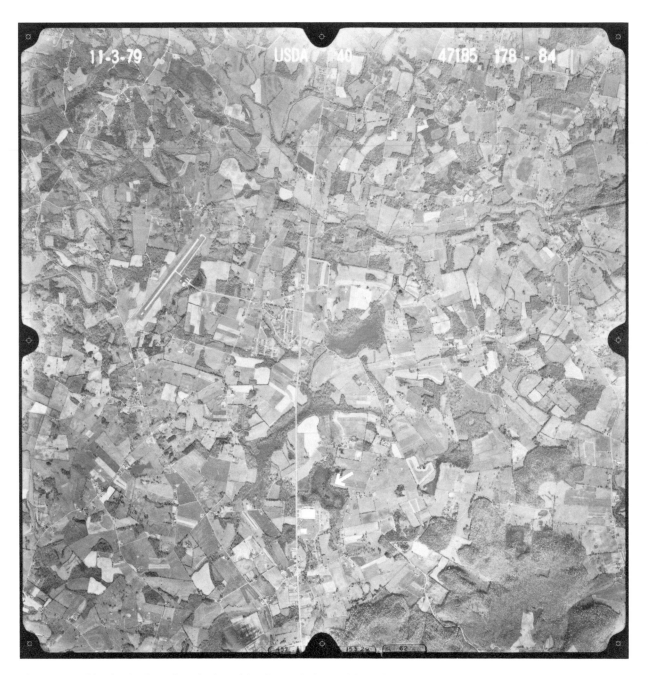

Figure 37. This checkerboard agricultural landscape is located in White County, Tennessee. Anderson Pond is an approximately 70-acre, relatively undisturbed, permanently wet, karst sinkhole swamp located in the lower center, one of the best remaining in the Eastern Highland Rim Subsection of the Interior Low Plateaus physiographic province. When selecting areas for potential nature reserves, a regional "landscape ecology" perspective is needed. (This U.S. Department of Agriculture 1:40,000 scale photo was taken 11-3-79.)

hood of extinction of a species in all patches at the same time is remote. The "natural disturbance regime" determines the size, density, and temporal frequency of patches, while the internal structure of patches is determined by species composition and population densities and dispersion. Pickett and Thompson suggested that "internal disturbance dynamics" may become a critical part of reserve design. White and Bratton (1980) discussed types and scales of disturbances that can influence a reserve.

Arnold (1983) found that habitat island size was not linearly correlated with butterfly population size, while density, patchiness, and quality of resources were more significant. In contrast, Smith (1974, 1980) studying pikas and Fritz (1979) studying spruce grouse did observe a linear correlation. Arnold found the minimum dynamic areas for five endangered butterflies difficult to estimate accurately because all five species had suffered habitat loss, and urbanization surrounded their remaining habitat islands. Nevertheless, he thought that their available habitats had far less than the minimum dynamic areas necessary for the insects' perpetuation. Therefore Arnold could not address all the recommendations about reserve design made by Pickett and Thompson (1978): reserves should be larger than the largest disturbance patch size, including rare patches, should include internal recolonization sources, and should represent different ages of disturbance-generated patches. As Arnold (1983) pointed out, additional considerations are species mobility, resources requirements, and patch longevity. It remains uncertain whether minimum dynamic areas can be achieved in single reserves for many species (White 1987).

J   An Autecological Approach

It may be that the question of reserve size can be answered better on a species by species basis, contrary to the MacArthur and Wilson equilibrium model, which implies that all species are equivalent. A return to autecological studies of individual species was suggested (Simberloff and Abele 1976b; Abele and Connor 1979; McCoy 1982, 1983; Graves and Gotelli 1983; Boecklen and Gotelli 1984), but the current rate of species loss does not permit such a luxury (Diamond 1984b). Any valid models that provide insight for preserving species assemblages should be used. The validity of using the equilibrium theory and the species-area relationship has been questioned and an autecological approach stressed (Zimmerman and Bierregaard 1986). Bennett (1987) incorporated both insular biogeography and autecological thinking in studying mammals in Australian forest fragments for insights about reserve design. We will now examine the requirements of individual species rather than species assemblages.

1   HOME-RANGE REQUIREMENTS

Sullivan and Shaffer (1975) used home-range requirements to estimate the area needed for just eight grizzly bears (600 km²), eight mountain lions (760 km²), and eight wolves (600 km²). They concluded that few reserves in the United States were large enough for just eight individuals (600–760 km²) and that no reserves east of the Mississippi River were large enough to support the most transient of large carnivore populations. Pelton (1986) suggested black bears in the eastern United States are being restricted to large blocks of Federal land due to loss of corridors for movement. Obviously "eight" individuals is modest compared to the "500 rule" discussed in Section IVE4 for long-term "genetic" fitness.

The grizzly bear population in Yellowstone National Park, Wyoming-Idaho-Montana, moves freely out of the park and into adjacent national forests, which raises questions as to whether the acreage of the park alone is sufficient to support a viable population over time, irrespective of other considerations such as persecution outside the park. Some demographic data suggested the grizzly bear population is declining (Knight and Eberhardt 1985). Leopold (1949) recognized some national parks are not large enough to accommodate certain wide-ranging large mammals like the wolf, so adjoining national forests must be viewed as part of the reserve unit. If there are only 1,000 bears in six major populations remaining in the United States (Allendorf and Servheen 1986), then interagency cooperation is essential to their survival.

However, home-range requirements are often poorly known. Thiollay and Meyburg (1988) estimated that two forest hawk eagles on the island of Java may have home ranges of about 20–30 km² and may not survive in forest patches smaller than 20–100 km². No 10,000-ha and few 100,000-ha tracts would include all 27 primary forest raptors in

French Guiana (Thiollay 1989), a circumstance that also introduces the sample effect.

2 LARGE CARNIVORES AS INDICATORS: AUTECOLOGY FOR DEFINING ENTIRE COMMUNITIES

Large carnivore ranges might be used as indicators to estimate reserve area for species assemblages. Eisenberg (1980) suggested that large carnivores are sensitive indicators of the condition of an entire ecological community in the tropics and thus defined the minimum landscape area needed to preserve an intact ecosystem. East (1981b) thought that reserves large enough to ensure minimum viable populations of the African hunting dog and cheetah, because of their large home ranges, should be sufficient for the long-term survival of large African faunal communities. Both authors assumed that protecting the largest and widest-ranging species in an ecosystem may provide adequate safety for all species. Such large carnivores could conceivably be "keystone" species (Section VB).

L. E. Gilbert (1980) doubted that reserves designed to maintain large predators would automatically maintain smaller organisms unless "patch dynamics" is considered. Murphy and Wilcox (1986) commented that the habitat needs of vertebrates are often unlike those of invertebrates, so protecting the one does not guarantee conserving the other. However, I do not think such admissions invalidate the use of large carnivores for prescribing theoretical reserve size.

Eisenberg and Harris (1989) argued that large herbivores and carnivores with high space requirements are the most valuable elements of an ecosystem. If so, designing reserves to accommodate them would conserve the most valuable elements, some perhaps keystone species, *and* conserve many or most of the smaller organisms in the ecosystem.

3 MIGRATORY ANIMALS

Salmon moving upriver to spawn and Neotropical birds are familiar examples of animals that often migrate to and from protected reserves. But large mammals are more germane to this discussion and will receive our attention.

Houston (1971) pointed out a problem in some U.S. national parks: they do not contain all of the historical range of migratory ungulates, which must roam outside park boundaries for resources on land not under park jurisdiction. The problem was appreciated early, and it was also recognized that adjusting the boundary of parks could make them more self-sustaining (Wright et al. 1933). In fact, Nelson (1917) noted that Yellowstone National Park boundaries did not encompass all the winter range needed by its elk population.

In Africa, Myers (1972) observed that the wildebeest herd in the vicinity of Serengeti National Park often migrates 25 miles outside its boundaries during a drought. Such problems arise when all ecological requirements of the resident biota are not considered at the time boundaries are established and are not confined only to animals more traditionally regarded as migratory. For example, the grizzly bear is known to wander 25 miles out of Yellowstone National Park into adjacent national forests and then return (Knight et al. 1984). Seidensticker (1987) reported that tigers wander well outside their reserves in Indonesia and Bangladesh.

Large reserves, therefore, that cannot completely enclose their dynamic large mammal populations can cause management problems. Such populations include the elephants in the 21,000-km² Tsavo National Park in Kenya, where seasonal fluctuations can influence the availability of food and water (Myers 1972; May 1975a; Diamond and May 1976), and the elephants, buffaloes, zebras, wildebeests, and gazelles in Kenya's Amboseli National Park (Western 1982). But Myers (1972) reasoned that it may not be fair to directly compare temperate zone parks with African parks whose savannas undergo great seasonal fluctuations. He remarked that "in some senses, a park in savannah Africa could hardly ever be big enough."

The Alaskan caribou with the largest range, the Arctic herd, migrate over an approximately 140,000-km² landscape. The area overlaps so many units of the U.S. National Park System in Alaska that no single unit could realistically be expected to accommodate the travels of this herd (Hemming 1971). Juday (1983) discussed other problems encountered when selecting reserves for large mammals in Alaska. Thus, for practical reasons, parks may not always be able to accommodate the migratory movements of animals like the caribou. It may be more reasonable to expect reserves to be able to accommodate the migrations of large mammals like the elk and perhaps the grizzly bear. Where possible, parks should be designed to supply all the seasonal needs of their populations, for example, embracing their feeding range and protecting migratory routes.

The discussion of migratory mammals gives just one indication that a park's boundaries do not always coincide with the ecological requirements of its biota. This has long been recognized and is still being pointed out (Wilcove and May 1986). One U.S. conservation organization called for an adjustment of national park boundaries based on ecological considerations (National Parks and Conservation Association 1988). The request is sound but difficult to satisfy because the concept of "complete ecosystems," contrary to what many assume, is not easy to delimit (e.g., Gordon 1989). However, complete watersheds are more quantifiable, and we should consider the benefits of managing reserves on the basis of encompassing watersheds where possible (Sudia, pers. com.). Manu National Park in Peru contains a whole river drainage inside its 1,600,000 ha, though opportunities to establish such large reserves are becoming rarer.

4 MINIMUM VIABLE POPULATION SIZES: EARLY PAPERS

East (1981b) used estimates of minimum viable population size to determine needed reserve area. Assuming that the numbers exceeded 100 for herbivores and 25 for carnivores, he reasoned that reserves larger than 10,000 km² are needed to secure the survival of large mammal communities on African savannas, but that small reserves could be important if "managed." He thought that very large reserves (over 10,000 km²) are needed if large carnivores like lion, leopard, cheetah, spotted hyena, and wild dog are to be represented by at least a few hundred individuals. Main and Yadov (1971) estimated that some species of kangaroos and wallabies in Australia have a minimum viable population size of 200–300 individuals. They concluded that reserves larger than 202 km² are needed to maintain representatives of all the regional fauna in Australia over long periods and must include the diversity of topography and soils found in the region.

The methods these authors used to arrive at minimum viable population size and then reserve size are very rough. They focus on one species and do not rely on the theory of biogeography, which ad-

dresses species assemblages where least-squares estimation also is rough (Section IIC5). The methods are reportedly simple to apply *if* the information needed on minimum viable population size is available: first identify a species for conservation; then, if habitat homogeneity and other factors are equal, the area requirements for one individual multiplied by the "long-term" minimum viable population size equals the area requirement for a minimum viable population (Slatyer 1975; Frankel and Soulé 1981).

Minimum viable population size is not easy to ascertain. For instance, the U.S. Forest Service had to conduct extensive studies to determine how much land a breeding pair of northern spotted owls used for feeding and nesting in the Pacific Northwest (Salwasser et al. 1984). It has resulted in attempts to refine such estimates (Simberloff 1987; Doak 1989). Lawsuits have been brought against the U.S. Forest Service over the question of how much habitat the spotted owl needs to survive (Booth 1989). The method of estimating reserve size based on minimum viable population size is a sound autecological approach but more factors must be taken into account before this elusive entity of minimum population size can be more accurately calculated. The central problem is that the determinant of minimum viable population size is environmental stochasticity, including catastrophes, which is so idiosyncratic and inherently random that it precludes simple models giving simple answers (Section VIIJ6). Demographic stochasticity by itself allows the construction of such models.

The notion of minimum viable population size is not new. Wright et al. (1933), for example, said that each U.S. national park "shall include sufficient areas in all these required habitats to maintain at least the minimum population of each species necessary to insure its perpetuation." Although Gilpin and Soulé (1986) provided an interesting theoretical model to help determine minimum viable population size, it should be emphasized that no such determination has yet been made with confidence for any species, taking into account various demographic, environmental, and genetic stochasticities and catastrophes. Currently, genetic, demographic, and environmental factors must be considered separately despite an awareness that these factors interact.

Shaffer and Samson (1985) implied that the complexity necessary in a model for estimating minimum viable population size is beyond analytical model capabilities. They also said that the necessary data exists for few animal species. For instance, using computer simulation modeling and relying on only demographic and environmental stochasticity data (there were no data on genetic factors), Shaffer (1983) concluded that grizzly bear populations smaller than 50–90 occupying less than 1,000–13,500 km² have less than a 95 percent chance of surviving for even 100 years.

The estimate may vary from one population to another due to differences in population characteristics and habitat quality. What are the implications of this? Of the four tracts of land in the lower 48 states proposed by the U.S. Fish and Wildlife Service as official "critical habitat" for the grizzly bear on November 5, 1976 (this old proposal was officially withdrawn on March 6, 1979), only two were definitely large enough to accommodate 50 bears on at least 2,500 km² (Shaffer pers. com.). Shaffer and Samson (1985) did further analysis with the model. Their simulation indicated that the average period to extinction was 114 years for a landscape with a carrying capacity of 50 individuals, or in 300 years 94 of 100 simulated populations would have gone extinct. They judged their simulation unlikely to be accurate but realistic enough to give closer approximations than are available with any general model (Fig. 25).

Wright and Hubbell (1983) also used a stochastic model, but to determine whether one large reserve or two small reserves of the same total area would be better able to prevent or delay extinction of a focal species, assuming initial similarity of the reserves. The better strategy depended on immigration: When the reserve was closed to immigration of the focal species, one large reserve was best; when the reserve was open to immigration, the difference between the two strategies was negligible. It was possible to specify a "minimum critical reserve size" above which the focal species will almost always be present. Their concept of minimum critical reserve size, based solely on consideration of demographic stochasticity and ignoring all other pertinent factors, should not be confused with Lovejoy and Oren's (1981) "minimum critical size" (Section VIIG). Wright and Hubbell thought that increasing numbers of rare species are being confined to reserves with no possibility of immigration, so that knowing the minimum critical reserve size is crucial. They maintained that a narrow range of reserve sizes exists for a focal species, providing an almost "never present" option at the small end to an "almost always

present" option at the large end. Their work is also related to the sloss debate treated in Chapter IX.

5 EFFECTIVE POPULATION SIZE

Genetics should be another consideration when designing nature reserves (Frankel 1970). For example, on a genetic basis Tyndale-Biscoe and Calaby (1975) recommended a minimum reserve size of only 60 km² for a common Australian mammal species, the greater glider. Reserve sizes should be based on the concept of effective population size. In fact, the whole area of the relationship between genetics and the management of wild plants and animals had been greatly neglected until Schonewald-Cox et al. (1983) focused attention on it.

Soulé (1972) concluded that a population of 10,000 is needed to retain genetic variation in lizards over the long term, but has subsequently changed his estimate. Soulé (1980) adopted the 500-individual recommendation of Franklin (1980) for long-term fitness and said it is the one needed to guide nature reserve management and allow for speciation and adaptation. On this basis, for example, Soulé (Frankel and Soulé 1981) estimated that mountain lions need a minimum of 13,000 km² to survive (allotting 26 km² per individual, which may be very conservative). He thought that wolves, which require about the same area per individual as mountain lions but with adjustments for nonbreeding adults, need a minimum of 39,000–78,000 km² to survive. By comparison, the area of Yellowstone National Park, Wyoming-Montana-Idaho, is approximately 9,000 km².

Seidensticker (1987), using a crude tiger density of 1 individual/50 km², estimated a requirement of 25,000–50,000 km² of habitat for an N_e of only 250. Soulé et al. (1986) considered the difference in genetic advantage between effective population sizes of 500 and 250 probably insignificant. Estimates of reserve size based on long-term genetic fitness requirements are thus different (usually larger) from many estimates based on land-bridge island extrapolations. Park size based on N_e is not necessarily the same thing as size of available good quality habitat for a species, though Schonewald-Cox (1983) demonstrates the close relationship between population size and reserve size for many herbivores and large carnivores.

Newmark (1985) defined the biotic, as opposed to

legal, boundaries of a national park as a hypothetical perimeter encompassing the complete local watershed plus sufficient extra area to sustain a minimum viable population (MVP) of the terrestrial nonvolant species with the largest range. He presumably meant "effective population size," but called it "minimum viable population size" (Section IV). He found that the legal boundaries for seven of the eight parks/park assemblages enclosed smaller areas than the biotic boundaries by factors of 1.2–9.6 for MVP = 50 and of 6.0–96.0 for MVP = 500. He concluded that 7 percent of all the mammals, ignoring chiropterans, found in seven of the eight national park/park assemblages required an area of MVP = 50 × home range, exceeding the legal boundaries. For MVP values of 50 and 500 it became obvious that legal and biotic boundaries are unlikely to be congruent.

Salwasser et al. (1987) identified specific huge conservation tracts around ten North American national parks adequate to accommodate large carnivores on the basis of the "500 individuals rule" for long-term genetic fitness, following Newmark (1985). Their management demands multi-institutional cooperation. They concluded that the Greater Yellowstone Ecosystem may be the only place where 2,500 carnivore individuals like grizzly bears can be accommodated, assuming that Wilcox's (1986) 0.25 ratio of effective population size to actual size (N_e/N) can be used as a rule of thumb.

Soulé (Frankel and Soulé 1981) earlier observed that not only do the largest national parks in the world hold too few of many of the large predators and herbivores to meet the long-term fitness criterion of 500 individuals, but many fell below Franklin's (1980) minimum number of 50 individuals for short-term fitness. For example, the area of the approximately 14,000-km² Serengeti National Park in Tanzania, one of the biggest in East Africa, may be of sufficient size for the genetic fitness of its 2,000 lions, but the approximately 30 adult African hunting dogs that reportedly inhabit the park clearly fall below the necessary population for short-term genetic fitness. Soulé earlier elaborated on this example by pointing out only 10 of the dogs, presumably divided among five packs, could be expected to breed in any one year (they made up only 20 percent of the short-term effective population size of 50). This produced an inbreeding rate of 5 percent, which demands immediate intervention to induce gene flow to maintain existing variability. Hence, he

concluded, they appear to be in immediate danger of decline in fitness, not to mention loss of variation and with it some evolutionary potential.

Active management to create artificial and not natural situations presents a different perspective. East (1983) thought that under intensive management the total population of a species in a "regional network of reserves" would become a single population for purposes of genetic conservation, less grim a condition than Soulé portrayed. With artificial management, the total population would be greater than 500 individuals for almost all East African ungulate species (Western and Ssemakula 1981). Intraspecific mixing could be a concern (Section IXD1).

The 50/500 rule for genetic fitness now seems somewhat entrenched in conservation thinking (see Soulé 1987a). Lande and Barrowclough (1987) advised otherwise:

> *It is clearly not going to be possible to maintain large quantities of single-locus polymorphism in many managed populations, at least in those of larger vertebrates. On the other hand, large amounts of such variation ($H > 0.1$) are not routinely found in many natural populations (Nevo 1978). Many undisturbed vertebrate populations have observed heterozygosities of less than three to four percent. Consequently, managers should not necessarily be alarmed by such values in populations of birds and mammals. It does seem both realistic and desirable, however, to maintain evolutionarily important amounts of quantitative genetic variation in most managed populations by maintaining effective population sizes on the order of at least several hundreds of individuals.*

All such attempts at providing rules of thumb are valuable. However, the 50/500 rule is now being presented as a guideline for conservation (Salwasser et al. 1984; Wilcox 1986). We should remember that it has a very slim empirical basis. Franklin (1980) used Lande's data to formulate the 500 rule, and Lande (1988) stated that "this figure (500) may be roughly correct even for characters under stabilizing natural selection favoring an intermediate optimal phenotype, but this does not justify its blanket application to species conservation." He added that "this number is of dubious value as a general rule for managing wild populations." As indicated in Section IVE4, effective population size really cannot be calculated from the data at hand. To ascertain its difficulty, see Wood (1987).

6 MINIMUM VIABLE POPULATION SIZE: RECENT CONCLUSIONS

Some previously described models attempt to evaluate the effects of chance environmental variations and catastrophes. One recent stochastic population model was proposed to explore the relationship of body size to population growth rate and density and to estimate the sizes of population and habitat that would allow mammals a 95 percent chance of persistence for 1,000 years. The results indicated that small mammals may have a viable population size of a million individuals but need a habitat of only tens of square kilometers, while large mammals may have a viable population size of hundreds of individuals but require a habitat of a million square kilometers (Belovsky 1987). Shaffer (1987), on the basis of Soulé (1987a), synthesized what we know about this concept, especially in regard to large mammals:

> But, as we have already seen earlier in this section, environmental and catastrophic uncertainty may require very much larger population sizes for a high level of security in the mid- to long-term (e.g. 95% probability of persistence for 100 to 1000 years) . . . . Although a clear picture of the functional form of the relationship of population size under the effects of genetic uncertainty is still highly desirable, it

> now appears that, for the single, isolated, unsubdivided population, genetic considerations will not always, perhaps not often, set the lower limit to acceptable population size. . . .

> More importantly, a comprehensive model of the relationship of population persistence to population size under the combined effects of all forms of uncertainty, including genetic uncertainty, is still lacking. Consequently, the machinery to provide comprehensive estimates of population persistence is still not available, at least not in an integrated form. . . .

> Demographic uncertainty poses the least threat while catastrophes pose the greatest; environmental uncertainty being somewhere in between. . . .

> Initial attempts to estimate MVPs (minimum viable populations) and MARs (minimum areas required) for unsubdivided populations of mammals provide a range of population sizes of 100s or 1,000,000s and areas up to millions of km² for high level to mid- to long-term security (i.e., 95% probability of persistence for 100 or 1000 years, respectively). The range is set by population growth rates, their variability, and population density. These estimates of MVPs and MARs compare unfavorably with the size class distribution of current reserves but may be reduced by further theoretical, empirical, and experimental developments or by comprehensive planning and management providing multiple reserves for most species.

VIII

Nature Reserve Isolation: Planning Options

A   The Problem

If some national parks and reserves are too small for the long-term perpetuation of some species, what could the response of managers be? Could we realistically expect to expand their sizes at this late date? Perhaps at some localities. Newmark (1986) estimated that 85 percent of the land adjacent to western North American national parks is in public ownership, providing opportunities for possible expansion.

What about areas that are becoming more restricted and isolated due to landscape alteration outside their boundaries? Some biota in such areas are expected to be affected by isolation from nearby habitat. Common sense and experience allow us to recognize that landscape alteration can eliminate resources outside park boundaries on which some species in the park may depend. Buffer zones and external influences are intertwined (Chapter XIII). Therefore, what can be done?

B   Potential Solutions

1   BUFFER ZONES

Perhaps we should have been more diligent in creating buffer zones around more national parks and reserves as well as participating in more cooperative regional planning of the kind advocated by K. R. Miller (1978) for all of Latin America. Buffer zones for U.S. national parks were urged in 1935 (Wright and Thompson 1935). Nature reserves could be included in zoning systems encompassed by buffering compartments (van der Maarel 1982). Such recommendations for buffer zones and zoning systems could still be applied for certain U.S. national parks and other reserves. While a buffer zone by itself can be helpful, the primary need is to control human activities that impact the adjacent reserve, which a buffer zone may or may not accomplish. Buffer zones around U.S. national parks could regulate land use (Hiscock 1986).

2 LAND-USE REGULATIONS

We could also try various approaches to achieve more compatibility between the use of land adjacent to U.S. national parks and the parks themselves (Shands 1979; Conservation Foundation 1985), including land-use regulations. One option is promoting more applications of conservation easements (Madden 1983). Hiscock (1986) proposed a legislative model to protect against adverse land uses adjacent to park boundaries. Frank and Eckhardt (1983) provided other insights. Legal issues also become important (see Section XIIIB2). The National Parks and Conservation Association (1988), though not recommending buffer zones per se, described a few options to create a "zone of influence" around a U.S. national park. But buffer zones can do more than this. For example, Dobson and May (1986) recommended such zones for African parks as a "firebreak" to stop the spread of rinderpest. The zones can also function as corridors or stepping stones to other reserves (Section IXB).

3 BIOSPHERE RESERVES

The concept of a "biosphere reserve" (Fig. 38) should be energetically promoted throughout the world. It promotes the sound use of adjacent lands, thus decreasing the probability of isolation (UNESCO 1974). It potentially combines the concepts of buffer zones with land-use regulations. Subsequent symposia have examined the land-use conflicts inevitable when adjacent land-use zones are not created at the time the national park or biosphere reserve is first established (Scace and Martinka 1983).

Although concentric zoning is conceptually sound, Eisenberg (pers. com.) indicated that the idea is not original. The British long ago designed national parks in India and Sri Lanka, and probably elsewhere, with concentric rings around a central core. Hart (1966) pointed out that French national parks in West Africa are designed to include concentric "rings": the inner ring contains the most biologically important areas, the next ring has controlled resources management, and the outer ring has agriculture. The Adirondack Forest Preserve in New York was created in 1885 and the larger Adirondack Park in 1892 for the purpose of concentrating state land acquisition within its boundaries, although it did not illustrate a true ring pattern.

The original concept of a biosphere reserve out-

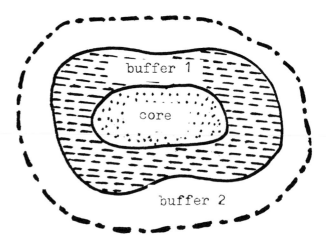

Figure 38. A simplified diagram suggesting the idealized basic design of a "biosphere reserve." The core is the least disturbed zone, where development is not permitted and uses are strictly controlled. The buffer zone(s) was intended to shield the core area from the direct impact of human activity. The founders of the biosphere reserve concept admonished that reserve establishers be aware of important environmental, social, and economic issues in the surrounding area. Such considerations, if implemented, could protect the core area from progressive isolation and human exploitation. (From UNESCO 1974.)

lined in UNESCO (1974) followed this ring pattern. The core area was for strict protection, research, and education. The buffer zones were intended not only to shield the core area from the direct impact of human activity, but for other purposes such as to provide space for wide-ranging species, such as large herbivores with seasonal migrations, and for rare species for which the core may be too small to permit an adequate population size, to set aside an area for manipulative research that could be compared to nonmanipulative research in the core, and to segregate some recreation or tourism activities to avoid adverse effects on the more protected inner core. Biosphere reserves could also include "varied or harmonious landscapes" (i.e., landscapes created by past pastoral or agricultural activities) as well as "modified or degraded landscapes." Therefore, it was implied, indigenous people and their long established patterns of land use were not incompatible with the biosphere reserve concept. Also, reserve planning and zoning should be based on the carrying capacities of the different zones.

The wisdom of biosphere reserves seems better appreciated and articulated now. One conference participant, Eidsvik, in Peine (1985) indicated that the "buffer zone" is now for the protection of indig-

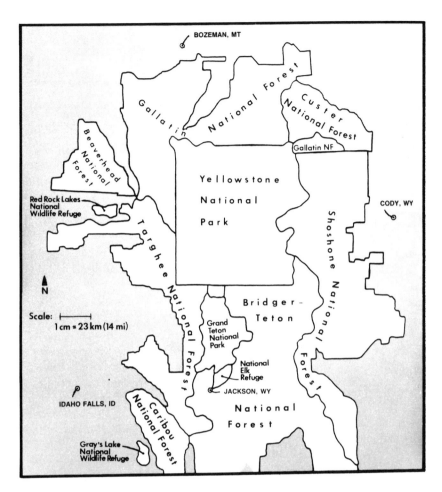

Figure 39. The approximate region known as the Greater Yellowstone Ecosystem. Yellowstone National Park is surrounded by seven national forests and other types of reserves. (From Norse et al. 1986; reprinted by permission of The Wilderness Society.)

enous people practicing traditional land use, while an outer "multiple use zone" can in some cases accommodate cattle grazing, farming, forestry, settlements, etc. He called the outer multiple use zone an "area of cooperation." This is the same concept Lusigi (1981) and Western (1982) espoused for Kenya. For a good articulation, elaboration, and extension of the biosphere reserve concept, see Batisse (1986) and Gregg and McGean (1985). The newest version of biosphere reserves therefore incorporated the idea of graded zones of cooperation, which appears to have been absent or poorly articulated when the concept was originated. For a recent account of its virtues, see Gregg et al. (1989).

As of May 1989, we had 276 biosphere reserves in 71 countries. However, there is a wide gap between the model biosphere reserve concept and its implementation (Tangley 1988). For instance, a 1982 survey revealed that 84 percent of all biosphere reserves consist simply of preexisting national parks or other reserves. The core and buffer zones could have legal protection, and the buffer zones must be more clearly defined. Section XIVC$_3$ also describes a biosphere reserve.

4   BROAD-SCALE U.S. REGIONAL PLANNING

In the United States, as in Great Britain (see Ratcliffe 1977), restricting the role of nature conservation organizations to exclude land-use planning outside reserves can increase rather than reduce conflicts with other land users. Therefore, setting aside and protecting nature reserves over time really involves overall wise land-use policies. Eagles (1984) presented a planning strategy and philosophy to protect environmentally sensitive areas in general, including parks and nature reserves. Fabos (1979) presented another planning perspective.

A former director of the U.S. National Park Service described a pertinent policy (Hartzog 1974):

> *And it is highly important that parks should not be treated as isolated reserves, but as integral parts of the complex economic, social, and ecological relationships of the region in which they exist. Joint planning, then, with all levels of government and the private sector, is essential.*

For example, Yellowstone National Park (about 9,000 km²) is centered within the approximately 20,000-km² informal administrative designation called the Greater Yellowstone Ecosystem (Fig. 39). The larger area encompasses two national parks, seven national forests, two national wildlife refuges, and various state, corporate, and private lands. Some grizzly bears leave Yellowstone National Park and wander over much of the Greater Yellowstone Ecosystem. Therefore, the conservation of the grizzly bear demands coordination of many political and administrative entities. In spite of characterizations to the contrary, such as National Park Service and Forest Service (1987), coordination is not sufficient. Schneebeck (1986) studied some of the legal aspects of this issue in relationship to the grizzly bear. Eidsvik's (1984) statement seems to me an accurate perception of the future of integrated planning outside national parks in the United States:

> *While there is a definite need to integrate the planning of national parks and other protected areas with regional plans, this need is not perceived by managers as being critical in North America. Long-established traditions have fixed a management style in which governments and non-government organizations have confidence that the parks can best achieve their objectives under present management regimes. It is therefore unlikely that major changes in management style will occur in North America in the next decade. Integrated planning does not appear to be a feasible approach at this time.*

However, the above perception of the present situation is not impossible to change. For instance, three major U.S. land management agencies, the National Park Service, U.S. Forest Service, and Bureau of Land Management, already have authority or mandates to coordinate their land-use plans with those of state or local governments. The long-term future of national parks and reserves may hinge heavily on whether such cooperative endeavors are truly carried out at all levels: federal, state, local, and private. This is a marked change from how U.S. national parks were viewed in the early days of their establishment: park boundaries were walls to shut out destructive influences. Nelson (1978) considered the relationships or interdependencies between reserves and their adjacent areas as probably the major management challenge of parks and reserves today. Other countries are establishing their own forms of zoning and areas of cooperation to serve their own needs (Conservation Foundation 1984).

IX

Single Large, or Several Small Reserves (SLOSS) and Beyond

A   Introduction

1   A REVIEW OF THE DEBATE

A question related to reserve size is SLOSS: Will a single *l*arge *o*r *s*everal *s*mall reserves of equal total area contain more species? The conclusions of some key papers will be described.

Simberloff and Abele (1976a), Diamond (1976a), Terborgh (1976), Whitcomb et al. (1976), and Simberloff and Abele (1976b) began the debate. Simberloff and Abele (1976a,b) said that species-area relationships are too ambiguous to indicate whether two small reserves, each half the size of a larger reserve, will contain more species than the single large one. They thought it depends on how many species the two reserves share and the slope of the species-area regression line. It also depends on the gradient of dispersal and survival abilities of the species considered, according to Shaffer and Samson (1985). Diamond, Terborgh, and Whitcomb argued for single large reserves, citing a variety of convincing considerations, including managerial aspects, but did not deal explicitly with all the points made by Simberloff and Abele. Abele and Connor (1979) restated the position of Simberloff and Abele (1976a,b). Figure 40 represents

their early thinking in the controversy, but by no means has the issue proved so simple.

Helliwell (1976b) thought that much depended on whether the area required by the particular species is large or small. Simberloff (1978c) judged large areas preferable to prevent local population extinctions of insects, but all the area need not be contiguous. Nilsson (1978) preferred large reserves over several small ones, on the basis of plant and bird observations. Higgs and Usher (1980) considered the best strategy, at least for plants on limestone outcrops, to be several small reserves, and Gilpin and Diamond (1980) supported this view on the basis of an examination of real New Hebrides islands. Cole (1981) maintained that a single reserve or island will preserve more species than several small ones of equivalent area, and thought the conclusion of Simberloff and Abele (1976a,b) accurate only for islands containing a very small part of the total available pool of species, such areas being inappropriate as permanent refuges. Simberloff (1982b) thought the theory of island biogeography did not favor a single large reserve over several small ones. Kindlmann (1983), from a consideration of incidence functions, concluded that the number of re-

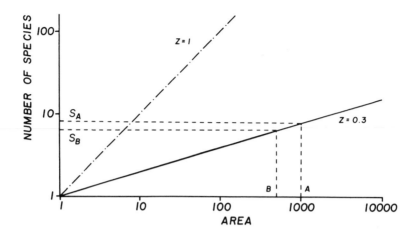

Figure 40. Plot of a species-area relationship using log transformed species numbers and areas (i.e., a log-log plot). The dot-dash line is a species-area relationship with a slope of 1 ($z = 1$), reflecting a constant return in species number regardless of tract size. The solid line with a slope of 0.3 ($z = 0.3$) is the situation frequently found in real landscapes. A slope less than 1 indicates a decreasing return in number of species per unit area with increasing area.

Point A on the *x*-axis represents a nature reserve with area A, and point B on the *x*-axis a reserve with area $B = A/2$. The dashed lines project these areas onto the species-area curve of $z = 0.3$ and then to the vertical axis so the number of species in each reserve can be found as points S_A and S_B on the *y*-axis. The small distance between points A and B on the *x*-axis indicates that setting aside half the area will conserve more than half the species; therefore, two small reserves of area $B = A/2$ may harbor more species than a reserve of area A. Abele and Connor's (1979) above argument was an early one in the subsequent long controversy known as Single Large Or Several Small reserves (SLOSS). (From Abele and Connor 1979.)

fuges is limited for optimal species number, the exact number depending on the value of the functions and the area to be protected. Simberloff and Gotelli (1984) presented plant data that implied there is no reason to preserve single large sites rather than an archipelago of small ones making up the same area. Blake and Karr (1984) examined twelve forest habitat islands in east-central Illinois and concluded that two smaller tracts are more likely to have a greater number of bird species but that a single larger tract will retain more long-distance migrants and forest-interior species that are dependent on forest area. The "edge effect" is another variable, as Williamson (1975) pointed out. If the reserve is intended to maintain "interior" rather than ecotonal species (the internal and external species of Kendeigh 1944), then its virtual size is smaller than its physical size.

Other authors have tried to consider both the species-area influence and managerial factors together. Higgs (1981) concluded that theoretical and managerial considerations give conflicting advice, pointing to no clearly superior strategy, so each situation demands an individual assessment. Simberloff and Abele (1982) and Simberloff (1982a) continued to view the species-area relationship as either neutral or favoring several small reserves, though different management considerations could favor one or the other strategy. Willis (1984) thought that on average it seemed sounder not to dismember or subdivide a reserve, although there are bound to be exceptions.

Patterson and Atmar's (1986) nested-subset hypothesis has implications for SLOSS: Several small fragments of a single biota can be expected to support nested subsets for the species originally present or expected to be retained in a single reserve. They thought it possible for reserves with different initial biota to have the capacity to converge under selective extinction pressures toward a common species composition. Boecklen and Bell (1987) judged faunal collapse models neutral with respect to SLOSS, but under certain circumstances an archipelago of refuges could preserve more species than a single large refuge. Woolhouse (1987) found that the question does not lend itself to general solutions. Some experiments assessing the effect of fragmentation on extinction rates were inconclusive (Quinn et al. 1989), but Burkey's (1989) simulation model, which dealt only with demographic stochasticity, consistently demonstrated that a species is more likely to persist in a continuous habitat tract than in one that is subdivided into isolated fragments.

Shaffer and Samson (1985) suggested that the debate, except for management considerations, involved a two-part question relating to both the colonization and extinction stages of reserve design, and there is no reason to assume that answers to both parts will be the same. Soulé and Simberloff (1986) thought the SLOSS debate is no longer an issue for determining optimal reserve size, which must rely on minimum viable population size. The debate continues nevertheless. For example, Deshayne and Morisset (1989) show that there are more species on a single island than on several small ones in northern Quebec, but only if the area is small (less than 12 ha).

The issue may not have a clear and simple answer. I suspect workers are growing more weary of it than approaching any agreement on its resolution. However, it is not just an academic debate without real potential application (see Recher et al. 1987). It has been described as a red herring with little relevance to practical conservation (e.g., Murphy 1989).

2 SOME PRACTICAL GUIDANCE

Most ecologists probably agree that the optimal strategy for large mammals is "many large" reserves. However, everything else being equal, the maximization of species number for some organisms may be achieved by greater numbers of small reserves, for example, plants in Lincolnshire, England (Game and Peterken 1984), or in the prairie-forest ecotone of the United States (Simberloff and Gotelli 1984), or, as Woolhouse (1987) indicated, for birds in United Kingdom woodlands if they are not isolated. We can only say that a large reserve *may* save more species than would several small reserves of equal total area (Odum 1989). We should still establish small parks and reserves since they serve certain purposes such as preserving endemic spe-

cies or unique habitats and providing "stepping stones" between reserves (Terborgh 1974; Whitcomb et al. 1976; Lovejoy 1982). Both large and small scattered forest remnants have shown value as reserves for some Australian birds on 10–150-ha patches (Loyn 1987). Small reserves (less than 5,000 ha) can preserve many such animals that have modest space requirements and can thrive at high densities (Eisenberg and Harris 1989). But a single small reserve often is not an acceptable substitute for a single large one. This point apparently has never been debated (Simberloff and Abele 1984). What can we say about this issue?

"Many reserves," if dispersed, can have broad landscape diversity with consequently many species, accommodate distributional patchiness, for example, for tropical forest birds (see Diamond 1980a), and insure against demographic stochastic events, disease, and catastrophe (e.g., hurricanes, tornadoes, and fire). "Large reserves" can enclose many species by virtue of larger habitat area. But Simberloff and Gotelli (1984) suggested that the habitat explanation for the species-area relationship indicated that scattered small reserves might encompass more habitats than a single large one. Also, Abele and Connor (1979) pointed out the relative rise in number of species with increasing area (slope of the species-area curve) may be lower for large reserves than for small ones.

Nevertheless, we can say that large reserves will tend to preserve both whole ecological systems and their processes (however hard geographically to define this abstraction) and entire ecological communities (also hard to define). Large reserves could also help to: minimize competition and predation from species residing in habitats adjacent to the reserve; better meet the area requirements of large carnivores and other wide-ranging species; provide more environments and so allow organisms to adjust to long-term environmental change, as Hunter et al. (1988) suggested; and be more likely to contain subdivided populations and therefore to conserve more genetic diversity within a species, as Futuyma (1983) indicated (Section IXB1). Also, large reserves would presumably be better buffered against outside influences and human perturbations. This last point requires elaboration, which it has not yet received in the SLOSS debate (Section IXF1).

However, the pluses and minuses of "many" and "large" should be considered together. For instance, Simberloff and Abele (1976a) thought that more reserves, at the expense of average size, could in some instances decrease the probability of overall species extinctions in the reserve system because of increased opportunities for inhabitants to escape from stressful influences such as disease, predators, and catastrophes without leaving the system. Quinn and Hastings (1987) developed a simple model according to which a certain degree of habitat fragmentation may increase the ability of threatened species to survive, leading the authors to advise caution about recommendations for only a few very large reserves to conserve threatened species.

Gilpin and Diamond (1988) challenged the theoretical basis for Quinn and Hastings's assertion. However, Goodman (1987c) stated that a series of reserves, equal in total area to one large reserve, would have fewer extinctions than the large one due to environmental perturbations as long as there was some migration between them. "Many" and "large" should be considered in conjunction with other issues that parallel the sloss debate: proximity/barriers, corridors, coverage, genetics, and shape (next sections).

B Reserve Proximity/Barriers

1 CLUSTERING

How should reserves be arrayed? The advice usually given is that they should be near enough to each other to allow faunal migration between them. Small populations could thus be bolstered by immigrants, decreasing the probability of local extinction due to random or other events. Brown and Kodric-Brown (1977) hypothesized and demonstrated for arthropods on thistle plants that a declining population of a species on an island might be "rescued" by immigrants of the species from nearly islands; hence extinction rates may fall when immigration rates are high and not depend simply on area as MacArthur and Wilson (1963, 1967) implied. Brown and Kodric-Brown's "rescue effect" needs verification for other species.

Bekele (1980) concluded that the distance between conservation units is generally not important for large mammals except as it relates to mass migrations, but his conclusion is open to question because of the difficulty in studying this variable. Soulé (Frankel and Soulé 1981) pointed out that proximity has disadvantages as a guideline: The order of extinctions predicted by some scientists could be similar in nearby reserves as noted by Terborgh and Winter (1980); scattered reserves are likely to offer more habitat diversity and thus contain more species; and management considerations concerning disease and catastrophe hypothetically argue against close proximity. Dobson and May (1986) cited data to show how fast disease can spread in game animals throughout much of Africa: Rinderpest spread from northern Somalia to the Cape in just eight years (1889–1897).

Also, Slatyer (1975) observed that dispersed reserves are likely to preserve more genetic variation within a species. This stems from a presumption that genetic variation within a species is more likely to increase in heterogeneous environments, such as larger landscapes tend to have, than in homogeneous ones. Although substantial circumstantial evidence indicates that genetic polymorphisms are related to environmental heterogeneity, experimental evidence is meager (Hedrick et al. 1976) but increasing (Hedrick 1986). We know that genetic differentiation within a species does not always correspond to barriers or environmental changes (Endler 1977). But if reserves are widely dispersed, we know that ecologically unstable populations—frequently at the limits of their geographical ranges—can contain combinations of chromosomal and genic diversity not always present in central populations (Lewontin 1974; Soulé 1973).

2 BARRIERS TO DISPERSAL

Soulé (Frankel and Soulé 1981) further suggested that migration between nearby reserves is possible only for species (such as insects, bats, and birds) accustomed to traversing inhospitable landscapes, while many species (such as fish, amphibians, reptiles, and nonflying mammals) are ill-equipped for such travel. Nevertheless, Soulé (1972), using simplifying assumptions, indicated it would take 500–

5,000 years for a gene in a lizard population of the genus *Uta* to move from one end to the other of Angel de la Guardia Island in the Gulf of California (a 75-km distance)!

Psychological barriers also can retard emigration. Terborgh (1975) presumed psychological factors to underlie the reluctance of many tropical forest bird species to cross even a few kilometers of unsuitable terrestrial habitat. Diamond (1972) had earlier found that water gaps also presented such a barrier. Lynch and Whigham (1984) perceived a similar reluctance of forest interior birds to cross small fields in parts of the U.S. Eastern Deciduous Forest, and Yahner (1983) observed one small mammal group living in shelterbeds reluctant to move into adjacent fields.

Roads also may serve as psychological barriers. Diamond (1972) found that some tropical birds resist crossing a road only a few yards wide. Diamond (1973), Willis (1974), May (1975a), and Diamond and May (1976) thought that the reluctance of some species to cross major highways means that putting a wide road in a park cuts in half the park's effectiveness for maintaining species. Oxley et al. (1974) regarded divided highways with clearances of 90 m or more as possibly the equal of freshwater bodies twice as wide in barring the passage of small forest mammals. Mader (1984) reviewed the subject of barriers. Some large mammals like mule deer and red fox simply avoid getting close to highways, though they will cross them (Rost and Bailey 1979; Storm et al. 1976). Roads, irrespective of their potential isolating influence, may be overall predictors of the absence or presence of some species such as wolves and mountain lions (Thiel 1985; Van Dyke et al. 1986). Dispersal barriers at the edges of reserves will be discussed in Section XIIIC2.

3 CORRIDORS

The term "corridors" was used early by Simpson (1936) in the context of dispersal between continents. The paleontological record is a testament to the value of intercontinental corridors. Corridors envisioned today for nature reserves are quite different. It is interesting to speculate as to whether the idea was influenced by an earlier perception that biota dispersed along river valleys, broad physiographic features like the U.S. Atlantic Coastal Plain, and other such "highways" in the southeastern United States (Adams 1902).

Leopold (1949) noted that "many animals, for reasons unknown, do not seem to thrive as detached populations," but it was Preston (1962) who recommended corridors between reserves. Corridors should allow the increase of size and enhance the chance of survival of smaller populations. Even if size were adequate, populations should benefit from the recolonization that corridors permit as individuals are locally lost. As was discussed under clustering (Section IXB1), corridors can also reduce inbreeding depression. Forman (1983) categorized and described the origins of various types of corridors: remnant (hedgerows), spot disturbance (railroad and powerline strips), environmental resource (streams), planted (shelterbeds), and regenerated (regrowth of a disturbed strip). Forman (1987a) said we really know little about what constitutes a good corridor, though we assume width and connectivity to be primary controlling characteristics. Wide and sufficiently habitat-diverse corridors between reserves will be difficult to create, let alone maintain.

Meager actual data exist on the use of corridors. Wegner and Merriam (1979) found that small mammals and birds used fencerows as habitat corridors within an isolating agricultural mosaic. Henderson et al. (1985) studied chipmunks in patches of woods separated by farmland, but connected by fencerows, and found that chipmunk extinctions in a single patch were soon followed by recolonization by animals from other patches traveling along the fencerows. Noss (1983) and Forman and Godron (1986) reviewed some literature on the interconnections between habitat patches. Harris (1989) voluminously documented statements by procorridor advocates and work that appears supportive. However, wide advocacy seems to be based more on intuition and casual observation than scientific documentation. Controlled laboratory experiments with flies do argue for corridors (Forney and Gilpin 1989), and the value of such small experimental systems to the broader issue of habitat fragmentation on large temporal and spatial scales has been applauded (Ims and Stenseth 1989).

Soulé thought the degree to which many species would use corridors is questionable (Frankel and Soulé 1981). He suggested that large predators may use corridors of adequate design but that nonriparian species may not find a riparian habitat corridor to their liking. Forman (1983) thought that large mammals and some birds move along corridors well, while small mammals and plants may have problems. Forman and Godron (1986) showed how assumptions about what constitutes a barrier or a corridor for a species can be incorrect. The question of what factors influence the movement of a species requires detailed field study.

In some extreme cases, any realistic opportunity to use corridors may be gone, especially for small remnants (Fig. 41). All remnants have value, but their future in terms of the survival of all native species is poor. They require appreciation and special management (Saunders et al. 1987b).

Corridors will promote gene flow through dispersal of individuals between reserves. The establishment of corridors, where none previously existed, could cause loss of locally adapted genotypes due to gene flow, but not a loss of alleles. Therefore, the questions surrounding the pros and cons of genetic mixing (Section IXD) also relate to corridor design. Corridor disadvantages include transmitting diseases and pests, facilitating poaching and predation, and encouraging exposure to domestic animals and their diseases (Simberloff and Cox 1987). Ambuel and Temple (1983) also advised that corridors between woodlots in forests of eastern North America could be deleterious, if their proposed biotic interaction model is correct.

Nevertheless, I think the need for corridors outweighs their potential disadvantages. Ideally each situation should be assessed individually, although this will be unrealistic in many cases. Corridors may be one of the most important single challenges we face. If individual assessments demand corridors, then, as Harris (1985) points out, riparian woods are probably our single best opportunity (Fig. 42), but we must not overlook others:

Numerous cultural artifacts can also help meet our design criteria. Abandoned railroad rights-of-way, and powerline, pipeline, and other easements can be used by mammals. Canopy roads, wooded median strips of interstate highways, windbreaks, greenbelts, and wooded visual screens will be used as corridors by birds. The Florida Trail, equestrian trails, jogging trails, and bicycle routes should be of value through urban areas, just as wooded fencerows play a role in rural landscapes. All of these represent linear connectives that permeate the landscape; all have a role to play in the interconnected habitat island system.

Such recommendations are turning up in the form of Presidential commission recommendations—Alexander (1986) recommended the establishment of connecting corridors or greenbelts between national parks and other U.S. reserves.

However, as Simberloff and Cox (1987) pointed out, it would be wise to first consider cost-benefit analyses, for example, in some cases it might be cheaper to manage some species by moving them between reserves rather than buying and maintaining corridors. They also remarked that decisions about corridors should "be based on data or well-founded inference, not on overarching generalities." Noss (1987a) provided a rebuttal to Simberloff and Cox (1987) and a concise summary of the pros and cons of corridors.

To paraphrase Noss, the potential advantages of corridors include 1) higher immigration rate that will maintain species number, increase population size, prevent inbreeding, and encourage the retention of genetic variation; 2) increased foraging area for wide-ranging species; 3) predator escape cover for movement between patches; 4) a mix of habitats and environmental stages for species that require them; 5) provision of refugia from large disturbances; and 6) greenbelts to limit urban sprawl, abate pollution, and provide recreation and scenery. Potential disadvantages include 1) higher immigration rate that could spread disease, insect pests, exotic species, and weeds, and decrease genetic variation in local populations or disrupt local adaptations; 2) easier spread of fire and abiotic disturbances; 3) exposure of wildlife to hunters, poachers, and predators; 4) riparian strips might not be used by upland species; and 5) "cost, and possible conflicts with land preservation strategies to protect endangered species habitat if corridor quality is low."

I agree with Noss's statement that "in the face of scientific ignorance about these phenomena, maintenance of habitat connectively would seem to be the prudent course." We must presume they are the best overall long-term alternative we have to thwart the effects of habitat isolation.

Maintaining or reestablishing native connectivity should be distinguished from creating previously nonexisting connections. The former incurs fewer risks. Loss of natural connectivity is causing the "island dilemma." Fortunately, some countries such as Australia are more aware of this problem and are looking for solutions (see Saunders et al. 1987a).

4   THE PROBLEM OF SIMPLE PRINCIPLES

If national park and other reserve managers were to adopt the principles of nearness and connected-

Figure 41. Tall-grass black-soil prairie once covered more than 13 million acres in eastern Illinois and northwestern Indiana. According to a 1985 report, only about 200 acres remain of which some 20 acres are essentially undisturbed. The rectangular block in the lower right corner is Weston Cemetery where 5 of these 20 acres remain near Pontiac, McLean County, Illinois. This is the largest tract remaining, embedded in an agricultural matrix. Another 1-acre tract exists in another cemetery near Hammond, Lake County, Indiana. Hypothetically speaking, if an animal species were restricted to undisturbed tall-grass black-soil prairie in this 1-acre cemetery, it would have to traverse approximately 70 miles of predominantly agricultural landscape in order to colonize the largest remaining (5-acre) remnant of this habitat type. This example illustrates how drastic habitat fragmentation has been in some parts of the U.S. (This U.S. Geological Survey 1:15,000 scale aerial photo was taken on 3-8-77.)

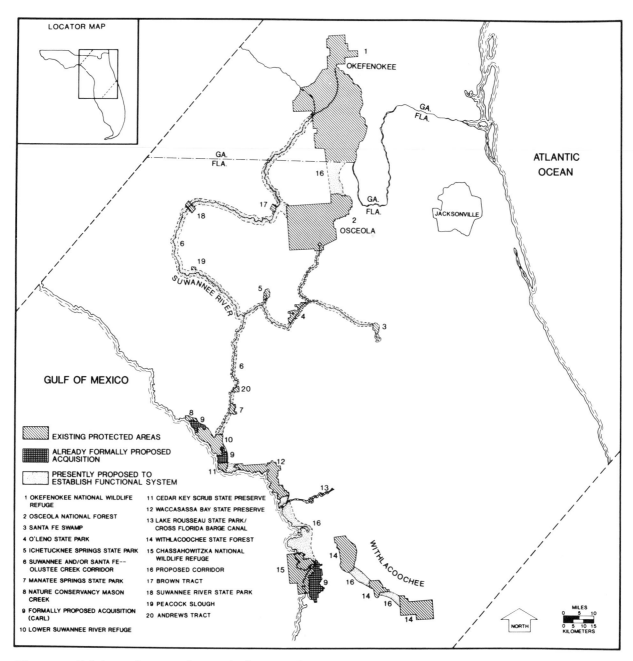

Figure 42. Existing and proposed network of protected areas and corridors into a regional system in north Florida and south Georgia. (From Noss and Harris 1986; reprinted with permission of Springer-Verlag.)

ness/corridors as a guideline for system planning, then the establishment of all future national parks and reserves would take into account the distribution of all other nearby reserves. Some simple reserve design principles such as proximity and size apparently were applied when new units of the U.S. National Park System, National Wildlife Refuge System, and others were established in Alaska. For large mammals requiring more land than any one of these reserves provides, such a design is one more advantage.

Unfortunately, the determination of what is "positive" may not be so simple, since many considerations argue for widely spaced reserves. Soulé (Frankel and Soulé 1981), at least, thought that the weight of such considerations favors wide spacing. The more space between reserves the greater the difficulty in providing connecting corridors, if they are deemed essential. Thus, simple principles may not hold up in the face of complex phenomena and practical realities that require the balancing of too many factors in individual situations. Simberloff (1978c) noted that the optimal size and spacing of reserves must rest on detailed field study of the dispersal characteristics and population dynamics of a particular species.

For instance, Harris (1984) recommended corridors for protected natural areas in the U.S. Western Cascades where forest harvest is a big industry, timbering is routinely conducted on U.S. national forests, and much uncut forest and riparian habitat still exist. He proposed that the islands of old-growth forest be surrounded by zones of long-rotation and low-harvest timbering, and that islands created by timber harvest also be connected by corridors. This ingenious design concept would perhaps allow large carnivores to move between old-growth forest islands. Such a planning scheme is theoretically sound if corridors are deemed essential. However, its across-the-board application for many species is still premature. A study is needed of individual species' dispersal characteristics, as well as of the pros and cons of corridors in various situations. Unfortunately, we may not have the time or opportunity.

C Reserve Numbers and Coverage

1 SPECIES AND AREA: $S = cA^z$

How many reserves should there be? Or, how much land area should be set aside for reserves? Darlington (1957) found that the number of reptile species in the West Indies doubles when area increases by a factor of ten and corresponds to a z value of 0.301 (Fig. 19). Preston (1962) later expressed the species-area equation $S = cA^z$, with $z = 0.263$. Preston (1962) and MacArthur and Wilson (1967) found that a tenfold increase in island area gave a 1.86 increase in number of species. Wilcox (1980) later explained the relationship as a 30 percent exclusion of regional fauna for each tenfold decrease in area, extrapolating from z values. Pimm (1986) suggested that a twentyfold reduction in area will reduce the species number by 50 percent. Williams (1943) much earlier concluded that doubling the number of flowering plant species required multiplying the area by 32. This may indicate only that z values vary between ecosystems, but recommendations also vary widely. The important point is that Darlington's data on West Indian reptiles have been generalized by others into a rough conservation rule of thumb: Given the most typical slope of the species-area equation, then setting aside 10 percent of the area of a habitat type may still conserve only 50 percent of its existing species, even if absolute preservation were achieved (e.g., Diamond 1975b; Wilson and Willis 1975; May 1975a). This is based on typical z values around 0.3. Note that a small change in z can cause a large change in dependent variables (Fig. 43).

Williamson (1981) considered the 10-times-area-two-times-species rule a useful starting point for picturing the effects of area on "real islands." The rule has been extended by some to an expanse of habitat (e.g., Diamond 1976b) or to landscapes in general (Wilson 1985b, 1988). As guidance to a nontechnical forest planning audience, Norse et al. (1986) cited a 30 percent exclusion of fauna for each tenfold decrease in area. Nobody, as far as I know, has yet extended this thinking to biogeographical provinces like those described by Udvardy (1975), but I expect that someone will.

The rough tenfold area-twofold species guideline is now regarded as insupportable by Simberloff (1978c), on the basis of work by colleagues. Only about 45 percent of the variation in species on a logarithmic graph can be attributed to the logarithm of area (Connor and McCoy 1979). Boecklen and Gotelli (1984) did an analysis of species-area regression that supported their point that species number is poorly modeled solely by area and sug-

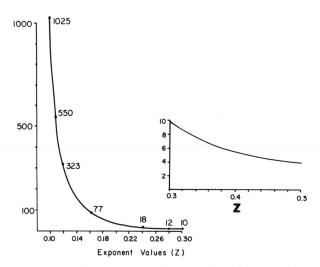

Figure 43. The relationship between the value of z in the species-area equation $S = cA^z$ and the increase in area required to double the number of species. If the z value is 0.30, the graph indicates that a tenfold increase in area would be needed to double the number of species; if the z value is 0.50, a fourfold area increase would be needed. Changes in z, because it is an exponent, have a dramatic effect on the dependent variable. However, concerns have been expressed as to whether certain ranges of z values (0.2–.04) are due to statistical artifact (see Connor and McCoy 1979; Connor et al. 1983). (From Harris 1984; reprinted by permission of The University of Chicago Press. ©1984.)

gested that the species-area relationship illustrates only that the number of species generally increases with area.

2   SOME PRACTICAL GUIDANCE

The species-area relationship can therefore be used as a conservation guideline in an imprecise way: Species numbers usually increase with area but approach diminishing returns at a certain point. Consequently, it takes a large amount of land in a country, and judiciously set aside in many biotic community types, to preserve a large percentage of the species that dwell there.

Slatyer (1975) legitimately questioned the IUCN recommendation that a minimum of 5 percent of a nation's land should be set aside for reserves, which he believed to be shortsighted without a prior determination that all biomes are adequately covered. Myers (1979, 1986) insisted that 10–20 percent of tropical moist forest in select localities (with 10 percent the absolute minimum) must be set aside to

preserve sample biotic communities and endemic species. This might have been based on the 10 percent-gives-50 percent rule, or may simply be an optimistic number at which to shoot during a time of alarming concern over tropical forest destruction rates. Similarly, Miller (1984) advised 10 percent of a nation's land area as a reserve guideline for the world, but his rationale also was unclear. Ecologist Paul Sears recommended that 25 percent of a nation's land be set aside, and some modern environmentalists recommend 50 percent.

Specific recommendations for the whole world have been given, for instance, Wolf's (1987) that the 425 million hectares within the world's protected reserves be trebled. But such recommendations are best based on biogeographical provinces and their existing protected area average, rather than broadly on country or world acreage. Western (1989) indicated that IUCN's goal is to increase the earth's present coverage of 2.8 percent to 8–10 percent in a cross section of all major ecosystems.

Wilcox's (1984a) warning was valid: In the absence of good information about the distribution of biological diversity on which to base reserve selection, even extensive systems of nature reserves may not contain a significant portion of that diversity. This was due to what Wilcox (1980) called the "sample effect." This means that a random sample of one reserve may not contain all the species one might expect to capture because individuals of a species may be found in clusters. Even relatively evenly distributed individuals of a species may by chance occur at low, perhaps nonviable, densities. This "sample effect" was probably derived from Preston's (1962) concept of a "sample," which does not contain a complete log-normal distribution of species because of small sample (tract) size (Section IIB1). The sample effect is a good conservation concept.

The sample effect implies that reserves should be located where species diversity and endemism are high. Diamond (1986) and Terborgh and Winter (1983) used concentrations of endemic species to identify potential reserves in New Guinea and Colombia/Ecuador, respectively. Scott et al. (1987) recommended the use of geographic information systems to determine how many species are contained in reserves and where future reserves would protect the most species. Identifying gaps in reserve networks in a methodical way is the best approach to retaining maximum biological diversity in minimal area (Scott et al. 1988). Duffey and Schonewald-Cox (1989) described some alternative approaches to the typical ad hoc subjective procedure of selecting reserves in Australia (and in other countries), including systematic ranking and scoring procedures.

Countries developing new or "rounding out" older nature reserve systems should be aware of the need to include many biotic communities and should follow a legitimate scientific plan. Furthermore, the selection of individual reserves ideally should be based on a systematic survey of many important design goals. Margules and Usher (1981) focused mostly on diversity and rarity, but naturalness, representativeness, and size are other considerations. They described how to attempt to maximize biological diversity in reserve systems (Margules et al. 1988). In the Macleay Valley flood plain, Australia, they found that to capture every plant species at least once, only 4.6 percent of the total number of wetlands is needed, constituting 44.9 percent of total wetland area, but to capture all varieties of wetland *and* all plant species 75.3 percent of the total wetland area is needed.

Noss (1987b) described the efficient system of elements-of-diversity inventory and evaluation used by The Nature Conservancy (TNC), USA. TNC uses a "fine filter" for species inventory and a "coarse filter" for community-type inventory. TNC maintains that the coarse filter will preserve maybe 85–90 percent of the species in a state, without the necessity of focusing on each species individually. Species not captured in the coarse filter are captured in the fine filter of threatened and endangered species locality listings. As anyone involved in biotic inventories knows, species are easier than community types to describe and inventory.

Noss, stressing the importance of heterogeneous landscapes or landscape mosaics, suggested that this inventory approach could be improved by an even coarser filter that would identify levels of biological organization above the homogeneous community type. He indicated that such considerations are important not only for determining the conservation value of large sites but for assessing the effects of habitats surrounding the sites. In other words, guidelines for reserve design need to take into consideration landscape structure and dynamics.

3 EXISTING RESERVE COVERAGE

The U.S. Situation. As of December 1985 the major subset of the U.S. National Park System owned in fee,

described as national parks, monuments, preserves, seashores, lakeshores, and recreation areas, occupied 3.24 percent of the U.S. land base (50 states and possessions), while the entire U.S. National Park System occupied 3.26 percent. The system's units, however, are not evenly distributed. Similarly, as of July 1986 the net U.S. National Wilderness Preservation System, also unevenly distributed, took up 3.82 percent of the U.S. land base. Sullivan and Shaffer (1975) concluded that if only eight individuals need a minimum reserve size of 600–760 km^2 (they maintained that eight is much too small for the survival of large carnivores such as grizzly bear, wolf, or mountain lion), and if the minimum size is multiplied by the minimum 66 U.S. Kuchler vegetation types (there are now 135), then required area, the 40,000–50,000 km^2, is 1 percent of the U.S. land base. This analysis suggested that the existing size of the U.S. National Park System or U.S. National Wilderness Preservation System would be too small for the hypothetical eight bears to reside in each of the U.S. Kuchler vegetation types.

The U.S. National Park System still does not have at least one large natural area in each of the country's major physiographic provinces, let alone finer landscape divisions like Kuchler vegetation types; 42 percent of the Kuchler vegetation types are missing from the National Park System, although units smaller than 5,000 ha had to be excluded from the analysis (Crumpacker and Hodge 1988). According to Davis (1987 and in Wilcove 1988), of the 261 ecosystem types using a Bailey-Kuchler classification scheme, 104 are not in the National Wilderness Preservation System. However, the situation appears somewhat less grim if the distribution of all protected natural areas in the United States, regardless of ownership or administration, is taken into account. Since no centralized information base gives the exact location and distribution of all the various types of U.S. protected natural areas, administered at the federal, state, and private level, we cannot yet confidently calculate how much of the U.S. land base consists of protected reserves, but progress is being made (Jenkins 1988). Crumpacker (1985) concluded that the number of additional reserves needed for a comprehensive U.S. system cannot be known until nationwide inventories and their level of protection are more completely known.

Sullivan and Shaffer (1975) pointed out that existing "wilderness and primitive areas" in the United States at that time seemed inadequate in number, size, and distribution,[4] and Shaffer (1987) thought they were still too small and too few over a decade later. Although the number of larger wilderness areas has markedly increased since 1975, their clustered distribution has changed little because additions were made only in Alaska and Florida (Sierra Club 1983) and Pennsylvania (The Wilderness Society, pers. com. 1986).

The World Situation. Myers (1985) pointed out that some poor countries have set aside remarkable amounts of their land base into reserves. Harrison et al. (1982) reported on 11 countries larger than 20,000 km² with over 10 percent of their land area protected. Of the 11, Tanzania had one of the largest total reserve areas set aside in Africa, but Botswana was the largest in percentage of total land base and per capita of population. Including all of Tanzania's national parks, game reserves, and game-controlled areas, its total was 30 percent (Program for International Development 1984).

Harrison et al. (1982) gave the following data for the world: as of June 1982, 2,611 protected areas, covering nearly 4 million km², had been set aside by 124 countries. The number of reserves and the percentage of landscape set aside varied widely. Sixteen of the 193 biogeographical provinces (using the UN list) had no protected areas, and 33 biogeographical provinces had less than 5 protected areas totaling less than 100,000 ha. The percentage coverage in each biogeographical province has not yet been determined (Harrison et al. 1982, 1984; IUCN 1985).

4   CONCLUSION

The answer to the question—How many reserves?—thus evades a precise answer. Shaffer and Samson (1985) implied that how much is enough for a particular species is a goal of future research. Ignoring the issue of allocating limited resources, we can say that, ideally, the answer is as many as possible, as large as possible, and representing as many biotic community types as possible. With so many of the world's 3–30 million species (Erwin 1983; Wilson 1985) facing extinction, we could hardly have too many reserves in the tropics.

D   *Genetic Translocations*

As habitat becomes more fragmented, isolated populations can become very small. Since this is a deleterious condition, moving individuals from one location to another is a future management option. Therefore, a familiarity with all aspects of such translocations is imperative.

Theoretically, translocations should bolster populations only with similar demes or ecotypes, if one accepts the dogma of racial purity in conservation relative to intraspecific mixing, but this has been questioned, for example, by Frankel (Frankel and Soulé 1981). Mixing of "intraspecific" gene pools conceivably could be either harmful or beneficial, but little evidence points to harm. Plants may exhibit some outbreeding depression (Antonovics and Bradshaw 1970; Price and Waser 1979), and Templeton et al. (1986) advised avoiding outbreeding depression in animals by not encouraging hybridization between different coadapted gene complexes, but Templeton (1986) also saw no long-term

harmful effects resulting from animal intraspecific outbreeding. We do not yet know enough to make generalizations about outbreeding depression for specific situations.

1   CONCERNS ABOUT MIXING AND DETERMINING GENETIC SIMILARITY

Intraspecific mixing theoretically could be more harmful than helpful if it 1) resulted in loss of adaptive fitness due to "swamping" or outbreeding depression (Templeton et al. 1986), or 2) introduced deleterious genes. Either could result from well-intended but misguided management action. The following discussion will focus on the literature relating to outbreeding depression.

Ehrlich and Raven (1969) thought that natural

migration between demes in some species may be limited to short distances, so translocations between more separated demes may interrupt the natural gene flow. Slatkin (1985) felt that gene flow varies greatly between species and cannot account for morphological stasis, and that we know little about its evolutionary role. Most of what we assume about gene flow is based on theory. The outcrossing rates observed by Schemske and Lande (1985) for natural plant populations led them to suggest that outcrossing is favored by selection in large outcrossing populations with inbreeding depression, and then selection favors selfing when outcrossing reduces the observed inbreeding depression.

Greig (1979) made a strong plea against mixing of subspecies or locally adapted ecotypes when translocations (introductions and reintroductions) are conducted by conservation programs, a warning given long before and less eloquently for U.S. national parks (Wright et al. 1933). Shields (1982) thought that hybridization between animals with differing local adaptations can influence offspring fitness. Conant (1988) believed translocations in general could have undesirable consequences, such as discouraging differentiation through mixing. Since we know so little about the consequences of intraspecific mixing, such warnings probably should be heeded, at least until we know more.

Caution should be applied when intraspecific or interspecific gene pools are mixed, either by intentional management, accidental human disruption, or the elimination of natural geographic barriers. However, the determination of genetic dissimilarity within intraspecific gene pools before contemplating mixing, although technologically feasible via genetic and karyotypic surveys (see Chambers and Bayless 1983), will not be easy in practice. Templeton et al. (1986) said that locally adapted and coadapted populations are best detected through studying natural populations, which can be augmented for captive animals by observations of mate choice, pedigree analysis, and genetic lab analysis. The application of simple rules to the results of electrophoresis, as a sole indication of taxonomic relationships, is naive (Nei 1987).

Because of the desirability of retaining the full range of genetic variation within a species, efforts should focus below the level of species, I think, but not on subspecies, which have been regarded as unreliable (Wilson and Brown 1953). The practical problem is that subspecific designations are not always dependable keys to biologically significant sub-

division (Templeton et al. 1986), so it is hard to proceed without extensive field and laboratory investigations. The subspecies is therefore not an appropriate evolutionary category for genetic management (Wiley 1981).

2   HOW MUCH GENE FLOW IS ENOUGH?

Some addition of new genes to a population could be regarded as healthy, as is natural immigration, and could counteract the potentially deleterious influence of small population sizes and increase evolutionary potential. This recognition stems from the Wahlund Principle: Fusion of isolated populations reduces the frequency of homozygous genotypes (Wahlund 1928).

Population geneticists are not in agreement on how much gene flow is necessary to counteract adaptation of peripheral populations for many organisms. For instance, some modeling has shown that neighboring demes can maintain their genetic differences while exchanging genes, providing a gene in a deme is selectively favored in its habitat, and gene flow is not great enough to dilute the effect of selection (May et al. 1975). These conditions may rarely be met, and Nagylaki (1975) thought that a small population could not be able to genetically differentiate through natural selection if swamped by immigrants from neighboring populations where other alleles are favored. Lacy's (1988) computer simulation modeling concluded that genetic drift was the overriding factor influencing the loss of genetic variation, confirming the importance of immigration to counter such loss. Roughgarden (1979) suggested that the immigration of a few individuals into a small population can result in "fusion" or "homogenization" of immigrant and recipient gene pools and counteract their further divergence due to genetic drift. However, such a model must assume the absence of natural selection. Large populations will demand even less immigration for fusion. In fact, Lewontin (1974) indicated that a migration rate of one individual per thousand individuals per generation will cause panmixis between two populations in the order of 10^4 (cited by Frankel and Soulé 1981). Allendorf (1983) maintained that one successfully reproducing migrant individual among demes per generation would prevent allele loss due to genetic drift but allow alleles in demes to respond to local adaptation.

3 GENETIC VARIATION: INDIVIDUALS VS. POPULATIONS

Knowledge of how much of the total genetic variation is contained within a certain number of individuals from a local population would also be useful before undertaking deliberate mixing, but generalizations should be regarded as suspect. Denniston (1978) made an imprecise projection that one individual contains half the genetic diversity (as represented by the statistical variance σ^2) of a small population, and 10 individuals contain 95 percent. Seal (1985) largely supported this projection, indicating that each individual contains 50 percent, two have 75 percent, and ten have 95 percent. Since an asymptote is approached at 92 percent with six individuals, he explained that the biblical choice of six animals, or three pairs, was a sound absolute minimum number for Noah's ark if they all lived and produced young.

4 THE GENETIC DILEMMA

Fisher (1930) demonstrates a direct correlation between the quantity of genetic variation in a group of plants or animals and the rate of natural selection. This "fundamental theorem of natural selection" can be applied today. As the landscape becomes more fragmented, artificial mixing may be more needed but theoretically could retard speciation and adaptation (Franklin 1980; Soulé 1980). One dramatic prediction addresses this dilemma (Chapter XVI). Franklin (1980) judged that it is better to sacrifice evolutionary change now if doing so conserves genetic variation for future evolutionary change. Therefore, the resolution of the dilemma may lie in strategies that retain as much natural genetic variation as possible within a population.

5 AFTERTHOUGHTS

Genetic management questions are only starting to be addressed, in part because of our ignorance about nature. As Frankel (1970) pointed out about the world community, "we have acquired evolutionary responsibility." Therefore, national park and reserve managers might start viewing their wards as potential donors to as well as recipients from species gene pools existing outside their own park or reserve systems, provided that information first exists to make intelligent management decisions. Such decisions must be based on a clearly defined policy of genetic management, constituting a problem all reserve managers worldwide must confront, but which few have confronted up to now (Lacy 1988). Unfortunately, the theory and implementation of genetic manipulation are still very young (Varvio et al. 1986).

Some local genetic variations result from local adaptation, while others may conceivably be due to chance events associated with random mutation, genetic drift, or the founder effect (Simberloff and Cox 1987). Should we try to maintain all this variation, as current conservation philosophy seems to imply? As Soulé (1980) pointed out, even if genetic considerations are ignored (genetic management), artificial migration is still needed to prevent stochastic events from causing local extinctions in reserves (demographic management). Demographic stochasticity (Section IVC) is now considered more important overall than genetic stochasticity, at least for the short term, since genetic variation becomes irrelevant once a population goes extinct (Lande and Barrowclough 1987).

E   *Other Translocations*

Whether communities are in equilibrium is a recurrent question we will look at often, but see Wiens (1986) about expectations. For instance, in regard to interspecific mixing from a nongenetic standpoint, the concept of "assembly rules," derived from studies of tropical forest birds on islands, is relevant to tropical reserves on real islands (Diamond 1975a) and could be applicable to continental reserves if the rules were better understood. The hypothesis is that, through diffuse competition, species in a community are selected and adjusted relative to one another in terms of niche and abundance, so they all "fit" together and resist invaders. The conservation implications are that certain species combinations may be forbidden. These concepts have subsequently been impugned (Connor and Simberloff 1979; Simberloff and Connor 1981), rebutted (Diamond and Gilpin 1982; Gilpin and Diamond 1982), and challenged (Connor and Simberloff 1983). Such assembly-rule concerns of Diamond (1975a), if valid, would perhaps have more weight if all other things were equal, but such is rarely the case.

F   Perimeters and Shape

1   RESERVE SIZE AND EXTERNAL INFLUENCES

Wright et al. (1933) suggested smaller size made a reserve more endangered by external influences. Nelson (1978) suggested that large size does not necessarily diminish outside-inside effects, and a large boundary might even accentuate them. Willis (1984) argued that influences involving people or their activities outside a reserve (e.g., poachers, exotic species, and pesticides) depend on the number of access points for humans, which large reserves might reduce! Diamond and May (1976) suggested that the area-to-perimeter ratio is a measure of exposure to the outside (small reserves and long thin ones with low a/p ratios are most exposed), and Schonewald-Cox and Bayless (1986) and Soulé (1986) also theorized that small and long thin habitats are most vulnerable to outside influences.

Wright and Machlis (1987) attempted to test the hypothesis, using survey data from 100 parks in 49 countries (Machlis and Tichnell 1985). Although larger parks generally reported more threats to wildlife than did smaller parks, in only two cases did threats vary significantly with park size (involving nonnative species and the management of migratory species). The data are somewhat problematical, so the case for larger size and external influences remains open.

2   RESERVE SHAPE

Reserve shape is also much debated. A round reserve has been widely declared superior to any other shape (e.g., Diamond and May 1976) on the basis of a biogeographic generalization called the "peninsular effect," described by Simpson (1964): The number of species often diminishes as one proceeds to the end of a peninsula. Local extinctions at the end of a peninsula were assumed to be counteracted by individuals migrating from more central regions but probably at a slow rate.

But as Simberloff (1978c, 1982a, 1983a) pointed out, some research, such as Taylor and Regal (1978), offered alternative explanations for the peninsular effect: not slow migration but habitat differences. Furthermore, no research has demonstrated that round reserves hold more species than long thin ones. Seib (1980) concluded that the number of lizard species on Baja California depended upon limiting factors and competitive exclusion instead of geometric shape. Busack and Hedges (1984), in data from four major peninsulas, found no z values significantly different from those on the nearby mainland and only one peninsula (Florida) with a decreasing gradient in species density for lizards and snakes. For other studies showing no evidence that the decrease in species number toward the tip of a peninsula is an immigration-extinction phenomenon, see Simberloff and Abele (1984) and Means and Simberloff (1987).

Simberloff (1982a) commented that narrower refuges may be more visible to immigrants, and larger perimeters can have more "edge effect" (after Williamson 1975). Game (1980) demonstrated mathematically that if immigration rate more than extinction rate depends on shape, then the optimal reserve shape in all situations is not necessarily round. Blouin and Connor (1985) examined the relationship between species number and habitat shape on oceanic islands for 33 data sets and concluded that if similar mechanisms govern species number on both oceanic islands and habitat islands, then shape should not be a major concern in nature reserve design. However, such mechanisms are unlikely to be the same. Reserve shape may be unimportant, depending on the species-area relationship and its influence on species numbers, so long as reserves are not very thin (e.g., 200 m), in which case edge effect becomes overwhelming. But reserve shape could be important for other reasons, such as external influences (previous section). It could also be important for animal movements across boundaries (Section XIIIC2).

G   *Nature Reserve System Design Simplified*

PRINCIPLES FOR DESIGN OF FAUNAL PRESERVES

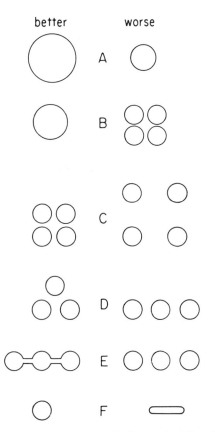

Figure 44. Nature reserve design principles that have been advanced reportedly based on the theory of island biogeography. Principles B, C, and F are still being debated. Simberloff (1983b) and Simberloff and Abele (1984) maintain that some principles are not derivable from the theory of island biogeography (e.g., B) or are unrelated to it (e.g., F). (From Diamond 1975b; reprinted by permission of Elsevier Applied Science Publishers Ltd., England.)

Some aspects of nature reserve design have already been discussed. Diamond (1975b) and Wilson and Willis (1975) advanced various geometric design guidelines for reserve systems, reportedly all derivable from the theory of island biogeography. These guidelines have apparently been adopted without reservation or additional explanation; for example, the 1980 IUCN *World Conservation Strategy* (IUCN 1980) adopted those put forth by Diamond (1975b). Simberloff (1982b) first pointed out the lack of adequate scrutiny, since the empirical support for some of the guidelines is contestable (Fig. 44). Although Margules et al. (1982) concluded that these specific guidelines should be used with caution, if at all, they have been adopted as gospel in environmental planning books (Eagles 1984), in textbooks (Krebs 1985), in strategies to create African reserves (IUCN/UNEP 1986), and in environmental symposiums (Mintzer 1988). Even Diamond (1981) later indicted it is difficult to formulate universal principles for reserve design and management. I think this represents an example of premature adoption of world nature reserve conservation policy. There may be no absolute hierarchy of conservation goals, or any "right" list of reserve system selection guidelines (Cocks and Baird 1989).

Note

[4]In 1975, among 89 designated wilderness and primitive areas in the United States, only 10 were larger than 1,000 km² and 26 larger than 600 km², with all 36 clustered in 11 western states according to Sullivan and Shaffer (1975). As of September 1983, among 269 designated wilderness areas, 48 were larger than 1,000 km² and 20 larger than 600 km², with 66 clustered in 10 western states plus 1 each in Georgia and Florida.

X

Research and Policy

A   Some Policy Questions

Many policy questions require a close look by managers and planners of parks and nature reserves. Can we manage to prevent possible future extinctions caused by reserve size or insularity (Soulé et al. 1979), and what should we do when we suspect that reserves harbor smaller than viable populations? (See Sections VIIJ6, VIII, IXB3.) How much should, or indeed must, the habitat in U.S. national parks be manipulated to comply with a guiding principle that the parks represent a "vignette of primitive America" and is such a laudable goal realistic? (See Section XIVD.) Can preservation efforts easily deal below the level of the species, as Greig (1979) admonishes? (See Section IXD1.) Should the goal of management continue to be one of ensuring that natural ecosystem processes operate unimpaired (as adopted once by the U.S. National Park Service) or one of preserving maximum species

number, as implied by applications of the theory of island biogeography (see Margules et al. 1988). Also, should single-species management ever take precedence over either of the above (Kushlan 1979)? I think this review supports the old U.S. National Park Service policy of ensuring that natural ecosystem processes operate unimpaired for existing national parks, but the other two options might be preferable for managing or locating reserves, depending on circumstances.

Such policy questions are often difficult to answer and some require continuing study to gather more and dependable scientific data. Even policies derived from a good empirical foundation should not necessarily be cast in stone but regarded as flexible, responsive to future new findings, rather than a bureaucratic refuge.

B   Policy Formulation

Recommendations are one thing, the practical realities of implementation another. Nevertheless, we can never intelligently implement management directives however difficult without the information only additional research can provide. As Leopold et al. (1963) indicated, "management without knowledge would be a dangerous policy indeed." But adequate knowledge is not always possible, and decisions still have to be made.

Soulé (1985) thought that the discipline of conservation biology demands the making of recommendations before one is "completely comfortable with the theoretical and empirical bases of the analysis." Even if we accept this as the reality, we must also acknowledge that some conservation guidelines already put forth are insupportable, despite their reception as gospel by nonexperts. Invoking irrelevant theory is potentially detrimental to conservation (Simberloff 1986b).

May (1984, in Slobodkin 1988) said that "Unfortunately, in many . . . practical situations, decisions must be made today. . . . The choice is not between perfect and imperfect advice to managers, but between crudely imperfect advice and no advice at all." However, Slobodkin (1988) stated that "it is by no means obvious that 'crudely imperfect advice' from a supposed expert is more or less valuable than 'no advice at all'." Long-term policy should preferably not be based on crudely imperfect advice. Nature reserve planners and managers should seek out the advice of scientists. But caution is warranted because of the immaturity of the field and its extensive controversy, not excluding this review.

The problems being faced do not always allow the luxury of conclusive research. This is the "policy dilemma" part of the "island dilemma." Also, the best and most empirically sufficient advice is not often amenable to easy application. This is the "implementation dilemma" aspect of the "island dilemma." In light of these various dilemmas, nature reserve planners and managers do not have an enviable position, which scientists must appreciate more fully. Nature reserve planners and managers must also appreciate the difficulties scientists face.

XI

Nature Reserve Size/Design and Management: National Contrasts

A *European Examples*

1 CHARACTERISTICALLY SMALL RESERVES

Duffey (1971) reported that the 129 National Nature Reserves then in Great Britain averaged approximately 8.6 km², while the 62 in England alone (excluding Scotland and Wales) averaged approximately 4.1 km². By 1977 the reserves in Great Britain numbered 150 and averaged 8.0 km² (Ratcliffe 1977), by 1978 161 averaged 7.8 km² (Poore and Gryn-Ambroes 1980), and by 1984 182 averaged 7.6 km² (Foster et al. 1984). However, 29 percent of the National Nature Reserves in England and Wales are in 10 national parks with a mean size of 100.6 km² (Brotherton 1982), all in IUCN management category V: protected landscape. For a more complete description of various protected area categories in the British Isles, see Foster et al. (1984). The Netherlands had 1,270 nature reserves in 1982, occupying 6 percent of the country's land base, but only 9 were as large as 40 km², and 275 were smaller than 0.04 km² (van der Maarel 1982).

2 FRAGMENTATION AND INSULARIZATION

Size and isolation of nature reserves in Great Britain is thought to be influencing their species numbers. Moore (1962) studied the heaths in Dorset and concluded that the effects of increased isolation were observed because of slight impoverishment of the fauna in outlying heaths. Duffey (1974) indicated that the main environmental factors affecting wildlife on the Breckland heath reserves are reduction in size, fragmentation, and isolation. But in samples of invertebrates, Mader (1981), Hopkins and Webb (1984), and Webb (1989) found more rather than fewer species on small isolated patches of heathland. Webb (1989) observed that invertebrate species number depended more on the structure and composition of the vegetation surrounding the heath fragment than on fragment size or isolation.

Muggleton and Benham (1975) argued that fragmentation of habitat and consequent inbreeding had been responsible for the decline of the large blue butterfly in Great Britain. Duffey (1977) suggested an intensive management program to maintain the large copper butterfly on part of a reserve in England regarded as much too small (0.3 km²) for its long-term survival. Duffey (1971), in a discussion of reserves for insects, described the British experience of intensive management of small, sometimes compartmentalized reserves. In Great Britain many large mammals were long ago extirpated, and insect populations enjoy the luxury of much attention (e.g., Ratcliffe 1979).

3   RESERVE DESIGN REALITIES

L. E. Gilbert (1980) noticed a relative scarcity of British literature on the design aspects of the theory of island biogeography and suggested that the longer British history of land use, compared to that of the United States, may have given them less opportunity for better reserve design. This may have been so, but publications on the design of British nature reserves have increased significantly since then (e.g., Higgs and Usher 1980; Margules and Usher 1981; Reed 1983; Woolhouse 1983, 1987). Nevertheless, their longer land-use history could preclude some design options, and the British more

than younger countries may be constrained to managing what they have. Foster et al. (1984) commented that "since the total protection of extensive area of unaltered natural environment is not an option in the U.K., it has been necessary to find ways of integrating conservation with other land uses." As an example of the antiquity of their land-use history, Rackham (1980) traced the location of some English woodlands back to the Roman period. Forest reduction and fragmentation in Great Britain began 5,000 years ago (Wilcove et al. 1986).

Green (1989) depicted the historical decline of wildlife in Great Britain. By the late nineteenth century, the typical countryside patchwork of fields, farms, meadows, ponds, and heaths was in place. Habitat fragmentation and species extinctions grew rapidly (Fig. 2) up to the present. The resulting habitats have more variety than the original forest, though this is little consolation for the native species lost. With the need for more agricultural productivity, Green argued for designation of such rural landscapes as some form of reserve, to encourage more conservation. Such an integration of conservation and agriculture, though not easy to resolve and implement, offers an alternative approach toward the goal of maximum preservation of biological diversity. This concept has relevance well beyond Great Britain.

B   U.S. Examples

1   LARGEST U.S. RESERVES

Small reserves are abundant in the United States. For example, as of July 1987 the 78 sites in the Ohio Nature Preserve System had a mean size of 200 acres, the 154 sites in the Illinois Nature Preserve System averaged 166 acres, the 214 sites in the Wisconsin System of State Natural Areas averaged 164 acres, and the 96 sites in the Indiana Nature Preserve System averaged 124 acres.

However, unlike Great Britain and The Netherlands, the United States also has many large reserves. How do the data portrayed in Figure 35 relate to the U.S. National Park System and U.S. National Wilderness Preservation System? Yellowstone National Park has a gross area of 8,982 km², the largest single unit of the National Park System in

the lower 48 states and the world's first national park, established in 1872. Only 2.3 percent of the reserves in the world are larger. Nine units of the National Park System exceed 10,000 km², all in Alaska, representing only 2.8 percent of all units. Three units of the National Wilderness Preservation System in Alaska exceed 10,000 km², and are not part of the nine in the National Park System. The largest unit, both a national park and a wilderness, is Wrangell-Saint Elias National Park and Preserve with a gross area of 53,365 km².

2   RESERVE DESIGN REALITIES

Although U.S. national parks and other reserves are generally much larger than Great Britain's and

The Netherlands', our opportunities for larger sizes, or better designs, may have vanished in many cases and, in the conceivable future, we may bemoan the fact that better scientific guidance was unavailable when reserve boundaries were first established. Nevertheless, regional cooperation still offers a chance to alleviate this problem (Sections VIIIB and XIIK, Chapters XIII and XIV).

The Nature Conservancy (TNC) manages a large system of nature reserves throughout the United States. They advise the selection of good ecological boundaries, for example, that take into account hydrological systems, the incorporation of multiple habitats, the negative effects of edge, and the recognition that small reserves are probably more vulnerable and need more intervention than large ones. However, noticeably lacking at present is formal advice on the scientific aspects of nature reserve design (not inventory). Advice is now mostly procedural and administrative. TNC (1987) stated:

None of these materials (the scientific literature), however, will quite give you the answers you want or tell you how to design a preserve for the particular elements and there is nothing in them that can be distilled into a set of generally recognized and incontrovertible rules. In fact, beyond what is common sense, virtually all the complicated matters having a bearing on preserve design are still under considerable dispute.

There is much truth in this analysis, but the prospect for potential guidance is not quite that bleak (Chapters XII and XVII). Real-world experience in nature reserve establishment often contrasts with advice provided by academia. TNC (1987) illustrated this point:

Both shape and juxtaposition of preserves are generally matters outside our hands. Element occurrence boundaries and ownership patterns inevitably determine preserve shape. And we put our preserves where the element occurrence are, regardless of their proximity to or distance from other occurrences. As for corridors, we have to recognize that in most cases in the heavily settled areas of the United States, they cannot be created or maintained. If a targeted element on a preserve becomes extirpated, we will have to evaluate reintroducing it from elsewhere.

C Summary

The sizes of the largest national parks and nature reserves in different developed countries differ strikingly. Countries with some of the largest reserves, like the United States, still have many nature reserves that are very small. Intensive management of these small reserves seems a projected challenge for many countries. As of 1985 the 14 million-ha Western Australian wheatbelt had 626 nature reserves ranging in area from 0.4 ha to 309,000 ha, with a median of 120 ha (Wallace and Moore 1987). Older countries like Great Britain have lost some planning options because the landscape has long been occupied, but the options of even younger countries like the United States and Australia may well be on the verge of being precluded.

D Urban Habitats

Another contrast, alluded to in Section IIB3, is growing steadily "within" all countries: rural versus suburban-urban environments. Cities typically contain fragmented natural habitat and could be managed and designed for optimum wildlife abundance (Adams and Dove 1989). Adams and Dove cited studies that indicate the importance of habitat area and isolation in various locales and for different species, for example, city parks, cemeteries, and remnant woodlots in Bratislava, Czechoslovakia, for amphibians, reptiles, birds, and mammals (Vizyová 1986); in habitat patches in Oxford, England, for amphibians, reptiles, and mammals (Dickman 1987); in forest patches in metropolitan Milwaukee, Wisconsin, for mammals (Matthiae and Stearns 1981) and plants (Levenson 1981); for insects in

Cincinnati, Ohio (Faeth and Kane 1978); and for birds in Seattle, Washington (Gavareski 1976). Most of these habitat patches ranged in size from 0.5 to 45 ha. Some biological diversity can be protected at this scale, and such small patches have a role to play for some species. Cities could be a granite garden (Spirn 1984) and augment national strategies for biological conservation or just provide opportunities for human enjoyment of nature. An awareness of the role cities can play in this regard is in-creasing (see Adams and Leedy 1987). However, our ignorance of the dynamics of animal populations is perhaps greater for fragmented city habitats than for rural environments. For example, Poynton and Roberts (1985) stated, "In our present lack of knowledge, evaluation of what constitutes an 'effective dispersal corridor' in any particular city, even for the most obvious natural species, has to rest largely on guesswork."

XII

Conservation Guidance in the 1990s: Where Do We Stand Now?

Simberloff (1978a,b,c, 1982a) translated the scientific literature for presentation in popular forums, presumably to improve its digestibility and its accessibility to nonscientists. Some efforts give the impression that recommended guidelines have drawn little controversy (e.g., Conservation Foundation 1984). Attempts to summarize this field concisely for a general audience are applauded, but they understandably sacrifice important detail (e.g., Office of Technology Assessment 1987). Therefore, what can we now offer with confidence as conservation guidelines?

A   The Theory of Island Biogeography

It is in some ways reassuring to see scientists and land managers increasingly conscious of the potential applications of MacArthur and Wilson's (1963, 1967) theory of island biogeography. But exactly what new insights from the theory and its associated species-area relationship (Chapter II) can be unequivocally applied to the conservation of animals by means of nature reserves? Before answering this question, let us first clearly review what the theory's equilibrium model says.

As outlined by Crowell (1986), the equilibrium model rests on two assumptions: 1) the rate of extinction decreases monotonically with area, and 2) the rate of immigration decreases with isolation. Its predictions are: 1) the number of species will increase directly with area; 2) species richness will decrease with distance from a source of replenishment; 3) the numbers of species will fluctuate about an equilibrium level; 4) there will be species turnover, with extinction balanced by colonization; and 5) successful colonization will be nonrandom, determined by the dispersal abilities and demographic characteristics of the source species.

In my view, only prediction 1 is unarguable: the more land we set aside, the more species we will preserve. Simberloff (1978b) pointed this out for conservation planners, but ecologists, amateur naturalists, and many laymen intuitively and deductively recognized it long before the theory of island biogeography appeared in 1963. Assumption 1 was verified by Rey (1981) for arthropods on *Spartina* islands, but evidence for larger habitat islands is mostly inferential (Diamond 1984b).

The species-area equation, including relative

abundance, is as yet too poorly understood and controversial for confident application to nature reserves. Whether an equilibrium number of species for nature reserves exists is unclear, and even MacArthur and Wilson were not sure that a perfect balance could be reached. The expectation by theory adherents, of finding an equilibrium number of species in a natural system, is perhaps a pursuit of uncritical dogma (Wiens 1986).

In the view of Miller and Harris (1977, 1979), no part of the equilibrium aspect of the theory of island biogeography had then been shown to apply to nature reserves. I think their conclusion is still correct. Newmark (1986, 1987) supposedly demonstrated validation for an area effect but Section VIH indicates uncertainty.

The theory of island biogeography did provide a framework within which to view a large number of interrelated ideas and still serves this useful purpose. It adopted the concepts of stochastic variations in population size and probability of extinction and proposed such ideas as differential extinction of species on islands, stepping-stone colonization, and clustering (Section IIA2), all apparently supported by enough evidence on real islands to be useful as guidance to nature reserve planners. Some controversy may revolve around definitions of what the theory says.

I would, however, agree with Simberloff (1982b) that the abundance of publications on the theory of island biogeography and applications has misled many scientists and conservationists into believing we now have a ready-to-wear guide to natural area preservation. We do not, yet. He further pointed out that the proliferation of uncritical publications can have the unfortunate effect of diverting research into wrong directions and management attention away from more pressing problems. The long-appreciated need for a better understanding of the habitat requirements of individual species, as Simberloff (1986b) pointed out, is an example of a relatively neglected area. Zimmerman and Bierregaard (1986) concluded, on the basis of the world's largest experiment to test it (Section VIi), that focusing on the details of the theory is misguided without accompanying autecological information on the species being studied.

We also must distinguish between application of the theory of island biogeography (as in MacArthur and Wilson 1967) and, more generally, of island biogeography (as in Williamson 1981). We desperately need more studies of reserve size, habitat isolation, minimum viable population size, nature reserve system design, genetic mixing, and many other related questions that still lack a good overall title, other than perhaps the "island dilemma" (terminology Diamond 1975b). Wilcox (1980) introduced what I perceive as a more restrictive term—"insular ecology." As Pielou (1981) remarked, "it is not the resemblance between models and reality that lead to new discoveries, but the discrepancies between them."

B   *Minimum Populations*

Minimum viable population size involves a complex of considerations, including demographic stochasticity, environmental stochasticity, genetics, and social dysfunction. It is presently poorly understood and estimated. It has not been confidently calculated for any species (Section VIIJ4). As Hooper (1971) explained, it has meaning only if a probability of extinction is accepted and a time period defined. Shaffer and Samson (1985) concluded that "some reserves will necessarily be very large and there is no simple, universal critical population size that, if achieved, will remove area requirements or the effects of subdivision as issues from the design of nature reserves." Although the concept has great potential use for nature reserve design on a species by species approach, its application will be delayed by the lack of better estimates. The best available thinking is found in Soulé (1987a). Present tentative estimates make it questionable whether it can be successfully achieved for many wide-ranging species, given the small size of many reserves (Sections VIIJ6 and XIIIA,C3). Shaffer (1987) summarized Soulé (1987a):

Many a mammalian species, particularly the larger, more spectacular and immediately useful or interesting to man, will require reserves on the order of 100,000–1,000,000's of km² for a high probability (0.95) of persistence for even a century. This is assuming that each reserve is intended to support a full complement of its native mammalian fauna and does so independently of all other reserves or of surrounding, non-reserve areas without active management.

C   *Habitat Size and Species Loss*

Here we will examine both equilibrium and non-equilibrium (in the sense of Brown 1971) conditions. As discussed in Section VIB, forest size is undoubtedly related to the number of breeding bird species in the U.S. Eastern Deciduous Forest (e.g., Whitcomb et al. 1981) and elsewhere. Area also correlated with species declines in the U.S. Eastern Deciduous Forest, Southeastern Brazilian woodlots, an Ecuadorian field station, and elsewhere. But original species compositions before decline usually had to be inferred, though some plots were periodically surveyed over long periods after isolation started. It is now uncertain whether species declines in all such studies are real (Boecklen and Simberloff 1986). Soulé et al. (1988) presented data showing that habitat area and time since isolation significantly correlated with the current number of surviving species of chaparral birds in isolated canyons in San Diego, but admitted that they did not unequivocally demonstrate that missing species had become extinct. Assuming that some of the extinctions are real, to what degree area alone is responsible is not surely known. Lack of recolonization may play a role in reported declines.

The Barro Colorado Island study did not clearly determine the relative contribution of area alone to the decline of bird species (Karr 1982a,b). Lovejoy et al. (1986) had good evidence of species loss in small (1–10 ha) plots due to either an area or edge effect. As far as I know, none of the habitat island studies have demonstrated true insularity. Simberloff (1978b) thought that Vuilleumier's (1970) study of birds in natural paramo habitat islands in the northern Andes came closest: the number of species on an island was a function of its area, and the proportion of endemic species for any paramo island was best explained by distance to the closest large island (an indication of isolation). The influence of isolation is another matter: Lynch and Whigham (1984) and Opdam et al. (1985) demonstrated the effect of isolation on bird species confined to woodlots, and Opdam, van Dorp, and ter Braak (1984) showed evidence that bird species abundance was influenced by *both* area and isolation. None except Lovejoy et al. (1986) apparently had good knowledge of the species composition before fragmentation or isolation occurred, including on Barro Colorado Island as Willis (1979) pointed out.

Proponents of land-bridge island relaxation theory claimed that the rate of local extinctions for some species was inversely related to island size (e.g., Diamond 1972; Terborgh 1974; Wilcox 1978; Soulé et al. 1979; Hope 1973; Heaney and Patterson 1986). The conclusions of these earliest studies were challenged (Simberloff and Abele 1976b; Abele and Connor 1979; F. S. Gilbert 1980). Boecklen and Simberloff (1986) indicated conceptual and statistical flaws, for example, regarding birds (Terborgh 1974), lizards (Case 1975), and mammals (Soulé et al. 1979). However, the studies varied considerably in approach, so extinctions may have been as claimed for some mammals (Heaney and Patterson 1986) and some birds (Diamond 1984b).

F. S. Gilbert (1980) commented that evidence still did not link extinctions in reserves to a decrease in area. Rey (1981, 1984) thought that the predicted effect of area was confirmed for arthropods on tiny *Spartina* islands, but the effect of isolation on immigration rates and numbers of species was not. However, there is inferential evidence for the area effect on both larger habitat islands and nature reserves. An important and ambitious experimental study of the habitat-island effect is underway, and the results for mammals are significant (Lovejoy et al. 1983, 1984, 1986; Lovejoy 1987), but it has a drawback in that the patches being studied are surrounded by secondary successional habitat and not by an inhospitable matrix that cannot be traversed. However, Schwarzkopf and Rylands (1989) reported that some 10-ha forest fragments still support three species of primates. Habitat structural diversity, rather than period of isolation or distance to the primary forest, seemed to influence primate species number.

The difficulty in doing the necessary experimentation must be recognized. Separating the effects of area from all other factors in sites the size of small habitat islands or nature reserves is probably impossible even with multivariate techniques (see Bennett 1987). Area vs. isolation vs. habitat heterogeneity vs. internal impacts vs. external influences simply present too complex an array. It may also prove impossible to separate the effects of humans from those of so-called natural processes (Brown 1986).

We should remember the arguments of the theory of island biogeography for the importance of large nonisolated reserves, but also that available habitat of adequate quality for a selected species and a diversity of quality habitats for many species may be just as influential as area per se. Bekele (1980) found a highly significant correlation between numbers of large mammals and habitat diversity in western U. S., Ethiopian, and Indian reserves but a correlation with reserve size only in the western United States.

Brown (1986) indicated that U.S. national parks could not contain their present mammalian fauna if all the matrix between the parks were converted to uninhabitable landscape. This is a prediction of the theory of island biogeography with which I concur, even in the absence of good supporting data. The present size and potential for isolation of the world's parks and reserves are a cause for uneasiness as to the long-term future of their fauna.

D   *Nature Reserve Size*

For species assemblages, terrestrial habitat fragmentation studies will provide some insight for some species, especially birds, but are unlikely to disentangle area from other influences. Some land-bridge island extrapolations are suspect; Boecklen and Simberloff (1986) estimated such wide confidence limits for predictions derived from relaxation and faunal-collapse models that the models seem to be a problematic source of specific recommendations about reserve size. Lawlor (1986) did illustrate how species-area relationships can provide important biogeographic information about a species in some cases. Incidence functions hold promise as a tool, but few have been calculated.

If the long-term effective population size (N_e) is actually near 500, as suggested by Franklin (1980), then I would concur with Soulé (Frankel and Soulé 1981) that the largest reserves in the world contain too few of many of their large predators and herbivores to retain genetic variation over the long term, and some reserves are too small for even short-term fitness. Support for this contention comes from Wilcox and Murphy (1985), who pointed out that both East (1981b, 1983) and Schonewald-Cox (1983) had shown that many large mammal populations in reserves have fewer than 100 individuals, and more than half the populations are in the range of 100–1,000.

The "500 rule" has been widely adopted in the literature, though Seal (1985) proposes 250–500 for captive vertebrates. Lande and Barrowclough (1987) thought the number is closer to several hundred for quantitative traits. But how much influence such predicted genetic erosion will have on a possible local extinction and how soon it will become

manifest is uncertain. However, Shaffer (1987) saw genetic considerations as the least of our worries for minimum viable population size (Section VIIJ6). Lande (1988) argued that demography may usually be of more significance than population genetics in determining minimum viable population size, but said a realistic integration of demography and genetics has so far eluded us.

Until minimum viable population sizes for certain species can be better estimated, we may have to use other approaches to estimate reserve size. We can still concentrate on defining the more general and familiar autecological considerations for individual species. This is the approach presumably used to conserve some large carnivores and herbivores, for example, in parts of Africa. Area requirements for these large vertebrates will provide an area-umbrella for smaller species. The theory of island biogeography cannot tell us how much area is required to conserve a species or set of species; this can be derived only by studying a species' natural history (Simberloff 1978b). Good estimates of minimum viable population size are much needed but does not have to be viewed as prohibiting any estimate of needed area. As Wilcox (1984b) indicated, we can identify a species with the greatest or most comprehensive habitat needs and then consider the pathway:

species → minimum viable population →
habitat requirement → minimum area requirement

Additionally, the needs of migratory animals (see Section VIIJ3) and the concept of entire functioning ecological systems (see Sections XIIIB2,C3) also should be considered in determining reserve size. In other words, knowledge of the life history of a species and its ecosystem is equally if not more critical to reserve size and design than is application of ecological theories and general models (Franklin 1985).

Schonewald-Cox and Bayless (1986) suggested

that reserve size, specifically perimeter-to-area ratios (Section IXF1), is important for external influences, but real data are meager. A large buffer zone, as described in Section VIIIB, presently seems a wise solution for various reasons (Chapters XIII and XIV).

E Nature Reserve Shape

The shape of an individual reserve is not an important consideration, at least in terms of the species-area relationship and its influence on species number. Simulation models suggest it may be important for animal movements across boundaries (Stamps et al. 1987; Buechner 1987; see Section XIIIC2). The suggestion by Schonewald-Cox and Bayless (1986)

cited in the previous section, regarding the importance of perimeter-to-area ratios for external influences, relates to reserve shape as well as size. The edge effect can be an important influence for some species and also relates to both the shape and size of reserves.

F Nature Reserve System Spatial Configuration

In terms of geometric design principles for reserves, and ignoring practical realities and trade-offs, many large reserves are needed in as many biotic community types as possible (Chapter IX). Corridors between reserves will be useful for some species, but it is too early to advocate their use in all cases because their benefits and drawbacks are still being debated; ideally each situation should be assessed individually (Simberloff and Cox 1987). If corridors are opted for in individual or regional situations, they should be integrated with buffer zones into a regional landscape network, as envisioned by Noss and Harris (1986) and Noss (1987c).

However, dispersed reserves hypothetically have many advantages, as Soulé (Frankel and Soulé 1981) described. Replicates of individual reserves, although each reserve is unique, would be most desirable for the following reasons: some species are rare; replication insures against the unforeseen; and the

probability is greater of capturing more genetic variation occurring within a species' range (Slatyer 1975). However, I would agree with Game and Peterken (1984) that efforts to apply across-the-board rules (e.g., that a large reserve is preferable to several reserves with the same total area) to global strategies for reserve design will probably be wasted effort because the reverse of a rule may also be true for some species. For example, several reserves of the same total area as one larger reserve may sometimes be preferable, depending on species-area relationships and/or managerial considerations. What is optimal for mammals in the Arctic may be less so for plants in the tropics, which makes global strategies like that portrayed in Figure 44 too simplistic. For instance, different taxa respond differently to increases in area (Section IXC), and Miller and White (1986) maintained that no single species-area model will suffice even for one biogeographic region.

G Nature Reserve Numbers and Coverage

Since species number is modeled poorly as a function of area alone (Boecklen and Gotelli 1984), over-

reliance on the species-area equation to predict overall reserve coverage for a large region, especially quantitatively, is unwise (Sections IXC1,2). The equation may be more useful at the scale of continents (Section XVF). Of great importance is realizing that even extensive systems of reserves may not contain a significant portion of the species in a country if little is known about the distribution of their diversity (Diamond 1980b; Wilcox 1984a). Reserve coverage in the United States should be improved and is grossly inadequate in many of the world's biogeographical provinces (Section IXC3).

H   Management and Reserve Design

Soulé (Frankel and Soulé 1981) saw an over-emphasis on the "design" and an underemphasis on the need for "management" of natural reserves in the "island biogeography" types of literature. This was true but has been changing quickly. "Management" here means intervention not laissez-faire (terminology Frankel 1983). Soulé (Frankel and Soulé 1981) also thought that excessive emphasis on design by itself is highly myopic.

But L. E. Gilbert's (1980) point was also well made: "While sound design reduces the need for management, in many cases management will have to deal with mistakes in design and unforeseen complications." Sound design and informed foresight will be a foremost challenge, as many design options in some localities already may be precluded.

Ecological change in reserves was categorized by White and Bratton (1980) as ranging from natural to human-caused, beneficial to detrimental, and manageable to impossible to manage. We need to identify the things we can change and those we cannot. Management may be directly related, indirectly related, or unrelated to a reserve's design. Therefore, although many management problems can be attributed to poor reserve design, at least some—such as various external influences—may exist within the best reserve design (Chapter XIII).

I   Management and Genetic Considerations

The potential negative influences of inbreeding and genetic drift in small natural populations, inferred from captive studies, should be recognized in outcrossing species confined to reserves. Exceptions to the no-inbreeding rule may arise when the entire reserve system is considered (see Chesser and Ryman 1986), and inbreeding has been positively exploited through management (Templeton and Read 1983), but these are exceptions and not the rule.

Subdivided populations are potentially either helped or harmed by the subdivision (see Lacy 1988). Separation can be deleterious but may also increase the amount of genetic variation in a species through local adaptation (Chesser et al. 1980). Isolation (as in nature reserves) that enhances the maintenance of genetic variation for the species as a whole may reduce the fitness of a particular population (Chesser 1983). The simulations of Boecklen and Bell (1987) indicated that intact populations preserve more heterozygotes, while subdivided populations preserve more alleles (see Chapter XVI).

Although there are good reasons to bolster population sizes by adding individuals, the deliberate mixing of different intraspecific gene pools should proceed with caution until we know more about its consequences. Caution is recommended even though Frankel (Frankel and Soulé 1981) found little evidence that it is harmful. Templeton et al. (1986) warned against it, but Templeton (1986) concluded that outbreeding depression resulting from intrinsic coadaptation is only temporary. We do not yet know much about outbreeding depression. Regarding our genetic dilemma, I would agree with Franklin (1980) that it is better to sacrifice evolutionary change at present if by doing so we conserve genetic variation for future generations. Optimal reserve design will maximize alleles and minimize inbreeding depression by preserving heterozygosity (Boecklen and Bell 1987). How to accomplish both is not yet clear.

J Landscape Ecology

Ecologists are just starting to recognize the influence of regional processes on local community structure (Ricklefs 1987). I think a primary concern should be to develop an awareness of the science of "landscape ecology" and management principles derived from it (Hansson 1977; Burgess and Sharpe 1981b; Forman and Godron 1981; Tjallingii and de Veer 1982; Noss 1983; Risser et al. 1984; Forman and Godron 1986; Urban et al. 1987; see Fig. 35). Decisions should take into consideration species diversity, distributed on a local, regional, or continental scale, occurring in the mosaic of habitats in the landscape. They must also consider the size, shape, and connectedness of habitats, as well as the mosaic of land uses that created and surround the habitats. This is not a recommendation that planners learn the terminology or literature of the field of landscape ecology, but rather that they adopt its perspective, which integrates much of what we have discussed earlier. This perspective is just beginning to be applied to the debates about reserve design (see Means and Greene 1987).

For example, studies of invertebrate species numbers on heathland fragments in Dorset, England, suggested that the fragments should be viewed as parts of an interacting matrix (Webb and Hopkins 1984; Webb 1985, 1989). I think we can presume that larger-scale landscapes are also interacting matrixes. Levins (1970) defined "metapopulation" as a "population of populations which go extinct locally and recolonize." Some data suggest that populations in mosaic environments behave this way. Merriam (1984) defined "connectivity" as a "parameter of the interconnection of functionally related ecological elements of a landscape so that species can move among them" and included both physical features and species behavior. Connectivity is a fundamental aspect of landscape mosaics, including nature reserves, and their metapopulations.

Landscape ecology has its roots in Central and Eastern Europe where it has long been used as a basis for landscape planning and management (Naveh 1982; Naveh and Lieberman 1984). The United States and other countries urgently need to follow this lead. Natural area management in the United States and elsewhere will consist increasingly of managing a mosaic of remnant habitat patches. Indeed, the day has already arrived (Figs. 41 and 45). Risser (1986) reported that of 161 nature reserves containing some tallgrass prairie located in 14 U.S. states, almost half are under 100 acres in size. In Missouri only 0.5 percent of the original tallgrass prairie remains, appearing as islands surrounded by pastures and croplands (Risser 1988).

The existing theoretical and empirical foundation for a science of landscape ecology was clearly expounded by Forman and Godron (1986). It remains a challenge to apply this thinking to nature reserve management, and Forman (1987a) made an attempt. Forman (1987b) stated:

in land use decisions and actions it is unethical to evaluate an area in isolation from its surroundings or from its development over time. Ethics impel us to consider an area in its broadest spatial and temporal perspectives.

We should be mindful of both this philosophy and perspective in establishing and managing reserves. We have to think of the landscape in terms of patches, corridors, and matrix, not just for the small nature reserve systems (remnant habitat patches) common in Europe and elsewhere, but for the larger national park systems as well. Merriam's (1984) field data and model supported the intuitive notion that connectivity significantly affects abundance and extinction probabilities, but human activity is eliminating connectivity worldwide, for example, in Australia (Bridgewater 1987). We must be aware of this destruction and protect existing natural landscape connectivity and assemblages. This means that effective conservation considers the entire landscape and thus blends into regional planning.

Figure 45. The 86.5-acre Markham Prairie Nature Preserve, Cook County, Illinois, is located in the town of Markham, a suburb of Chicago. It is one of the largest high-quality tall-grass prairies in Illinois. Based on a 1986 report, in the Chicago Lake Plain natural region of Illinois, about one-hundredth of 1 percent remains of the once widespread original prairie. The state-owned preserve is a remnant habitat patch adjacent to suburban development. (This U.S. Department of Agriculture 1:40,000 scale aerial photograph was taken 10-10-74.)

K Regional Planning in the World

Regional planning must take into account land-use practices adjacent to reserves and, especially in developing countries, the social and economic needs of people living nearby. Myers (1972) and other authors have stressed the necessity to view the establishment of national parks not only in a broad ecological sense but also in relation to human needs outside the park. Otherwise, inevitable encroachment up to the park boundaries takes place progressively, and the park ultimately is viewed as an "island" by people living next to it (Chapters XIII and XIV). Lacking protection, some reserves will be reduced in size to accommodate such pressures, as has happened in East Africa. Lamprey (1974) indicated the importance of a preventive buffer zone:

> *In the experience of many African national park authorities, the presence of intensive settlement on the boundaries produces a de facto zone of "limited conservation" inside the park, within which some poaching, tree-felling, grazing, grass burning, and other illicit activities may occur, necessitating constant policing.*

In addition to "biosphere reserves" (Section VIIIB3), other categories of protected areas recognized by IUCN (1978, 1984), such as "multiple-use management area/managed resource area" and "natural biotic area/anthropological reserve," can accommodate indigenous people in a reserve concept. Regional and urban planning that integrates the natural and social sciences is urgently needed (e.g., di Castri et al. 1984). Western and Henry (1979) raised the concern that the complexity of regional and integrated land-use planning was be-

yond the capabilities of most third-world agencies that administer national parks. Before we criticize regional planning in third-world countries, however, Dasmann's (1987) comment about the United States is worth repeating:

> *The Park Service is responsible for all resources within the park, but its authority ends at the park boundary. Air, water, wildlife, seeds, nutrients, energy move in and out of the park, but once across the boundary some other agency assumes responsibility. The same kind of institutional barriers are found in developing countries, but they are often even more rigid. It is difficult for us to point the finger at their problems, or offer advice, when we have not been successful at home.*

Many third-world countries seem to be doing a much better job than the United States, including developing a model biosphere reserve (Section XIVC3).

Miller and Bratton (1987) believed that we do not yet know enough about the dynamic processes governing insularity to address it confidently in regional conservation planning. Until we know more about the consequences of park and reserve insularization, we would be wise to prevent the reduction of virtual sizes by means of landscape alteration outside park and reserve boundaries. Larger virtual size might be achieved by acquiring buffer zones or implementing land-use restrictions (Chapter VIII). Regardless of land-use alterations outside park and reserve boundaries, current stochastic models suggest the desirability of a large increase in size, possibly through regional cooperation (Section VIIJ6).

L The Current Demand

The design and management of national parks and nature reserves can be seen as involving a mix of theoretical considerations related to number of species, population sizes, autecology of individual species, interacting assemblages of species, genetic variation—spatial and temporal—within a species, and management concerns related to disease, catastrophe, emigration and immigration, annual migration across boundaries, ecosystem processes, regional planning, and, of course, human visitation

and exploitation. We are unlikely to be able to synthesize all such concerns and come up with a few simple all-inclusive design and management principles. More review is needed.

The primary dilemma is that we cannot afford to wait for impeccable evidence that can be translated into conservation guidelines. Decisions must be made with inadequate information. We must act now on the basis of whatever guidance we can glean from natural science, sociology, and economics.

M   *Where Have We Come Since 1962?*

As MacArthur and Wilson (1967) indicated, fundamental processes inherent in the discipline of biogeography are extremely challenging to study and understand: dispersal, invasion, competition, adaptation, and extinction. Also, the knowledge we do have of such processes is exceptionally difficult to apply to nature reserves. To arrive at some solid empirical foundation for conservation guidelines has been the real test. We have both succeeded and failed the test.

Success has been achieved in the sense that Preston (1962) and MacArthur and Wilson (1963, 1967) directly or indirectly instigated study on some relatively neglected topics, such as nature reserve size and insularity (Terborgh 1974); nature reserve system design (Diamond 1975b); minimum viable population size (Shaffer 1981); and patch dynamics (Pickett and Thompson 1978). More attention has been paid to other topics, such as the genetics of small populations, intraspecific genetic mixing, minimum size of a community, and dispersal barriers. An awareness has grown of the need for regional planning for nature.

Efforts to establish a viable theory failed only in the sense that empirical support for the theory of island biogeography itself is still too questionable for confident application to nature reserves. However, we know vastly more than we did then, including what we need most to study in the future. Many important questions were not even being asked in 1962–1963, nor was the complexity of their study appreciated. As MacArthur and Wilson (1967) indicated, "a good theory points to possible factors and relationships in the real world that would otherwise remain hidden and thus stimulates new forms of empirical research." This "failure" has thus generated a raving success.

XIII

Future Scenarios

After the above brief stock-taking of what we know, we will now look closely at two possible future scenarios, which we call the area-effects scenario and the external and internal influences scenario. Insufficient information precludes confident future projections for either one. However, the external and internal influences scenario has yet received little attention in the island biogeography literature, and I think it should be of more immediate concern.

A Area-Effects Scenario: Another Look

Preston (1962) predicted the loss of species in reserves over time due to inadequate area because of the hypothetical species-area relationship between isolates and samples. This model can address the loss of contiguous buffer zones of similar habitat and the consequently insufficient initial reserve size for some faunal species. None of this has been demonstrated to be due to the influence of area alone. However, we know that some species depend on resources outside reserve boundaries, and some reserves are too small to accommodate the feeding range of some large carnivores and herbivores.

Related projections stem from the species-area relationship and from stochastic theory. Soulé (1983) suggested that a decrease in area sets in motion a chain of events leading to population extinction by two pathways—habitat isolation and population size reduction—which is good theory. Lynch (1987) said that "a reduction in habitat area is causally related to an entire syndrome of physical and biotic change that may have a more direct influence than does area per se on populations."

Frankel's (1984) conclusion that the extinction of large vertebrates appears inevitable was presumably based on long-term genetic erosion. Schonewald-Cox (1983), from an examination of park size alone, predicted that most U.S. national parks will need intensive management to forestall the disappearance of large vertebrates. Shaffer (1987) based similar conclusions on recent overall stochastic theory but, unlike Frankel, had to involve extinction rates and probabilities (Section VIIJ6). Goodman (1987a,b) agreed with Shaffer (1987): A systematic program of management intervention will be needed to lower the extinction rate of many populations of both large and rare species, except in the largest reserves, because the effect of environmental variation on stochastic demography will not change significantly with modest changes in population size or growth rate.

The recognition that only about 2 percent of the reserves in the world are larger than 10,000 km² could be very significant for some species. Soulé (Frankel and Soulé 1981) warned that although the period of reserve acquisition may be over in many countries, the time of reserve attrition may just be starting. I agree, but I think area alone is most significant when all other things are equal, which is not the case. Ultimate and proximate causes of extinction aside (Sections VIH, VIIB), more clarity is needed on what does or could cause extinctions.

B External and Internal Influences Scenario: Another Viewpoint

1 INTRODUCTION

There is, I think, a more ominous scenario for local species extinctions in reserves, especially for the short term. National parks and nature reserves will not be "benignly neglected" from the outside or the inside. The impact of external and internal influences, both real and potential, could override that of area effects.

Potential extinctions due to area effects were first described as a natural process—relaxation (in the sense of Diamond 1972)—without human influence. The idea of internal and external influences is different: the impact on species by many other causes stemming from human actions. These could be correlates of area, but were largely ignored in the island biogeography literature that discussed area effects.

2 U.S. EXAMPLES

National Park Service (1980) listed many potential influences in seven major threat categories: air pollution, water quality/quantity, aesthetic degradation, physical removal of resources, exotic encroachment, visitor physical impacts, and park operations. Each category included specific examples from both inside and outside park boundaries. Subcategories included such items as exotic species, overcrowding, road and facility construction, poaching and collecting, mineral development, urban encroachment, timbering, agriculture, air pollution, water pollution, soil erosion, and oil and gas

extraction. The report stated that 75 percent of all influences, external and internal, lack scientific documentation as to harmful effects on park natural resources. This percentage is unreliable because of the way the data were gathered and the varying backgrounds of the contributors. The report probably represents mostly perceptions of threat. Nevertheless, it was a first assessment, however rough, of possible threats to U.S. national park resources, internal and external. It warrants thorough scientific analysis.

The U.S. National Park System is facing challenges from various threats according to Dickenson (1984), a former agency Director:

In the Nearctic Realm, we collectively face a wide variety of problems within or adjacent to our parks. These include aesthetic degradation (land development, urban encroachment, insect infestations, timber removal, pollution, acid rain, odors, suspended particulates, hydrocarbon pollutants), physical removal of resources (mineral extraction, poaching, grazing, collection of specimens), exotic encroachment (plants, animals, noise), physical impact of visitors (campfires, erosion, wildlife harassment, trampling) water quality and quantity changes, and others.

Although National Park Service (1980) had shortcomings, it dealt with real dangers. Damage to biota in U.S. national parks is soundly documented in various other sources for some categories of internal and external influences. For external influences, good data exist for the effects of such agents as air pollution, water pollution, water flow disruption, logging (erosion), and exotic species. Little progress has been made since National Park Service (1980) in tracking these perceived threats or in documenting or mitigating their impact (GAO 1987). Another warning of National Park Service (1980) was:

The 63 national park natural areas greater than 30,000 acres (121 km²) in size reported an average number of threats nearly double that of the Servicewide norm. Included in this category are units such as Yellowstone, Yosemite, Great Smoky Mountains, Everglades, and Glacier. Most of these great parks were at one time pristine areas surrounded and protected by vast wilderness regions. Today, with their surrounding buffer zones gradually disappearing, many of these parks are experiencing significant and widespread adverse effects associated with external encroachment.

How factual this report was remains uncertain. Some U.S. national parks, for example, Everglades, Rocky Mountain, Organ Pipe, Yellowstone, and Olympic, are experiencing significant landscape changes beyond their borders on one or two sides (see Figs. 5–7). However, the present or future impact on their biota is typically undocumented.

Fish and Wildlife Service (1983) surveyed 473 field stations by questionnaire asking for information on resource problems. Of the problems reported, 58 percent involved external sources, including soil erosion/sedimentation, water flow increase/ floods, industrial and commercial development projects, air pollution emissions, urban encroachment, right-of-way corridors, wildlife disturbance, and poaching/illegal collecting. Internal problems accounted for less than 20 percent, and about 25 percent cited both internal and external sources. The report claimed documentation of 82 percent of the internal and 62 percent of the external problems. The professional training and experience of the observers varied. Again, a thorough scientific analysis is needed.

National Park Service (1987) described natural areas on both public and private lands in the United States—given special recognition because of their uncommon or exemplary biotic communities or landforms—reported as threatened or damaged. Over a ten-year period the potential sources of harm most frequently reported were categorized as construction/operation of structures, water projects, agricultural/forestry activities, exploration/ extraction of geological resources, visitor use, and waste disposal and resource contamination, originating both inside and outside site boundaries.

National Park Service (1988b), which assessed the condition of the U.S. National Park System through a questionnaire survey, indicated that 60 percent of

the parks were considered to be threatened by an outside source. A third of all reported threats stemmed directly from an outside source, and another third involved the influence of conditions or activities outside park boundaries. The six major natural resource issues were encroachment by plants and animals not native to park environments; scars from past mining activities, agricultural practices, and erosion; impacts of intensive recreational use; depletion of park resources by legal and illegal hunting, commercial fishing, grazing, and authorized oil and gas activities; the degradation of air and water from outside sources; and urban development along park boundaries. The report presented an even more dismal picture than did National Park Service (1980) about the degree to which some national parks are being isolated by human activities.

All these examples of external and internal threats are thus far largely anecdotal and unscientific in documentation. However, they are numerous and consistent in their claims.

Even if we ignore the internal influences issue, it seems reasonable to predict that the impact of some external influences may increase as buffer zones around parks are gradually reduced or eliminated. Certain external influences (e.g., water flow disruption) may become more severe as a result of insufficient buffer zones around park boundaries, whereas others (e.g., acid rain) may persist even if buffer zones were drastically enlarged. Although the issue of external influences and their impact on biota in parks has a different focus from that of the issue of effects due solely to reserve size and insularity, the two are related in that both may be aggravated by increasing landscape alteration outside park boundaries. A big unanswered question is: Can all park biotic resources survive external influences over the long term without a buffer zone? We know little about the necessary character or width of buffer zones.

The issue of external influences, at least for U.S. national parks, has a longer history than some realize. In 1933 the influence of exotic plants and animals was recognized as originating outside park boundaries (Wright et al. 1933). Cahalane (1948) assumed that wildlife populations even in the largest parks were influenced by hunting, trapping, agriculture, and other practices on adjacent lands. In 1963 a committee of scientists warned of overall U.S. national park degradation and the potential impacts of economic activities on adjacent lands,

Figure 46. The 40-acre Gross Woods, Shelby County, Ohio, is an isolated old-growth mixed mesophytic eastern deciduous forest. The state-owned nature reserve is surrounded by a matrix of agricultural fields. (This 1:12,000 scale state-flown aerial photo was taken 7-18-78 and provided by the Ohio Department of Natural Resources.)

and called for long-term research (Robbins 1963). Kusler (1974) and National Parks and Conservation Association (1979) also concluded that external influences appeared to be a problem. But it was not until 1980 that serious questions were asked about the possible accuracy of these early inklings of problems for biota in U.S. national parks due to outside influences (National Park Service 1980), not to mention inside ones. An awareness of these influences by the public is now increasing due to the attention

Figure 47. An aerial photograph taken of prairie-pothole landscape in Cavalier County, North Dakota, about five miles south of Munich. The landscape matrix consists of pothole lakes, cultivated lands, and natural or planted grassland. The lakes are natural habitat patches with human landscape disturbance around them. (The 1:65,000 scale photograph, taken 6-4-79, was provided by National Aeronautics and Space Administration Ames Photography and secured from the U.S. Geological Survey Earth Resources Observation Satellite Data Center.)

being given them in semipopular literature (Conservation Foundation 1985) and in feature sections of journals (Elfring 1986; Sun 1985).

Keiter (1985) believed that the U.S. National Park Service seems to have inadequate authority to protect the national parks from the potentially adverse effects of external influences. Shepard (1984), in contrast, thought that a broad interpretation of the Property Clause of the U.S. Constitution gives Congress the potential authority to exercise vast legislative control over nonfederal property. Natural Resources Law Center (1986) discussed the mostly legal aspects of external threats affecting U.S. national parks. Keiter and Hubert (1987) and Sax and Keiter (1987) dealt specifically with the legal issues of external threats to Glacier National Park, Montana. Simon (1988) treated all the legal issues surrounding U.S. national park management.

How much might the process of local extinction, which some scientists have predicted over the long term due to area effects alone, accelerate due to external and internal influences? What must be undertaken is the technically and politically difficult task of managing or abating threatening influences outside park or reserve boundaries. As Vink (1983) suggested, nature reserve management necessarily must have two components—external and internal management.

3   AN AFRICAN EXAMPLE

In developed countries external influences on parks and reserves often include urban growth. In developing countries they more often include agricultural development and associated deforestation, and the foremost underlying external threat is probably the expansion of human populations outside park boundaries and the rising need for food, fuel, and other essentials of survival.

An example is the threat to the gorilla population of the Virunga Volcanoes Conservation Area in Zaire, Rwanda, and Uganda. Figure 48 shows land use at a reserve boundary. Harcourt and Fossey (1981) thought that habitat removal (the reserve was made smaller) probably accounted for most of the gorilla population decline over approximately 20 years, citing poaching and cattle grazing as additional factors. The gorilla population data of Weber and Vedder (1983) led them to conclude that habitat loss was significant, but less so than claimed by Harcourt and Fossey, and that poaching was pri-

Figure 48. In the middle of the photograph (taken March 1987) an abrupt transition in vegetation can be seen on the lower slopes of these volcanic mountains. The transition depicts agricultural fields directly adjacent to the boundary of Rwanda's Parc National des Volcans. The park is habitat for the mountain gorilla. (Photo courtesy of Wes Henry.)

marily responsible. Habitat encroachment, cattle grazing, and poaching are forms of external influences whose relative contributions will always be difficult to sort out.

Weber and Vedder correctly pointed out that ignoring the broader issues of human population growth and land use could result in a human wave that would eliminate the gorilla population forever. Human population and poverty are a great potential external threat here as in much of the developing world. For other examples of real world problems in managing wildlife in African parks and reserves, see Owen-Smith (1983).

C The Theory of Island Biogeography and the Real World: In Retrospect

1 PRESTON'S LEGACY

Preston suggested some mathematical and conceptual foundations for the MacArthur and Wilson (1963, 1967) theory of island biogeography that stimulated hundreds of scientific papers relating to basic and applied aspects. For instance, Preston (1962) had a notion about equilibrium in relation to immigration (Section IIA1), demonstrated the mathematical link between the species-area relationship and the canonical log-normal species-abundance curve (Section IIC6), expressed the species-area equation in its best-known form (Section IIC4), indicated that the equation might hold for continents and continental shelves in geological time (Section XVB), and conceived the idea of isolates and samples and therefore the importance of biotic fluxes across reserve boundaries (Section IIB1). Also in 1962 an international committee of the First World Conference on National Parks (National Park Service 1962) stated:

Few of the world's parks are large enough to be in fact self-regulatory ecological units but are more likely to be ecological islands subject to direct or indirect modification by activities and conditions in the surrounding area. These influences may involve such factors as immigration and/or emigration of animal and plant life, changes in the fire regime, and alterations in the surface or subsurface water.

The statement will also serve the purpose of introducing two critical questions that deserve recapitulation: Are national parks islands? Are they self-regulating?

2 ARE NATIONAL PARKS ISLANDS?

Contrary to the National Park Service (1962) statement and much current thinking, it is not at all clear whether most parks are already ecological islands. Dispersal barriers for some species are known (Section IXB2). Some parks could be islands only for some species, preventing emigration out to similar distant habitats or immigration in to provide the community with a full complement of species.

Stamps et al. (1987) theorized that habitat patches may be bounded by a "hard edge," an impenetrable boundary never crossed by dispersing individuals, or a "soft edge," permeable to certain species. From computer simulations they concluded that edge permeability and edge-to-size ratio are positively related to emigration. It remains a question whether either type of edge in a nature reserve has been demonstrated for large mammals (i.e., other than small mammals, reptiles, amphibians, and some birds), though one intuitively suspects that abundant examples are waiting for verification and that habitat traversability outside of reserves will get worse. Buechner's (1987) computer simulation models suggested that: perimeter-area ratios, edge permeability, the appearance, stopping patterns, and habitat preferences of moving animals, and the relative size of dispersal sinks and source pools may all influence the direction and magnitude of animal movement across reserve boundaries.

Preston's (1962) characterization of samples and isolates was an early recognition that animal movements across a sample's edge or boundary may influence the viability of its biota. In fact, Albright (1933) recognized that animals moving across national park boundaries will encounter conditions very different from those of their ancestors in the middle nineteenth century as a result of abutting civilization, thus necessitating research to determine what is actually happening.

One thing seems very clear: with respect to outside influences, no park is an island (terminology National Parks and Conservation Association 1979). This conclusion is consistent with Forman's (1987a) ethical principle and technical theory for landscape patches in general: "no boundary in a landscape is impermeable and no action is isolated."

3 ARE NATIONAL PARKS SELF-REGULATING?

Whether few parks are large enough to be self-regulating or self-sustaining is not certain, but some certainly are not, for example, Serengetti National Park with its large herbivores. Kushlan (1979, 1987) gave another obvious example: Everglades National Park and its source of water. He indicated that some U.S. national parks, like Everglades, are not self-contained ecosystems driven by endogenous processes; since ecosystem processes must also be considered, shape and total area by themselves are inadequate criteria for reserve design. These ecosystem processes can be interfered with from the outside. Even though it is awkward to address the question of what a "complete" ecosystem is, in terms of its geographical boundaries in the natural landscape, we recognize that some U.S. national parks and other reserves are not self-contained.

What about self-sustaining populations? Soulé (1987b), in summarizing a symposium, guessed at the lowest minimum viable population (MVP) for a vertebrate: the low thousands, assuming a 95 percent expectation of persistence without loss of fitness for several centuries. He stressed that a viability analysis should be conducted in each individual case and that his guess was a possible order-of-magnitude "lower boundary." If we use this stochastic extinction model as a guide, then many of the world's reserves containing large vertebrates are not self-sustaining because no one location has enough space, unless, of course, such species occur at several locations. Soulé stated:

> Probably within a decade or so, the experience of managers and field biologists, along with the continuing efforts of theoreticians and modelers, will facilitate the development of generalizable protocols for estimation of MVPs.

Since we cannot afford to wait, the guidance described in the previous paragraph probably is the best we can expect for now. However, as stressed throughout this review, I do not think size alone, while certainly very important, is the main criterion for short-term viability. Franklin (1985) indicated that "where conflicts do arise theoretical models will not substitute for judgment and prudence in the decision process." We have looked at, and will continue to look at, such conflicts.

4 THE WORLD'S NATIONAL PARKS: IMPACTS FROM OUTSIDE?

We do have more short-range concerns confronting us. We need to gather more factual data to see if Curry-Lindahl's (1974) perception of the situation in the world is supportable:

> There are few countries with national parks, where the latter have not been threatened by being overrun, reduced, altered, or even destroyed by external pressures. But there are also internal ones such as overuse by visitors.

Machlis and Tichnell (1985) reported on perceived threats to world parks revealed in 100 questionnaires returned out of 135 mailed to parks and reserves in more than 50 countries. Although only 60 percent of the returns claimed documentation of threat, 24 percent of the reported threats were exclusively from outside the park, 34 percent from inside, and 35 percent from a combination of both. The authors stated:

> Several of the 10 most reported threats in the study—illegal removal of animal life, removal of vegetation, local attitudes, and conflicting demands—can be attributed to interactions between parks and socioeconomic regions adjacent to them.

These threats are not unlike some described for U.S. national parks (Section XIIIB2). Therefore, movements across a park boundary not just of human products, as in developed countries, but of humans themselves, more often in the third world, were a concern not considered by Preston's (1962) simple model of animal movement across a "sample" boundary. Schonewald-Cox and Bayless (1986) and Schonewald-Cox (1988) proposed more elaborate boundary models.

An external influence that could affect all countries is human-induced global atmospheric warming (Houghton and Woodwell 1989). Experts predict that the average temperature could rise 1.5–4.5°C by the year 2000. Peters and Darling (1985) predicted that this could cause a northward shift in vegetation of some 300 km and that animals "trapped" in habitat-island nature reserves may not be able readily to move with it. This is based on the presumption that many nature reserves have impenetrable terrain outside their boundaries for some species.

This review will not treat the biological effects of global warming beyond reserve isolation (see Lovejoy and Peters in press). Hunter et al. (1988) suggested that nature reserves be connected to continental corridors to allow modifications in their geographic ranges due to climatic change. Thus, external influences can operate on very different scales: locally (e.g., water flow disruption or pollution), regionally or internationally (e.g., acid rain), and globally (e.g., atmospheric warming).

Some modeling literature, illustrated by Preston's important initiatives, often seems quite detached from many of the real world tasks of managing national parks and reserves, about which I think some in the scientific community may have received too little information.

XIV

Some Conservation Realities
and Philosophy

A   A Time Frame of Concern

Frankel (1974) recognized early the difficulty of making judgments in historical time, and making decisions on a sociopolitical time scale, for events that will happen in evolutionary time. Should we be concerned about the future welfare of biota in national parks and nature reserves into the distant future? Frankel thought so. He said that our answer hinges on what "time frame of concern" our society adopts for fauna in the reserves. This includes a consideration of the faunal genetic makeup, which constitutes a resource for continuing evolutionary options. Some of the stochastic extinction models in which genetics was only one component adopted as time frames of concern 100 or 1,000 years (Section VIIJ6). However, we should not forget that our actions in the next few years, ten at the outside, may largely determine whether much of the world's biota survives for us to be concerned about their long-term welfare.

B   Beyond Natural Science

Their experiences in East Africa induced Western and Ssemakula (1981) to remind us that, in the real world, whether national parks and reserves become faunal isolates will be dictated more by political and economic policies than by the application of any reserve design principles. Their warning about East Africa is also applicable to the United States and many other countries. Although most third world countries have had to deal with the externalities of park planning and management, while developing countries dwelled mostly on what happens within park boundaries, as Myers (1972) pointed out, this now must change.

Seidensticker (1987) indicated that conserving tigers in Indonesia and Bangladesh will involve protecting habitat outside reserves, thereby incorporating the tiger's habitat requirements in surrounding land management systems. Panwar (1984) described the establishment of buffer zones or multiple-use areas around many parks in India to accommodate the tiger. McNeeley and Miller (1984) described many examples of conflicts between wide-ranging large mammals and adjacent villages. Indeed, Frankel (1974) recognized early that the siting, design, and management of reserves will inevitably be affected by ecological, economic, social, and political circumstances. National parks also can provide real benefits to local people (McNeeley and Miller 1984; see Section XIVC).

I think L. E. Gilbert's (1980) view may be true in some situations but is overly pessimistic as a generalization:

> Biologists will probably not be given a significant role in land-use planning anywhere in the world. Ultimately most conservation programs will be the management of scraps of nature left untouched by various governments.

Mishra (1984) believed that the selection by land-use planners of marginal lands (defined as unsuitable for agriculture and human uses) for reserves in southern Asia would include most reserves already established there. These reserves may be defined as marginal, but many are well located even if they are scraps. Although some reserves were established because they were suboptimal habitat for humans, such as tsetse-fly-infested zones of East Africa, I think many biologists played an active role in establishing reserves in more desirable landscapes and can continue to do so. Our future success will depend on relating to the specific socioeconomic conditions of a country. Even strategies based on the best available technical expertise can fail if the important cultural context is not taken fully into account. Garratt (1984) stated:

> However it must always be remembered that a signature on a legal document or the drawing of a boundary line on a map do not suddenly change the nature of an area or erect a barrier between it and the surrounding land or cut cultural or economic links with the land which local people already have. . . .
> The message is clear that Nature does not recognize Man's laws and boundaries and that laws by themselves do not change human habits and traditions. Protected area management must therefore consider the physical and social environment of the broader region if it is to be effective.

Western (1989) maintained that land beyond national parks is our primary resource and main challenge in the protection of wildlife in Africa. I think he is correct and, along with corridors, such land offers us our primary opportunity to thwart the "island dilemma." His philosophy is worth repeating to the world:

> Wildlife conservation beyond the parks can only succeed by adapting philosophy and methodology to local conditions, whether cultural, economic, religious, or political. Human self-interest, tolerance, curiosity or just plain indifference may decide whether wildlife survives.

C   Nature Reserves and the Local Economy

Western and Henry (1979) declared that parks in most developing countries are enclaves whose visitors are economically advantaged compared with what people earn outside the park. They thought that the revenues earned by a country's parks can be increased and shared with adjacent landowners if the park is planned in conjunction with its surroundings. The following are five examples that support their views.

1   AMBOSELI NATIONAL PARK, KENYA

Western (1982) described the situation in the vicinity of the 488-km² Amboseli National Park in Kenya where large mammals disperse over 5,000 km² of landscape during the rainy season. Approximately 6,000 Maasai tribespeople, 48,000 cattle, and 18,000 sheep and goats use the same land and could not be relocated. Eighty percent of the migrant animals concentrated in the dry season in an area of only 600 km² and therefore used the same land as the Maasai cattle. The problem is now being alleviated by what Western recommended as a working model for African parks: demonstrating that wildlife conservation benefits exceed their costs by means of annual monetary compensation to the Maasai for any losses suffered by their cattle from migratory wildlife. Other forms of economic gain included plans for relocating some tourist camps outside the park, payment to gather firewood and road gravel outside the park, and employment by the park authorities. School and medical facilities were made available. Means to pump water out of the park for the cattle were being sought. Most importantly, by projecting tourism to full development, Western estimated, wildlife could generate revenue 18 times the annual income of a commercial and fully developed beef economy.

2   LUPANDE GAME MANAGEMENT AREA, ZAMBIA

The 32 Game Management Areas (GMA) in Zambia serve as multiple-use buffer zones adjacent to the country's national parks. Local people live and farm in the GMA, which they cannot do in the national parks, but their use of wildlife in the GMA is highly restricted, resulting in protein deficiencies in areas where tsetse-fly infestations affect cattle and in crop destruction by free-ranging animals. Because of poor local economies and no economic incentive to conserve wildlife, local residents reportedly sometimes encouraged poaching in exchange for meat to feed their families. Zambia's experimental Lupande Development Project, which began in 1981 in the Lupande GMA, is based on the expectation that revenue derived from wildlife can both meet the conservation goals of Zambia's National Parks and Wildlife Service (NPWS) and assist local economies. To achieve this, safari companies must now hire a minimum number of local people. Safari concession fees are paid into a fund used by both the NPWS and local chiefs for development projects. Funds are also used to employ residents as village scouts to guard against poachers. The NPWS shares decision making with the local people in the GMA. The World Wildlife Fund (WWF) is providing funds to extend this wildlife management system to more GMA in Zambia, in hopes of making them self-supporting, one example of the activities of the WWF's Wildlands and Human Needs Project (World Wildlife Fund 1988, 1989).

3   SIAN KA'AN BIOSPHERE RESERVE, MEXICO

The model biosphere reserve also can potentially be fully applied and bring economic returns to its inhabitants. The new Sian Ka'an Biosphere Reserve, created in 1986 by presidential decree, is located on the Caribbean coast of the Yucatan Peninsula in the state of Quintana Roo, Mexico, only 150 miles south of Cancun. The 1.2 million–acre reserve protects marshes, mangroves, lagoons, marine and reef environments, and tropical forests. A management plan bans disturbance in core zones but permits hunting, gathering, farming, and development for tourism in other parts of the reserve. Approximately 1,000 people, mostly lobster fishermen, live within the reserve, primarily in two villages. A growing number of Mayan subsistence farmers are settling outside the reserve's borders. The residents of the reserve manage it through a network of federal, state, and municipal officials, with nongovernmental groups as advisers. The reserve now has a lobster management program endorsed by the fishermen, a sustainable horticulture project, a palm research study, and experiments on sound cattle-raising techniques near the reserve. A nature tourism project is underway, based on the assumption that natural and cultural tours booked for visitors from Cancun and elsewhere will enhance the reserve's chances for economic self-sufficiency. An educational extension program is planned in the reserve buffer zone. All these projects are being promoted and subsidized by the World Wildlife Fund. Details are given in McCaffrey and Landazuri (1987) and Tangley (1988).

4   GIR SANCTUARY, INDIA

Saharia (1984) described another interesting park arrangement in the Gir Forest, a 1,500-km² woodland in the Saurashtra peninsula of Gujarat, India. Within the forest are 200 of the last Asiatic lions (*Panthera leo persica*) in the world. The Gir ecosystem in 1972 contained 129 settlements of Maldharis, with 845 families consisting of about 4,800 persons. The cattle population, mostly buffalo, was estimated at 16,800. The Maldharis and their cattle once were integrated with the needs of the lion. But because of cultivation and forest depletion next to the Gir sanctuary, 48,000 nonresident cattle would enter the sanctuary during the monsoon every year. The result was loss of cattle by predation and degradation of the landscape. In 1972 the government of Gujarat established the 1,412-km² Gir Sanctuary, and the 259-km² core area was made a national park in 1974. The Maldharis are being settled outside the sanctuary and given land, monetary subsidies, and health services. Sixty-three percent of the land next to the sanctuary is cultivated. This is essentially the early biosphere reserve concept, though it has not been so designated. It did require moving local people out of the core area. For more details, see Berwick (1976). The arrangement is similar to that of the Amboseli National Park in Kenya.

5 ROYAL CHITWAN NATIONAL PARK, NEPAL

Mishra (1984) described the complex human dilemma in Royal Chitwan National Park, Nepal. Tigers in the park were killing local people and livestock; rhinoceroses wandering out of the park were destroying crops; local people were forbidden to collect wood in the park. However, cash did flow into the local economy from tourism, local employment increased, and soil and water in the region were conserved because of the park. Thus, local people had economic incentives to cooperate with the park. However, Mishra believed that the economic returns from tourism in this case failed to motivate the local people to favor the national park.

The park is now adding buffer zones along some segments of its boundary, a very positive step. In some places it has also integrated local villages and their ways of making a living within the park. However, in other places the change in conditions between outside and inside the park is dramatic (Fig. 49), a pattern observable in many parts of the world. Also, some buffer zones were created inside rather than outside the park boundary to accommodate and promote good relations with the local villages (Fig. 50). This is an alternative to the de facto zone of "limited conservation," described by Lamprey (1974), inside some African parks (Section XIIK).

The above five examples, some more successful than others, conform to the goal expressed by Miller (1982):

As surrounding lands and waters become exploited for agriculture, grazing, forestry, fisheries and human settlements, the protected areas are called upon to relate in definable ways to human needs. Perhaps the most significant role protected areas can play in supporting adjacent lands is to contribute to the sustainability of the development process. . . . The salient point here is to question whether all possible efforts have been made to link protected areas economically and socially with the surrounding communities to provide tangible and visible support to the extent and in the form consistent with conservation goals.

In essence, the conservation of biological diversity and economic development are linked and may even be interdependent. This was the theme of the World Conservation Strategy (IUCN 1980) and the Third-World Conference on National Parks (McNeeley and Miller 1984): conservation for sustainable development. McNeely (1988) treated the relationship between economics and biological diversity in detail.

However, as previously indicated, economic incentive is not everything. Lusigi (1984) stated:

Effective conservation reflects a state of mind. In my judgment, the purely economic benefits now popularly advanced as a justification for nature conservation will not in themselves save the African natural heritage. A common failing in the implementation of conservation programmes in the past has been the scant regard that has been given to the so-called "human factor." The existence of a human population in a place presupposes a complex of ethnic, social and biological influences and interactions. If these are not understood and adequately incorporated into conservation plans, the consequences can be serious, and even disastrous.

The above examples illustrate how human uses have been integrated into reserve design and management. However, we also need information on how well total reserve management plans maintain biological diversity, the bottom line for judging the success of a reserve and its management plan.

D   U.S. National Park Policy Scrutinized

One of the policy questions identified in Section XA will be addressed in detail with regard to the U.S. National Park System, already used to illustrate many points. The Leopold et al. (1963) report was a landmark document that recommended badly needed guidance for managing U.S. national parks. It stated that "the goal of managing the national parks and monuments should be to preserve, and where necessary to recreate, the ecological scene as viewed by the first European visitors." The idea was encapsulated by the authors' much-quoted statement that "a national park should represent a vignette of primitive America," viewed by many as a management principle. However, confusion and mistranslation can distort a report's message in its passage toward popular perception and explanation. For example, other statements by the authors, such as "a reasonable illusion of primitive America could be recreated," are less often quoted. Such

statements can be taken too literally. The vignette concept needs judicious interpretation.

The report correctly indicated that national parks are affected by many conditions that did not exist in pre-Columbian times, for example, the absence of natural fire regimes, the presence of exotic species and new diseases, the absence of some natural predators, the absence of normal water level fluctuations, and, of course, the presence of heavy

Figure 49. Royal Chitwan National Park, Nepal, in some places illustrates dramatic land-use changes between the national park and land outside its boundary. The fenceline is the boundary as it existed in December 1988. (Photo by the author.)

Figure 50. Local villagers living just outside Royal Chitwan National Park, Nepal, daily bring their cattle just inside the park boundary to a narrow buffer zone for grazing and drinking, and then move them out of the park in the evening. Illustrated are cattle moving out of the park during December 1988. The villagers also bathe and wash their clothes in park waters. These practices, if judiciously allowed, can promote better relationships between the park and the local people. (Photo by the author.)

visitation. The report expressed the need for management to control changes resulting from human influences. Concerns that have arisen since 1963 include acid rain and climatic change.

We must not interpret the report as demanding management for "still-photography" museums, achieved by methods ranging from a hands-off approach, allowing the free play of natural processes, to active manipulation of natural processes to create a desired effect. The authors acknowledged the operation in parks of human-induced processes that are dynamic and cause resident species to change through succession. As the authors also pointed out, change is expected in the absence of human influences.

We should, I think, strive for the conservation of natural processes, but to do so, as the report endorsed, active manipulative resources management, and not simple protection, was, and still is, badly needed. But what should be the guidelines for manipulative management? The answer to this question is less clear.

Gordon (1989) concurs with my view that the Leopold report actually encouraged active management and not fixation on a static primitive condition; the National Park Service commitment to natural regulation did not dictate laissez-faire management. Leopold's perspective was declared as valuable today as it was in 1963.

Although the Leopold report did refer briefly to external park influences and possible cooperative efforts with other agencies outside park boundaries, it did not emphasize these questions. What seems needed now, which was not stressed by Leopold, is to view U.S. national parks more as integral parts of their surrounding landscape than as separate entities, and in the context of the socioeconomic conditions in which they occur. U.S. national parks were at first sited largely on the basis of scenery. An alternative approach is the systematic capturing of various natural landscape types. Locating high species diversity or abundance is another good principle (e.g., Miller and Bratton 1987). However, I think that the future selection of reserve sites, both in the United States and elsewhere in the world, must start to give due consideration to regional economic and social factors as well as the likelihood of being able to sustain holistic ecological systems in the chosen area. This may be what UNESCO (1974) intended, but did not clearly express, in advising that one criterion for

biosphere reserve selection should be "buffer-zone compatibility" with the surrounding area. Tangley (1988) better captured the current biosphere reserve philosophy:

Beyond the buffer zone, and lacking definite borders, is a reserve's transition area. . . . Because the transition area lacks borders, it potentially extends indefinitely and forms a link between the reserve and the surrounding region.

Fortunately, times are changing, at least for stated policy. I prepared a speech supported and delivered by a former Director of the U.S. National Park Service, Mott (1988a), from which the following were excerpted:

Many nature reserves, including national parks, may become habitat patches in a matrix of disturbed landscape, which could influence the viability of the biota within them. The study of landscape ecology has been in existence in Europe for a long time. It is a young discipline in the United States. We need to follow the European example and study the entire landscape more as a mosaic of habitat patches imbedded in a matrix of diverse land uses. Research should include patch or reserve shape, connectedness, and boundary permeability. For instance, what are the pros and cons of habitat corridors for individual nature reserve system situations and what is the optimal design for different species? . . .

Our previous view of stopping our concern at the national park or nature reserve boundary has got to be replaced with practical applications of buffer zones, regional planning, and consideration of the social and economic conditions adjacent to reserves. . . .

Our innovative thinking in these areas can set an example for the world, just as our predecessors did in 1872 when they created Yellowstone National Park. We must, however, recognize all aspects of the problem—technical, social, economic, and political. Our ultimate goal is holistic land use planning for national parks and nature reserves. To achieve this demands the viewpoint of "looking beyond" national park or nature reserve boundaries.

See also Mott (1988b) for more details in this speech. It took until 1988 to incorporate the need to consider and integrate land-use practices outside of U.S. national parks in official park management strategy and policy (National Park Service 1988a). The challenge and pressing need now is to translate such sound policy into action. This will require a national awareness, support, and effort.

E   *The Challenge Ahead*

Burgess and Sharpe (1981b) concluded that "a vast experiment is underway" encompassing both the progressive insularization of national parks and reserves and the potential impacts of "external influences." Unfortunately, we do not fully understand the processes and future results of this ongoing experiment. Marsh (1874) said "we are never justified in assuming a force to be insignificant because its measure is unknown." Because of external influences, Burgess and Sharpe indicated it may be impossible to maintain an ecosystem at 100 percent integrity, even with intensive management and ample increase in area.

Parks have been described as "islands of hope" (W. E. Brown 1971). Let us hope that Sigmund Freud's description of his world in his later cancer-tormented days is not a better analogy for the future of national parks and reserves in this country and elsewhere: "A little island of pain floating in a sea of indifference" (Jones 1961, cited by Klopfer 1981). In the third world, the pain of poverty outside some reserves and the potential danger such poverty poses to their biotic resources usually go unmentioned in island-biogeography literature.

In Africa below the Sahara, half the people use wildlife (including fish, insects, caterpillars, maggots, snails, and rodents) as a dietary supplement (Riney 1967). At least half of all wood cut in the world each year is burned as fuel (Eckholm 1976). World Resources Institute (1985) later indicated that up to 82 percent of the wood cut in developing countries is for fuel (often as charcoal), and FAO (1981) reported that two billion people, three-fourths the population in developing countries, rely on wood or charcoal as a domestic energy source (cited in Hyman 1988).

I think the greatest boundary-related threat to biota in reserves in some parts of the world is persecution outside reserve boundaries. Janzen (1986) theorized that the boundaries of some nature reserves could act as a unidirectional filter: Some animals leave but few return because of influences such as poaching.

I predict that, just as humans greatly accelerated the decline of species on real islands in the late Holocene, they will do the same on habitat islands in the form of nature reserves. Although the role of humans in reducing the Pleistocene megafauna on continents is debated (Martin 1984), if it was even partly responsible it is likely also to affect animals that are much more confined. Human population growth and environmental changes cannot continue to be studied as separate phenomena by narrow specialists. For instance, declining per capita production in all but a few African countries since 1965 (IIED/WRI 1987) may be the primary overall influence on the welfare of Africa's parks and reserves.

Mishra (1988) made the point:

> *If over-development, over-consumption and waste are the problems of developed countries, then poverty, hunger, apathy and lack of economic infrastructures are the seeds that breed environmental woes in the underdeveloped nations. It has been pointed out that people who are ill-fed, in ill-health and have no shelter or jobs cannot understand paternalistic concerns for conservation of their environment. When the source of their next meal is a major worry, lofty principles of nature conservation for sustainable development have little relevance to them.*

This review has identified people in relationship to reserves in various potential contexts: first, visitors who traditionally come for recreation, study, research, or simply to rest and leave a park or reserve exactly as they found it; second, indigenous people living in harmony with the biota in a park or its recognized buffer zone; third, floods of visitors whose numbers, as in some U.S. national parks, endanger natural resources unless controlled; fourth, people who are an external threat to the park, either residing outside where they poach or remove the biota for survival or profit, or whose industrial, domestic, or agricultural products are potentially harmful to the reserve. All these types are now active in various parts of the world, and the last is of especially great concern.

These human influences challenge the ability, or lack of ability, to integrate national parks into regional land-use planning. They engender an urge, often followed by action, to protect parks from people, rather than to design and integrate parks and uses for the benefit of local people. Human population is the fundamental problem. Parks will have to be protected from people until human pressures no longer threaten the biota either inside or outside park boundaries. This is the challenge of regional land-use planning.

Machlis and Tichnell (1985) expressed it this way:

The romantic vision of parks as protected paradises is widespread and, ironically, may threaten the permanence of national parks. This purely preservationist approach, where parks are considered "fortresses" under siege, invincible or soon eradicated, carries great political risks. It requires an essentially militaristic defense strategy, and will almost always heighten conflict (cited by McNeely 1989).

Most national park field-level natural-resource management in the United States seems to revolve around compensating for the influences of man (Houston 1971). This should come as no surprise. Leopold (1933a) implied that management principles could be applied to any living thing, which is what we advocate today by "biological diversity" conservation. Leopold's (1933b) pioneering work in game management also demanded "people" management, and biological diversity conservation today I think weighs largely on people management, though resources management is important too.

The grim reality is that each year less and less natural land remains and is subjected to more and more people pressure. We must now learn more about managing habitat patches in a disturbed landscape. The science of nature reserve management is just beginning but must already cope with an urgent need for intensive management and planning of national parks and nature reserves throughout the world, based on scientific principles and an awareness of many relevant concerns. The complexity of this applied discipline is great, demanding the best possible transfer of knowledge from scientific institutions and "planners and managers" with backgrounds similar to that of the "scientists."

The mandate of the Act of August 25, 1916, to the U.S. National Park Service directs the agency to "conserve . . . the wildlife therein . . . in such a manner . . . as will leave them unimpaired for . . . future generations." This is going to be exceedingly difficult as time goes on. It demands educating the general public about the most basic ideas of conservation biology (e.g., Stone and Stone 1989) as well as a synthesis of technical information for scientists (see Simberloff 1988). The challenge to all agencies and organizations that manage or administer national parks or nature reserves is to meet such a responsibility with the support of much research, sound management, and holistic regional planning. As Miller (1982) said, "The emerging 'protected areas enterprise' requires the best of ecological and social science, economic analysis, business management, regional planning and international relations."

The conservation of biological diversity in the world's national parks and nature reserves will require cooperation from the local to the international level, both to accommodate the movement of animals across political boundaries and to provide the technical assistance one nation can offer another. It demands a viewpoint broad enough to be concerned about the biota in a five-acre nature reserve in Fig. 41 and along our roadways, as well as the more charismatic grizzly bears in the Greater Yellowstone Ecosystem. They are all parts of the huge "checkerboard" that our now fragmented natural landscape has become. Some countries like Australia are already trying to integrate this perspective into nature reserve planning (Saunders et al. 1987a). We need to follow suite.

F Devastation of Present Tropical Forests: A Projection

A matter of paramount importance is that continued tropical deforestation will have a catastrophic effect. Simberloff (1986a and in Lewin 1983) used the species-area equation to model the impact of such forest loss, while pointing out some of the equation's drawbacks. Assuming the obliteration of all New World tropical forests sometime next century (except for 96,700 km² in existing parks and reserves in tropical America), he predicted the loss

of 66 percent of all species and 14 percent of all families of plants and 69 percent of all species and 26 percent of all families of birds. Simberloff (1984) projected that perhaps two-thirds of all tropical plant and animal species would be extinct within the next century. Such predictions are chilling. He thought that the fragmented New World tropical forests of the future would resemble the configuration in the Pleistocene refugia hypothesis in Figure

32. Since his estimates were conservative and based on the Neotropics, which are in the best condition, Simberloff (1986a) concluded that "the imminent catastrophe in tropical forests is commensurate with all the great mass extinctions except for that at the end of the Permian."

Cautions are necessary in using the species-area equation $S = cA^z$. Sections IXC1,2, and XVE point out that it gives inconclusive predictions of continental species diversity. Ideally we would like better confidence intervals than Simberloff (1986a) provided, a criticism he makes against applications of the theory of island biogeography (Boecklin and Simberloff 1986). Although this review has chastised crude models, they are sometimes better than none at all, but their inadequacies should be clearly set forth.

XV

A Paleobiological Perspective

Soulé (Frankel and Soulé 1981) invoked the fossil record to support his argument that a decrease in habitat area could result in a loss of species. He pointed to the work of Schopf (1974), who thought that the extinction of families of shallow-water marine invertebrates during the Permo-Triassic was due to a loss in total area of the continental shelves as a result of regression. Simberloff (1974b) estimates that shallow seas during this time decreased by 68 percent and that 52 percent of all families of marine animals went extinct, which Raup (1979) translated into an estimated loss of 96 percent of all species. Figure 51 illustrates Schopf's view of conti-

nental assembly and loss of peripheral shallow seas at that time. Schopf's (1974) hypothesis is plausible, but we will look at it in some detail. This also will serve the purpose of introducing extensions of the theory of island biogeography to evolutionary equilibria in geological time, and to areas the size of continents. MacArthur and Wilson (1967) suggested that a comprehensive theory of island biogeography should treat islands and continents together. This section is intended to challenge the reader, but can be skipped without significant loss to the overall theme of this review.

A   An Origination-Extinction Equilibrium

Fisher (1930) proposed that diversity was a balance between speciation in abundant rapidly evolving organisms and extinction of rare slowly evolving ones. Wright (1941) also suggested a possible balance between origination and extinction, as did Preston (1962), Williams (1964), Wilson and Taylor (1967), MacArthur (1969), and Wilson (1969). Simpson (1969) implied such a balance for higher taxa.

Although MacArthur and Wilson (1967) recognized both ecological and evolutionary equilibria, Wilson (1969) went further by proposing four "levels" of equilibrium, noninteractive, interactive, assortative, and evolutionary, which may shift from one to the other over time (Fig. 52). Interactive equilibrium involves competition and predation; assortative equilibrium refers to a combination of species

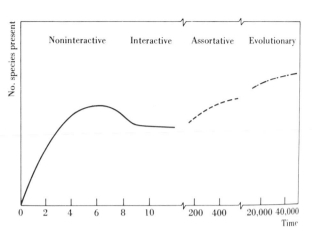

Figure 52. Hypothetical sequence of species equilibriums with time. Whether any of these various equilibriums exist is controversial. (From Wilson 1969.)

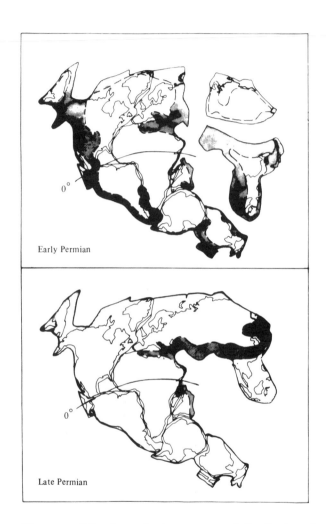

Figure 51. The change in the amount and distribution of shallow marine seas, from the Early Permian to the Late Permian, as depicted by Schopf (1974). The perceived consequent loss of habitable area for marine biota is one popular hypothetical explanation for the Permo-Triassic extinctions. (From Schopf 1974; reprinted by permission of The University of Chicago Press. ©1974.)

that appear indefinitely in ecological time; evolutionary equilibrium takes into account an evolutionary time frame. Other authors subsequently suggested the possibility of an origination-extinction equilibrium (May 1973; Simberloff 1974b; Rosenweig 1975; Flessa 1975).

Eldredge (1974) theorized that transgressions and regressions were primarily responsible for maintaining a speciation-extinction equilibrium in Paleozoic epeiric seas. Lillegraven (1972) thought a faunal equilibrium was responsible for the constancy of total familial and ordinal diversity of mammals on any continent throughout the Cenozoic, in spite of appreciable turnover. Webb (1969, 1976) applied the evolutionary equilibrium concept to land mammal genera in North America during the late Cenozoic, but his claims were impugned by Marshall and Hecht (1978) and rebutted by Webb (1978). Mark and Flessa (1977) assumed an evolutionary equilibrium for late Cenozoic mammals and Phanerozoic brachiopods, which was impugned by Cowen and Stockton (1978) and rebutted by Mark and Flessa (1978). Bretsky and Bretsky (1976) applied the equilibrium hypothesis to Ordovician benthic marine invertebrates, and Sepkoski (1978) applied it to marine invertebrate taxonomic diversity throughout the Phanerozoic.

B Species-Area Relationships for Continents

Preston (1962) thought the species-area equation might hold for continents. Flessa and Imbrie (1973), after speculative explorations using the equation, expected that "continental assembly" would result in extinction. Simberloff (1974b) thought Schopf's (1974) hypothesis was consistent with the species-area equation and therefore biologically plausible. Flessa (1975) found a relationship between continental size and mammalian diversity during the Pliocene-Pleistocene extinctions after the establishment of a land bridge between North and South America. However, Lillegraven (1972) found no correlation from the Oligocene to the Recent between numbers of mammalian orders/families and continent size. Sepkoski (1976) thought that the abundance of marine invertebrate species throughout the Phanerozoic correlated well with habitable area, while Flessa and Sepkoski (1978) were divided, optimistic and skeptical, respectively, regarding the explanatory power of Phanerozoic species-area relationships.

C Habitable Area Reduction

1 CONTINENTAL ASSEMBLY AND FRAGMENTATION

It is usually accepted that the supercontinent Pangaea existed 225 million years ago at the end of the Permian, but earlier continental positions are uncertain (Dietz and Holden 1970; Boucot and Gray 1975). Valentine and Moores (1970, 1972) thought that continental assembly culminated at the end of the Permian, a period accompanied by changes in environmental stability, nutrient supply, and provinciality. Their proposed model indicated that continental assembly is accompanied by regressions, continental fragmentation by transgressions, and they suggested that species-area effects could be significant for marine biota in expanding and shrinking epicontinental seas. One explanation for habitable area reduction is that continents assembled have less total periphery than continents disassembled. A second, related explanation is that continental assembly reduces subduction at plate margins. This decreases the rate at which oceanic ridges are built up, thus lessening the volume of mountain masses beneath the sea, which lowers sea level and drains shallow seas on the continents.

2 EPICONTINENTAL SEA REGRESSION

The possibility that reduction of epicontinental seas (regression) was responsible for marine faunal extinctions at the end of the Paleozoic Era was suggested very early (Chamberlin 1898) and later by others. Area is a powerful predictor of the number of species in marine benthic communities in the Recent (Abele and Walters 1979), although this was challenged (Stanley 1984). That area changes due to transgressions/regressions and continental assembly/disassembly should have a major impact on numbers of species is intuitively reasonable, but not all data are supportive. For instance, Jablonski (1980) outlined some of the controversy surrounding the biotic effects attributed to transgressions and regressions and thought that such effects on late Cretaceous bivalve and gastropod faunas could be more parsimoniously explained as a function of the type of facies sampled. His study followed Bambach's (1977) judgment that faunal responses can be ascertained only by sampling a single habitat, or across a series of habitats through time, thereby distinguishing within-habitat effects from between-habitat variations. Valentine (1969), previous to Schopf (1974), thought that a species-area effect could not by itself have accounted for the extinctions, although uncertainties in his calculations were great. Flessa (1980) indicated that although transgressions should reduce terrestrial diversity and increase marine diversity, and regressions should do the opposite, this land/sea reciprocity can not be seen in the fossil record.

D   Extinction Rates

A highly controversial but conceivable (and unsettling) idea is that the causes of extinction are so numerous and differ so over geological time that all biological groups are equally susceptible to extinction. Extinctions might then be random (but probabilistic), so that within ecologically homogeneous taxonomic groups (in the same adaptive zone), extinction rates may have been stochastically constant (Van Valen 1973, 1977; Raup 1975). The suggestion of constant extinction seems improbable, and the cited data have been impugned (e.g., McCune 1982). Van Valen's (1973) "Red Queen Hypothesis" claimed that species must continually evolve to keep pace with environmental change. Whether the Red Queen concept is true or not, we know that few species can evolve fast enough to keep pace with today's environmental changes and that the deleterious effects of small population size will counteract selection pressures anyway.

Raup and Sepkoski (1984) investigated major extinctions in fossil families of marine vertebrates, invertebrates, and protozoans over the past 250 million years and found 12 extinction events exhibiting a statistically significant periodicity with a mean interval of 26 million years. This finding has been challenged (Hoffman 1985). Two of the extinction events, at the terminal Cretaceous and late Eocene, correlated with meteorite impacts (Alvarez et al. 1980). Because the authors thought biological or earthbound physical cycles too unlikely a source of such periodicity, they wondered about extraterrestrial forces. Whitmore et al. (1984) and Davis et al. (1984) related the periodicity to meteor impacts, hypothesizing that gravitation toward an undiscovered solar body, called Nemesis, may influence comet and asteroid orbits into periodic collisions with the earth. Hallam (1987) refuted an extraterrestrial explanation for one major mass extinction. Modern paleobiology needs more data to test its theories about ancient extinctions. But man does not have to wonder today about extraterrestrial causes of extinctions to come; he is now his own catastrophe.

Some conclusions from the literature on extinctions are germane to conservation. Raup (1979) estimated the average species extinction rate for the Phanerozoic at 9 percent per million years. Increasing this one order of magnitude to account for preservation biases, he arrived at a figure of 2 species per year in a biosphere containing 2 million species (Raup 1988). Using such rough estimates and assuming 10 instead of 2 million species, Wilson (1988) estimated that current species extinction rates in tropical forests alone is 1,000 to 10,000 times higher than such "background" natural extinction rates.

E   Summary

Although some patterns found in the fossil record suggest a possible equilibrium between origination and extinction, they are not compelling evidence (Sepkoski 1978). Data that support the ability of the species-area equation to predict continental species diversity are inconclusive (Flessa and Sepkoski 1978), and so are predictions of the loss of species based on habitable area. We do not know if the number of species on earth has reached saturation. Thus the first of three points to be made in summing up is that extensions of the theory of island biogeography to continents are controversial.

Although regression, perhaps influenced by continental assembly, is a popular explanation for Permo-Triassic extinctions, Rhodes (1967) made the following points: no single cause is likely; the extinction pattern is not different from others in earth history; and many other explanations have been proposed, including trace-element poisoning, radiation, trophic resource fluctuations, and changes in temperature, salinity, and oxygen (Benson 1984). For example, Stanley (1984) considered reduced living space due to major regressions a trivial factor and temperature change a very important factor in marine mass extinctions during the Cenozoic and possibly in earlier times. Jablonski (1985, 1986) conceived of a test using modern biota whose results indicated that shallow water around islands could provide refugia for shallow-water species in a regression, so mass extinctions might not be due solely to the lowering of sea level.

Therefore, the hypothesis that changes in sea level were chiefly responsible for the Permo-Triassic mass extinction is only one of many, and Newell (1967) thought it unlikely that we will ever sort out all the causative factors. "Paleontology's outstanding dilemma" probably will long remain a subject for further study, conjecture, and argument. Newell (1984) stressed that the question of mass extinctions remains unsolved and that the Permian and Cretaceous extinctions were basically dissimilar and thus unlikely to have a common simple explanation.

F   Conclusion

Soulé (Frankel and Soulé 1981) warned that "the large terrestrial flora and fauna of this planet are just beginning a plunge into an unprecedented abyss of extinction" due to tropical deforestation and a consequent reduction in habitable area, comparing the current condition to the Permo-Triassic extinctions. This projection of impending massive extinction due to habitat destruction is certainly accurate (Section XIVF), but comparison with the causes of the Permo-Triassic extinctions is hypothetical. The fossil record cannot show a cause-effect relationship between reduction in area and species loss for this historical mass extinction, or any other.

If the Permo-Triassic extinctions were real, as evidence suggests (Raup 1979; Raup and Sepkoski 1982), they could have been due in part to a reduction in habitable area. Although area reduction consistently correlates with extinction it cannot account for all mass extinctions (Simberloff 1986a), or with certainty for any particular extinction. The second point to be made about extinctions therefore is that we should avoid casual reference to the fossil record and strive to separate fact from theory.

G   Paleobiology and Conservation

The third point is this: I think that paleobiology, dealing with the oldest aspects of natural history study, has much to teach us about current conservation crises that ecology, evolutionary biology, genetics, and ecological biogeography by themselves cannot. Raup (1988) said that "the fossil record has great untapped potential for contributing to our understanding of contemporary extinction." Biotic fossil data (e.g., Diamond 1984b) have yielded insights from Pleistocene refuges. Peters and Darling (1985) commented that we need to be mindful of modern climatic change, based on lessons that Pleistocene species range extensions provide. The reverse is also true: Diamond (1984a) asked whether knowledge derived from island extinctions can provide insights into prehistoric continental extinctions in the Pleistocene.

What has the deep paleontological record told us, as reviewed in this section? That area reduction, such as fragmentation, has been a consistent correlate of many mass extinctions and that connectivity allowed whole biotas to move and persist. The ancient scale and time frames differ greatly from those of the current nature reserve "island dilemma," but similarities in principle should be heeded.

Candolle, in 1855, thought that the breakup of a large landmass into smaller units would lead to extinction (Browne 1983). The breakup of tropical forests as big as small continents is well underway.

XVI

Evolutionary Arrest

A   Evolution and Insularization

The future of the evolutionary process in relationship to reserve size and isolation has not been widely discussed. Time frames here are roughly 10,000–100,000 years compared to hundreds of millions of years for the Permo-Triassic extinctions (Chapter XV).

Vermeij (1986) indicated that habitat fragmentation should favor speciation. Soulé and Wilcox (1980) and Soulé (1980 and in Frankel and Soulé 1981) thought that the eventual confinement of much of the world's biota in various reserves meant an end to the significant evolution of tropical plants (sometimes they specified large plants) and tropical animals (sometimes they specified terrestrial animals or higher vertebrates) because they considered such reserves too small to give the isolation necessary for autochthonous speciation (i.e., species or other taxa that originated in the region). Their projection was based on the assumption that isolation between reserves cannot make up for within-reserve isolation; extinction rates in the reserves will be too high, and the managed transfer of organisms between reserves to counteract the potential negative effects of small population sizes will inhibit genetic divergence.

Templeton (1986), although he did not advocate strong managerial interference with the genomes of species, did point out that managers might on occasion "use evolutionary change as a beneficial management tool rather than regard it as a deleterious situation that must be prevented at all costs." This possibility does not alter our basic concern: managed speciation in most nature reserves may not be what we should seek.

The Soulé and Wilcox prediction of an end to the evolutionary process for all these general groups of organisms is debatable. Frankel (1981) thought the historical evidence on minimum areas for speciation of different organisms too episodic for generalizations, but nonetheless saw an evident general trend: Larger mammals appear to require an area the size of Madagascar, as Soulé (1980) indicated (Fig. 53). The prediction may be true only for large vertebrates (Frankel pers. com.); thus, large nature reserves may still provide for continuing speciation, at least for lower vertebrates, invertebrates, and for most families of plants (Frankel in Frankel and Soulé 1981). Frankel (1984) indicated that speciation in plants and invertebrates may proceed, though "restricted," in large reserves.

Slatkin (1985) concluded that we still do not know whether gene flow has a primarily conservative or creative role in evolution, tending to retard local adaptation or to spread well-adapted combinations

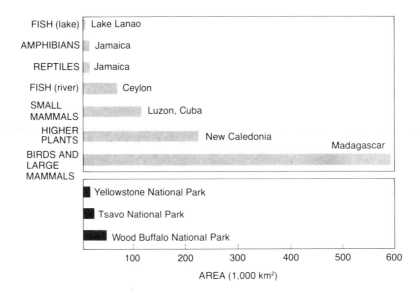

Figure 53. Smallest islands on which autochthonous speciation is known to have occurred for various taxa, according to data gathered by Soulé (1980). Three large nature reserves are shown for comparison. His interpretation and conclusion are if speciation is area dependent, the largest national parks in the world may be too small for the speciation of higher plants, birds, and mammals. (From Soulé 1980; reprinted by permission of Sinauer Associates, Inc.)

of genes. Boecklen's (1986) and Boecklen and Bell's (1987) computer simulations suggested that the two aims of genetic conservation (retention of both heterozygosity and alleles) may be mutually antagonistic from the standpoint of management. Alleles might best be retained in subdivided populations, with no interpopulation migration that would reduce alleles. The conclusion was that heterozygosity was best retained over the short term in single populations and over the long term in subdivided populations with high rates of interpopulation migration. Retention of alleles was assigned the higher priority, since heterozygosity can be reconstituted by increasing gene flow between subpopulations. Several reserves with occasional interrefuge migration was judged the optimal strategy for genetic conservation.

B   An Unsettling Prediction

A view expressed by Mayr (pers. com.) regarding Soulé and Wilcox (1980), specifically the quotation that ends this chapter, should be considered: Unless a sufficient number of insular areas (real islands) are protected, there is little hope for additional speciation via the allopatric speciation model, except for polyploidy in plants, and the above predictions by Soulé and Wilcox (1980) of severely restricted speciation will come to pass. Mayr's assessment was influenced by his view that animal speciation always proceeds via the allopatric speciation model, which has been challenged for many years. Nonallopatric speciation is possible though very unlikely (Felsenstein 1981), and evidence is not convincing enough to depart from the traditional view of speciation via the allopatric model (Futuyma and Mayer 1980).

Mayr further indicated that since speciation in large organisms may require more than hundreds of thousands of years, we cannot plan now regarding the cessation of speciation in some taxa. For example, the genera *Elephas* (Indian elephant), *Loxodonta* (African elephant), and *Mammuthus* (mammoths) probably were derived from *Primelephas* over about one million years in the Pleistocene (Maglio 1973, cited by Futuyma 1986). This is consistent with Brown's (1986) view that areas as large as the largest continents are necessary to maintain the largest living mammals over time frames necessary for differentiation and radiation at the level of genera. But more and more of the world's national parks and nature reserves could look like Figure 54 in the future.

Figure 54. The 220-square mile Loxahatchee National Wildlife Refuge is centered approximately 20 miles southwest of West Palm Beach, Palm Beach County, Florida. It is a fresh-water storage area surrounded by levees and canals, built by the U.S. Army Corps of Engineers. Water levels are actively managed. Note the urban development to the east, which is part of the lower east coast of Florida. To the west is approximately 700 square miles of agricultural fields planted in sugar cane. This is the second largest national wildlife refuge in the eastern United States, located in the midst of one of the fastest growing U.S. counties. (Image © 1989 CNES. Provided courtesy of SPOT Image Corporation, Reston, Virginia.)

Therefore, we really know little about how long speciation takes in large organisms, but we have some rough predictions. The role of gene flow in evolution is based more on assumption than data. The conditions necessary to cause speciation are relatively clear, but debate continues about different models. Consequently, the statement below by Soulé and Wilcox (1980) requires closer scrutiny and thought:

Perhaps even more shocking than the unprecedented wave of extinction is the cessation of significant evolution of new species of large plants and animals. Death is one thing—an end to birth is something else, and nature reserves are too small (not to mention, impermanent) to gestate new species of vertebrates. There is no escaping the conclusion that in our life times, this planet will see a suspension, if not an end, to many ecological and evolutionary processes which have been uninterrupted since the beginnings of paleontological time.

XVII

A Nature Reserve Strategy

A   Introduction

This review has attempted to take stock of our current knowledge about nature reserves (e.g., Chapter XII). The reader should now realize that overall general rules for nature reserve system design are risky. Individual situations usually demand auteocological data. Recommendations have too many "everything else being equal" provisos that never apply in the real world. Additionally, there are too few good research data, many special situations, and opposing strategies.

Ehrenfeld (1989) stated:

I feel obliged to point out that there is a widespread obsession with a search for general rules of scientific conservation, the genetic code of conservation so to speak, and this finds expression in very general statements about extinction rates, viable population sizes, ideal reserve designs, and so forth. . . . Yet this kind of generality is easily abused, especially when the would-be conservationists become bewitched by models of their own making. When this happens, the sight of otherwise intelligent people trying to extract nonobvious general rules about extinction from their own polished and highly simplified versions of reality

becomes a spectacle that would have interested Lewis Carroll. . . . We should not be surprised when different conservation problems call for qualitatively different solutions.

I do not think the above remarks were intended so much to belittle efforts at finding rules as to warn against becoming blinded by them. Modeling is badly needed and should continue. This review has implied that the critical design issues are reserve size, reserve numbers, distances between reserves, connectivity, location, and the relationship between reserves and surrounding lands and people. And they are, I believe, the key issues. As Franklin (1985) stated, "Any guidelines on size, shape, and other criteria must, of necessity, be general as each design problem is unique."

However, any good generalities that can be derived from the literature would be helpful. I will therefore propose some interrelated general guidance. Simplicity, where possible, may be useful when a field is shrouded by detail.

B General Guidelines

The more land you set aside, the more species you will preserve.

A larger area usually captures more species of plants and animals, but returns typically diminish as area increases beyond a certain point.

Habitat fragmentation and nature reserve insularization should be discouraged.

Nature reserve boundaries should not create abrupt transitions that discourage animal movement to surrounding habitat.

Buffer zones or areas of cooperation that permit gradual intergradation of a resource and its biota with adjacent human land uses are also desirable at reserve boundaries.

A large reserve is better than a small one, everything else being equal.

Many large reserves are needed in as many biotic communities as possible. Since opportunities may often be precluded by circumstances, especially the need to accommodate wide-ranging species, alternative options are more smaller reserves that are connected.

Small reserves can serve a useful purpose in any overall reserve system design to conserve some species or to facilitate migration of other larger or wider-ranging species.

Small populations should be avoided. Catastrophes or extreme environmental perturbations should dictate a lower threshold for survivorship, so populations should be as large as possible, and reserves should be replicated.

Models suggest that species of large vertebrates may need populations of several hundreds or even thousands to achieve long-term viability. Small populations in reserves can be viable if managed as a single population (metapopulation) whose combined size equals the desired number. However, this alternative demands natural migration or even deliberate movement of animals between segments.

Rare species, as well as large-bodied wide-ranging animals that are confined and unable to meet their energy needs, are likely to be the most vulnerable to extinction.

The establishment of corridors to facilitate animal movement should preferably be based first on an autecological study of individual species, and then ideally on a consideration of the pros and cons of corridors for individual situations. Otherwise, maintaining natural habitat connectivity appears to be the most prudent alternative course to follow.

The establishment of a new nature reserve should be based on studies of the distribution of species and communities in the host country or region, to avoid the sample effect.

Inbreeding should generally be avoided for typically outbreeding species.

Translocation of individuals should be preceded by studies indicating their degree of genetic similarity.

Present evolutionary change may be sacrificed if doing so conserves genetic variation for future generations.

Autecological studies of individual species and their relationship to other species in the ecosystem should be given a high priority. Such information can also supplement the application of some general models.

Nature reserves for large mammals should usually be increased in size where opportunities exist to do so. Buffer zones are an alternative.

Under ideal circumstances, nature reserve size should be such as to accommodate the largest widest-ranging mammals, on the basis of their life history and territorial behavior, and will then serve as an area umbrella for other species.

Reserve design should seek the theoretical ideal of maximizing alleles by preventing genetic drift in small populations, and of preserving heterozygosity by discouraging inbreeding.

Only a few individuals, compared to the source and recipient populations, need be allowed to migrate to ameliorate the potentially deleterious effects of fragmented habitat on gene pools.

It may now be impossible to separate natural from human influences in the study of populations in nature reserves, a difficulty some models ignore, so the human factor should be taken into account or recognized.

Smaller reserves probably will withstand less internal or external stress than larger ones.

To maintain biological diversity, laissez-faire management of nature reserves should be the exception, not the rule.

The design and management of nature reserves should be viewed as potentially an interactive regional matrix.

Regional planning for nature reserves must take human population growth into account and consider the social and economic conditions on adjacent lands.

XVIII

Epilogue

A Man in Nature

All things are ordered together somehow, but not all alike—both fishes and fowls and plants; and the world is not such that one thing has nothing to do with another, but they are connected.

ARISTOTLE, *METAPHYSICS*

Aristotle's comment represented an early inkling that organisms are subtly interconnected. Such biological interconnectedness is much better understood now that the science of ecology is well established.

Man evolved among other organisms. Modern man depends on nature for his scientific, economic, social, psychological, and spiritual well-being. Our recognition of these many connections between man and nature has a powerful significance. If we contribute to the loss of species, we destroy our own roots and well-being. Nature reserves play a major role in maintaining our relationship with nature.

Anne Morrow Lindbergh (in Dubos 1968) recalled her experience on an African safari:

Perhaps some of the tremendous renewal of energy one experiences in East Africa comes from being put back in one's place in the universe, as an animal alongside other animals—one of many miracles of life on earth, not the only miracle. Religion traditionally filled this function by giving us a sense of reverence before the mysterious forces around us; but the impact of science on our civilization had created the illusion that we are all-powerful and control the

universe. . . . The return to reality—whether in a regional power failure or in the African wilderness—comes as a shock, but it is a healthy one. . . In the blackout, many people rediscovered the strong web of human relatedness. In the African wilderness, man rediscovers his ancient and eternal kinship with nature and with animals.

Man is linked to nature in both time (coevolution) and space (natural habitat proximity). Not only is man's spatial relationship with nature being reduced, but man is severing the relationship of other biota to each other. Indeed, man is creating the "island dilemma" for both himself and the rest of nature. Connectivity needs to be maintained for both man's sake and the nature of which he is a part.

Our land, compared with what it was, is like the skeleton of a body wasted by disease. The plump soft parts have vanished and all that remains is the bare carcass.

PLATO, *CRITIAS*

Our natural landscape is becoming more like a huge patchwork "quilt" than a skeleton. Many of the soft parts have vanished due to urbanization and other consumptive uses, while other parts of the landscape have been wisely set aside as national parks and nature reserves. The degree to which these patches remain connected or buffered will influence the health of the world's terrestrial biota.

Figure 55. A view of the sphere of the earth taken December 1972 from the Apollo 17 spacecraft. The continent of Africa can be seen in the upper left and the Antarctic polar ice cap at the bottom. The large island off the southeastern coast of Africa is Madagascar. The Red Sea can be seen separating Africa from the Arabian Peninsula. The African Rift Valley can be barely seen trending south from the "L" where the Red Sea and the Gulf of Aden meet. The Rift Valley is where many famous East African game reserves are located. Scientists may still wonder whether such game reserves over time may come to resemble true islands like Madagascar, and whether explanations for organism distribution and abundance on Madagascar might also apply to these game reserves. (Image provided by the National Aeronautics and Space Administration.)

B   *Man and Nature Apart*

Mankind seems to be on the brink of one of the largest mass extinctions of living organisms the earth has seen since the end of the Cretaceous. This is due in large part to tropical forest destruction but also to habitat removal and fragmentation in many biomes of the world. It is the kind of challenge no other generation has faced, a situation that will not allow us a second chance.

We no longer have a right to view our alterations of the natural landscape as isolated from their surroundings. All our actions are intertwined, which we now realize as we become increasingly aware that we are part of a global environmental community. Indeed, as Figure 55 illustrates, the world is an island in space. Its natural resources are finite. Its natural landscape is finite. Its biota is finite. And opportunities to preserve this biota in nature reserves are becoming finite.

This "island dilemma" I think can be successfully resisted. Mankind has the wherewithal to do something about it and need not be resigned to large-scale extinctions. I hope we meet this challenge in a positive and enlightened manner. Too much is at stake if we do not.

The essence of the real problem underlying the "island dilemma" has been well stated by Western et al. (1989) in a pessimistic prognosis.

> *Protected areas are a seductively simple way to save nature from humanity. But sanctuaries admit a failure to save wildlife and natural habitat where they overlap with human interest, and that means 95 percent or more of the earth's surface. Conservation by segregation is the Noah's Ark solution, a belief that wildlife should be consigned to tiny land parcels for its own good and because it has no place in our world. The flaw in this view is obvious: those land parcels are not big enough to avert catastrophic species extinction by insularization or safe enough to protect resources from the poor and the greedy. Simply put, if we can't save nature outside protected areas, not much will survive inside; if we can, protected areas will cease to be arks.*

I think optimism is possible if we seek a better balance between setting strict nature reserve boundaries and integrating reserves with man and wildlife outside the boundaries. We also need to maintain connections between reserves, where feasible. We still have opportunities to make this a more common reality. I hope our societies have the wisdom to make this an international priority.

Since this review referred to the work of MacArthur and Wilson (1963, 1967) probably more than to any other, it is appropriate to end with a quote by Wilson (1984):

> *What event likely to happen during the next few years will our descendants most regret? Everyone agrees, defense ministers and environmentalists alike, that the worst thing possible is global nuclear war. If it occurs the entire human species is endangered; life as normal human beings wish to live it would come to an end. With that terrible truism acknowledged, it must be added that if no country pulls the trigger the worse thing that will probably happen—in fact is already well underway—is not energy depletion, economic collapse, conventional war, or even expansion of totalitarian governments. As tragic as these catastrophes would be for us, they can be repaired within a few generations. The one process now going on that will take millions of years to correct is the loss of genetic and species diversity by the destruction of natural habitats. That is the folly our descendants are least likely to forgive us.*

Acknowledgments

I would like to express special thanks to Beth F. Shafer for helping with the word processing of the various drafts of the manuscript and in innumerable other ways. Without her tireless help this book would not have been possible. Napier Shelton provided invaluable continuous counsel and moral support. I am grateful to Jean Mathews for greatly improving the writing of a late draft of the manuscript. The following reviewed very early drafts: Daniel S. Simberloff, Anthony G. Coates, Martin W. Buzas, Thomas E. Lovejoy, Christine M. Schonewald-Cox, Alan R. Weisbrod, and Napier Shelton. Mark L. Shaffer advised on minimum viable populations. Jonathan Ballou helped me better understand the inbreeding literature. Jonathan W. Bayless helped on some of the statistical aspects. Many anonymous reviewers read an older draft, and I am most indebted to them. However, the final interpretation and portrayal of the literature is entirely my responsibility. Nicholas J. Gotelli, Robert L. Peters, John Seidensticker, and David W. Crumpacker sent unpublished manuscripts. Maurice O. Nyquist, Harvey Fleet, Paul W. Rose, William Cibula, Mike McEnroe, Stephen Goodwin, Rose Hassoun, and John Richardson advised or assisted me with LANDSAT imagery or aerial photography. Jeremy D. Harrison provided additional data to supplement the 1985 IUCN List. I would also like to thank Theodore Sudia, Henry Merchant, Geza Tekeki, Jr., Robert Stottlemeyer, Douglas Houston, and James Kushlan for advice.

Many persons at the Smithsonian Institution Press were most supportive: Peter Cannell for his interest in the manuscript and his much appreciated guidance and advice, Theresa Slowik for getting the manuscript reviewed, and Ruth Spiegel for shepherding it through the production process. I would also like to thank Norman Rudnick for improving the final presentation of the manuscript immeasurably. I am grateful to Robb Reavill and Susan Abrams for their interest in the manuscript and their much appreciated help or counsel. There are many other friends, colleagues, or just concerned persons, too numerous to mention, who gave unselfishly of their time and knowledge, from which I benefited greatly. I wish to thank the U.S. National Park Service for the opportunity to work in the field of national park and nature reserve conservation, though the views here are my own.

Glossary

ABSCISSA. The horizontal (*x*) axis on a graph, or the horizontal coordinate of a point on that graph.

ADAPTIVE ZONE. A group of niches occupied or potentially occupied by a higher taxon or taxon member.

ALLELE. One of several forms of a gene.

ALLOMETRIC. Refers to the growth of part of an organism in proportion to the growth of the whole organism.

ALLOPATRIC. Occurring in different places; describing geographically separated populations (see sympatric).

AUTECOLOGY. An old term for the branch of ecology dealing with the study of individual organisms or individual species (see synecology).

AUTOCHTHONOUS. Describing a species or other taxon of regional origin.

AUTOSOME. A chromosome other than a sex chromosome.

BARRIER. Any feature that restricts movement of individuals from one place to another.

BIOGEOGRAPHIC PROVINCE. Biotic province; a large region containing a unique biota relative to other regions. Example: eastern deciduous forest.

BIOGEOGRAPHY. The science that studies the distribution of organisms (see historical biogeography, ecological biogeography).

BIOLOGICAL DIVERSITY. The variety and variability among living organisms and the ecological complexes in which they occur.

BIOTA. The plants and animals of an area.

BIOTIC COMMUNITY. Biological community or association, ecological community; an assemblage of species living in a prescribed area or physical habitat.

BOTTLENECK. Temporary decrease of a population to only a few individuals.

BUFFER ZONE. Collar of land designed to filter out harmful influences from surrounding activities.

CANONICAL DISTRIBUTION. A log-normal distribution of relative abundance according to the mathematical formulation developed by Preston (1962).

CARRYING CAPACITY. The number of individuals that can be supported by an environment and its resources.

CENTRAL LIMIT THEOREM. All distributions from a very wide class produce sample means that tend to be normally distributed.

CHIROPTERAN. Refers to a mammalian order that includes bats.

CLINE. Progressive change in characteristics of a population with geographic location, typically related to environmental changes.

COADAPTATION. Natural selection in which genes have positive or synergistic influences on a population.

CONTINENTAL ISLAND. Island formed as part of a continent (see oceanic island).

CORRIDOR. A route that allows movement of individuals or taxa from one region to another.

DEFAUNATION. The elimination of animal life from an area.

DEMOGRAPHY. The statistical study of a population with reference to its size, density, distribution, and vital statistics.

DETERMINISTIC. Not determined by chance (see stochastic).

DISPERSAL. The movement of organisms away from a location, such as their point of origin.

DISPERSION. The spatial distribution of individuals within a local population.

EASEMENT. An interest in the land of another that provides the easement holder specified rights without actual ownership.

ECOLOGICAL BIOGEOGRAPHY. The study of relationships between the distribution of organisms and physical and biological factors (see historical biogeography).

ECOLOGY. The branch of science that studies the distribution and abundance of organisms, and the relationship between organisms and their environment.

ECOTONE. A habitat created by abutment of very different habitats, or a transition area between them.

ECOTYPE. A genetically differentiated subpopulation restricted to a certain habitat.

EFFECTIVE POPULATION SIZE. The size of an "ideal" population whose decrease in genetic variation due to genetic drift or inbreeding equals that of the population being examined (see ideal population).

ENVIRONMENT. The complex of climatic, soil, and biotic factors acting upon organisms.

EPEIRIC SEA. Epicontinental sea; a large body of water that exists or once existed over part of a continent.

EQUILIBRIUM THEORY OF ISLAND BIOGEOGRAPHY. The theory of MacArthur and Wilson (1963, 1967).

EQUILIBRIUM TURNOVER. The change in species composition when immigration rate equals extinction rate.

EXTANT. Now living.

EXTINCTION. Dying out, usually global, of a species for any reason (see local extinction).

FACIES. Portions of a body of rock showing lateral changes in aspect.

FECUNDITY. Rate at which an individual produces offspring.

FITNESS. The average contribution of an allele or genotype to following generations, relative to other alleles or genotypes.

FLORISTIC. Relating to plants as elements of a flora.

GENE. The unit of heredity, transmitted in a chromosome.

GENE FLOW. Sharing of genes when two populations interbreed.

GENE POOL. The genetic complement of a population.

GENIC SELECTION. A form of natural selection by which an allele frequency in a population is determined by its increase relative to other alleles, and averaged over all gene types.

GENOME. The genetic complement of an individual.

GENOTYPE. The genetic structure of an organism (see phenotype).

GRAIN. Pertains to two or more resources distributed in such a way that a consumer species encounters them either in the same proportion as they actually occur (fine-grained) or a different proportion (coarse-grained).

HABITAT. The natural environment of an organism.

HABITAT ISLAND. A relative term indicating any geographically patchy or isolated habitat. Mountaintops and ponds are natural habitat islands. Forest fragments left by logging may be examples of man-created habitat islands. Resident organisms may or may not be able to leave.

HARDY-WEINBERG LAW. A prediction of gene frequencies on the basis of allele frequencies of a population.

HERMAPHRODITIC. Refers to an organism that has reproductive organs of both sexes.

HETEROZYGOUS. Containing two forms (alleles) of a gene, one from each parent (see homozygous).

HISTORICAL BIOGEOGRAPHY. The study of relationships between present and past organism distributions and physical earth history (see ecological biogeography).

HOME RANGE. The area enclosing most of an individual's activities.

HOMOTHERMAL. Refers to warm-bloodedness, the maintenance of a constant body temperature while environmental temperatures fluctuate (see poikilothermal).

HOMOZYGOUS. Containing two identical alleles at a gene locus (see heterozygous).

HYBRIDIZATION. Crossing of individuals of different populations, races, or sometimes species.

IDEAL POPULATION. A theoretical sexually reproducing population having random mating and no generation overlap. Additional assumptions include no migration, no selection, and no mutation.

IMPOVERISHMENT. A process that results in a severely diminished number of species or other measure of diversity.

INBREEDING. Mating of related individuals.

INBREEDING DEPRESSION. Reduction of fitness or vigor resulting from inbreeding by usually outbreeding organisms.

INTERSPECIFIC. Refers to individuals of different species (see intraspecific).

INTRASPECIFIC. Refers to individuals within a species (see interspecific).

KARYOTYPIC. Refers to the characteristics of the chromosomes of a species.

K-SELECTION. Selection for better utilization of resources (see *r*-selection).

LANDSCAPE. An areal entity that is a composite of all the characteristics that distinguish a certain area on the earth's surface from other areas.

LIMITING FACTOR. An environmental factor that limits a population's abundance or distribution.

LOCAL EXTINCTION. Elimination of a species in one area but not necessarily elsewhere. See extinction.

LOG-NORMAL DISTRIBUTION. A distribution that is normal (in a statistical sense) when one variable is plotted on a logarithmic scale along the *x*-axis, and the frequency on a linear scale along the *y*-axis.

LOG-TRANSFORMED. Refers to data changed by taking the log of each value.

MANAGEMENT. Human intervention.

MANAGERS. Land managers; those with the responsibility to manage land.

MARGINAL HABITAT. Habitats with few species due to adverse physical or other conditions.

MIGRATION. In genetics, gene flow between populations; often used more generally for broad-scale movement of organisms with or without gene flow.

MODEL. A conceptual or mathematical simulation of reality (e.g., biological) for purposes of describing, analyzing, or understanding nature.

MONOTONIC. Continuously increasing or decreasing without reversal.

MORPHOLOGY. Form and structure as a whole.

MUTUALISM. A mutually beneficial association between two different kinds of organisms.

NATURE RESERVE. Nature preserve, national park, natural reserve, etc. A tract of land set aside to preserve it in its natural condition.

NATURAL SELECTION. The differential survival or reproduction of organisms on the basis of varying genetic characteristics.

NULL HYPOTHESIS. A statistical hypothesis to be tested to see if an observed difference is due to chance alone as opposed to a systematic cause.

OCEANIC ISLAND. An island formed from the ocean floor as a result of volcanism that was never part of the mainland (see continental island).

OUTBREEDING. A mating habit in which close relatives do not usually breed.

PALEOECOLOGY. The science that tries to reconstruct the structure and function of ancient communities.

PANMIXIS. Random mating.

PARADIGM. Distinctive pattern of major assumptions, concepts, and propositions in a substantive area.

PATCHINESS. A characteristic of discontinuous and heterogeneous environments consisting of a patchwork of rather different resources, as opposed to homogeneous, or uniform, environments. Sometimes refers to a species distributed in an unexplainable fashion, maybe not where resources seem suitable.

PEDIGREE. A chart showing ancestral relationships.

PHANEROZOIC. The geological time from the Cambrian to the Recent (570 million years).

PHENOTYPE. Physical appearance of an organism (see genotype).

PHYSIOGNOMY. The study of form and structure in natural communities.

PHYSIOGRAPHY. The description of surface features of the earth such as bodies of air, water, and land.

PLAN. A predetermined course of action.

PLANNERS. Land-use planners; those with the responsibility to allocate tracts of land for specific uses or levels of protection.

POIKILOTHERMAL. Cold-bloodedness, the conformance of body and environmental temperatures (see homothermal).

POISSON DISTRIBUTION. One discrete probability distribution. The most common continuous probability distribution is the "normal" frequency distribution.

POLICY. A definite course or method of action selected by a government agency, institution, group, or individual.

POLYMORPHISM. The characteristic of having more than one form. In genetics, the occurrence in a population of several alternative alleles at a locus.

POLYPLOID. An organism or cell having three or more whole chromosome sets.

PROPAGULE. The smallest number of individuals of a species that can successfully colonize an island with a suitable habitat.

PROVINCIALISM. The occurrence of many distinct endemic organisms in a region.

PTERIDOPHYTES. An old term for one of the main divisions of the plant kingdom, including the ferns, horsetails, club mosses, and *Selaginella*.

QUADRAT. A square sample plot used usually to study vegetation.

REGRESSION. A statistical method of estimating the relationships between two variables by expressing one in terms of a linear (or more complex) function of the other. In geology, the retreat of ocean waters from over a continent in geological time (see transgression).

RELAXATION. The drop in number of species to a new sustainable level over time due to inadequate area.

RELICT. A regional remnant of a biotic community otherwise extinct. In evolutionary biology, the persistence of an ancient organism (phylogenetic relict).

RESCUE EFFECT. The arrival of individuals at an island in time to halt the local disappearance of a species.

r-SELECTION. Selection for a higher growth rate and productivity (see *K*-selection).

SIMULATION. An abstraction or simplification, for example, a model, of a real world situation (see model).

SPECIALIZED. Refers to evolved characteristics that permit an organism to adapt to a narrow environment.

SPECIATION. The process of deriving a new species from its ancestor.

SPECIES ABUNDANCE. In ecology, the relative distribution of the number of individuals of each species in a community.

SPECIES ABUNDANCE CURVE. The frequency curve of species with differing numbers of individuals in their populations, portrayed as a plot of species numbers (on the ordinate) against abundance of individuals per species (on the abscissa).

SPECIES-AREA CURVE. A plot of number of species against area traversed.

SPECIES DIVERSITY. Either the absolute number of species, or in ecology a measure that incorporates both the number of species and their relative abundance.

STOCHASTIC. Random or expected by chance (see deterministic).

SUCCESSION. An orderly process of biotic community development involving changes in species structure and community processes with time.

SYMPATRIC. Occurring in the same place; refers to areas where species distributions overlap (see allopatric).

SYNECOLOGY. An old term for the branch of ecology that deals with the study of groups of organisms associated together as a unit.

SYSTEMATICS. The study of the genetic and historical evolutionary relationships of organisms.

TAXONOMY. The naming of organisms and their assignment to taxa.

TRANSGRESSION. The movement of ocean waters over a continent in geological time (see regression).

TRANSLOCATION. The deliberate introduction or reintroduction of a species from another area by human intervention. In genetics, moving part of a chromosome to another chromosome.

TROPHIC LEVEL. Position in the food chain based on numbers of energy transfer steps (e.g., producer, herbivore, carnivore).

TURNOVER. Extinction of some species and their replacement by other species.

TURNOVER RATE. The number of species replaced by others per unit time.

VAGILITY. The ability to move from place to place.

VARIANCE. A statistical measure of the dispersion of values around the mean.

VEGETATION TYPE. A plant community with distinguishable characteristics (see biotic community).

VOLANT. Capable of flying.

ZONING. Land-use zoning; the demarcation of a planning area by ordinance into zones and the establishment of regulations to govern their use.

Bibliography

Abele, L.G., and E.F. Connor. 1979. Application of island biogeography theory to refuge design: making the right decision for the wrong reasons. In M. Linn (ed.), *Proceedings of the First Conference on Scientific Research in the National Parks* Volume I, *New Orleans, Louisiana, November 9–12, 1976,* pp. 89–94. National Park Service, U.S. Department of the Interior, Washington, D.C.

Abele, L.G., and W.K. Patton. 1976. The size of coral heads and the community biology of associated decapod crustaceans. *J. Biogeogr.,* 3:35–47.

Abele, L.G., and K. Walters. 1979. Marine benthic diversity: a critique and alternative explanation. *J. Biogeogr.,* 6:115–126.

Abbott, I. 1980. Theories dealing with the ecology of landbirds on islands. *Adv. Ecol. Res.,* 11:329–371.

———. 1983. The meaning of z in species/area regressions and the study of species turnover in island biogeography. *Oikos,* 41:385–390.

Adams, C.C. 1902. Southeastern United States as a center of geographical distribution of flora and fauna. *Biol. Bull. (Woods Hole),* 3:115–131.

———. 1925. Ecological conditions in national forests and in national parks. *Sci. Monthly,* 20:561–593.

Adams, L.W., and L.E. Dove. 1989. *Wildlife Reserves and Corridors in the Urban Environment.* National Institute for Urban Wildlife, Columbia, Md.

Adams, L.W., and D.L. Leedy (eds.). 1987. *Integrating Man and Nature in the Metropolitan Environment.* National Institute for Urban Wildlife, Columbia, Md.

Ahlen, I. 1983. The bat fauna of some isolated islands in Scandinavia. *Oikos,* 41:352–358.

Aho, J. 1978. Freshwater snail populations and the equilibrium theory of island biogeography. I. A case study in southern Finland. *Ann. Zool. Fenn.,* 15:146–154.

Albright, H. 1933. Research in the national parks. *Sci. Monthly* 36:483–501.

Alexander, L. (chairman). 1986. *Report and Recommendations to the President of the United States.* President's Commission on Americans Outdoors. U.S. Government Printing Office, Washington, D.C.

Allendorf, F.W. 1983. Isolation, gene flow, and genetic differentiation among populations. In C. Schonewald-Cox et al. (eds.), *Genetics and Conservation: A Reference for Managing Wild Animal and Plant Populations,* pp. 51–65. The Benjamin/Cummings Publishing Company, Inc., Menlo Park, Cal.

———. 1986. Genetic drift and the loss of alleles versus heterozygosity. *Zoo Biol.,* 5:181–190.

Allendorf, F.W., and R.F. Leary. 1986. Heterozygosity and fitness in natural populations of animals. In Soulé (ed.), *Conservation Biology: The Science of Scarcity and Diversity,* pp. 57–76. Sinauer Associates, Inc., Sunderland, Mass.

Allendorf, F.W., and C. Servheen. 1986. Genetics and conservation of grizzly bears. *Trends Ecol. & Evol.,* 1:88–89.

Alvarez, W., F. Asaro, and H.V. Michel. 1980. Extraterrestrial cause of the Cretaceous-Tertiary extinction. *Science,* 208:1095–1108.

Ambuel, B., and S.A. Temple. 1983. Area-dependent changes in the bird communities and vegetation of southern Wisconsin forests. *Ecology,* 64:1057–1068.

Antonovics, J., and A.D. Bradshaw. 1970. Evolution in closely adjacent plant populations. VIII. Clinal patterns at mine boundary. *Heredity,* 25:349–362.

Arnold, A.A. 1983. *Ecological Studies of Six Endangered Butterflies (Lepidoptera, Lycaenidae): Island Biogeography, Patch Dynamics, and the Design of Habitat Preserves.* University of California Press, Berkeley.

Arrhenius, O. 1921. Species and area. *J. Ecol.,* 9:95–99.

———. 1923. Statistical investigations in the constitution of plant associations. *Ecology,* 4:68–73.

Atkinson, A. 1989. Introduced animals and extinctions. In D. Western and M. Pearl (eds.), *Conservation for the Twenty-first Century,* pp. 54–69. Oxford University Press, New York.

Ayala, F.J. 1968. Genotype, environment, and population numbers. *Science,* 162:1453–1459.

Ballou, J., and K. Ralls. 1982. Inbreeding and juvenile mortality in small populations of ungulates: a detailed analysis. *Biol. Conserv.,* 24:239–272.

Bambach, R.K. 1977. Species richness in marine benthic habitats through the Phanerozoic. *Paleobiology,* 3:152–167.

Barbour, C.D., and J.H. Brown. 1974. Fish species diversity in lakes. *Am. Nat.,* 108:473–489.

Barnett, J., R. How, and W. Humphreys. 1978. The use of habitat components by small mammals in eastern Australia. *Aust. J. Ecol.,* 3:277–285.

Batisse, M. 1986. Developing and focusing the biosphere reserve concept. UNESCO *Nature and Resources,* 22:1–10.

Beaver, R.A. 1977. Non-equilibrium 'island' communities: Diptera breeding in dead snails. *J. Anim. Ecol.,* 46:783–798.

Behle, W.H. 1978. Avian biogeography of the Great Basin and Intermontane Region. *Great Basin Nat. Mem.,* 2:55–80.

Bekele, E. 1980. Island biogeography and guidelines for the selection of conservation units for large mammals. Ph.D. diss., Univ. of Michigan, Ann Arbor. Unpub.

Belovsky, G. 1987. Extinction models and mammalian persistence. In M. Soulé (ed.), *Viable Populations for Conservation,* pp. 35–58. Cambridge University Press.

Bennett, A.F. 1987. Conservation of mammals within a fragmented forest environment: the contributions of insular biogeography and autecology. In D. Saunders, G. Arnold, A. Burbridge, and A. Hopkins (eds.), *Nature Conservation: The Role of Remnants of Native Vegetation,* pp. 259–268. Surrey Beatty and Sons Pty. Limited, Chipping Norton, NSW, Australia.

Benson, R.H. 1984. The Phanerozoic "crisis" as viewed from the Miocene. In W.A. Berggren and J.A. Van Couvering (eds.), *Catastrophes and Earth History,* pp. 437–446. Princeton University Press, Princeton, N.J.

Berry, R.J. 1971. Conservation aspects of the genetical constitution of populations. In E. Duffey and A.S. Watt (eds.), *The Scientific Management of Animal and Plant Communities for Conservation,* pp. 177–206. Blackwell Scientific Publications, Oxford.

———. 1983. Genetics and conservation. In A. Warren and F.B. Goldsmith (eds.), *Conservation in Perspective,* pp. 141–156. John Wiley and Sons Ltd., Chichester, England.

Berwick, S. 1976. The Gir forest: an endangered ecosystem. *Am. Sci.,* 64:28–40.

Blake, J.G., and J.R. Karr. 1984. Species composition of bird communities and the conservation benefit of large versus small forests. *Biol. Conserv.,* 30:173–187.

Bliss, C.I. 1965. An analysis of some insect trap records. In G.P. Patil (ed.), *Classical and Contagious Discrete Distributions,* pp. 385–397. Statistical Publishing Society, Calcutta.

Bloch, N. 1987. Too small an ark. (Earthwatch) *Expedition News,* 8:9–14.

Blondel, J. 1987. From biogeography to life history theory: a multithematic approach illustrated by the biogeography of vertebrates. *J. Biogeogr.,* 14:405–422.

Blouin, M.S., and E.F. Connor. 1985. Is there a best shape for nature reserves? *Biol. Conserv.,* 32:277–288.

Boecklen, W.J. 1986. Optimal design of nature reserves: consequences of genetic drift. *Biol. Conserv.,* 38:323–338.

Boecklen, W.J., and G.W. Bell. 1987. Consequences of faunal collapse and genetic drift for the design of nature reserves. In D. Saunders, G. Arnold, A. Burbidge, and A. Hopkins (eds.), *Nature Conservation: The Role of Remnants of Native Vegetation,* pp. 141–149. Surrey Beatty and Sons Pty. Limited, Chipping Norton, NSW, Australia.

Boecklen, W.J., and N.J. Gotelli. 1984. Island biogeographic theory and conservation practice: species-area or specious-area relationships? *Biol. Conserv.*, 29:63–80.

Boecklen, W.J., and D. Simberloff. 1986. Area-based extinction models in conservation. In D.K. Elliott (ed.), *Dynamics of Extinctions*, pp. 247–276. John Wiley and Sons, New York.

Bolger, D.T., C.C. Biehl, M. Sorice, and M. Gilpin. 1987. Estimating effective population for the Yellowstone grizzly bear population: effects of non-poisson family size distribution and breeding sex ratio. In F. Singer (ed.), *Conference on Science in the National Parks* Volume 2, *July 13–18, 1986*, pp. 3–16. The George Wright Society and the U.S. National Park Service.

Bond, R.R. 1957. Ecological distribution of breeding birds in the upland forests of southern Wisconsin. *Ecol. Monogr.*, 27:351–384.

Bonnell, M.L., and R.K. Selander. 1974. Elephant seals: genetic variation and near extinction. *Science*, 184:908–909.

Booth, W. 1989. New thinking on old growth. *Science*, 244:141–143.

Boucot, A.J., and J.Gray. 1975. Epilogue: a Paleozoic Pangaea? In J. Gray and A.J. Boucot (eds.), *Historical Biogeography, Plate Tectonics, and the Changing Environment*, pp. 465–482. Oregon State University Press, Corvallis.

Bretsky, P.W., and S.S. Bretsky. 1976. The maintenance of evolutionary equilibrium in Late Ordovician benthic marine invertebrate faunas. *Lethaia*, 9:223–233.

Brian, M.V. 1953. Species frequencies in random samples from animal populations. *J. Anim. Ecol.*, 22:57–64.

Bridgewater, P.B. 1987. Connectivity: an Australian perspective. In D. Saunders, G. Arnold, A. Burbidge, and A. Hopkins (eds.), *Nature Conservation: The Role of Remnants of Native Vegetation*, pp. 195–200. Surrey Beatty and Sons Pty. Limited, Chipping Norton, NSW, Australia.

Brotherton, I. 1982. National parks in Great Britain and the achievement of nature conservation purposes. *Biol. Conserv.*, 22:85–100.

Brown, J.H. 1971. Mammals on mountaintops: nonequilibrium insular biogeography. *Am. Nat.*, 105:467–478.

———. 1978. The theory of insular biogeography and the distribution of boreal birds and mammals. In K.T. Kimball and J.L. Reveal (eds.), *Biogeography of the Intermountain West*, pp. 209–227. Brigham Young University Press, Provo, Utah.

———. 1981. Two decades of homage to Santa Rosalia: toward a general theory of diversity. *Am. Zool.*, 21:877–888.

———. 1986. Two decades of interaction between the MacArthur-Wilson model and the complexities of mammalian distributions. *Biol. J. Linn. Soc.*, 28:231–251.

Brown, J.H., and A.C. Gibson. 1983. *Biogeography*. The C.V. Mosby Company, St. Louis, Mo.

Brown, J.H., and A. Kodric-Brown. 1977. Turnover rates in insular biogeography: effect of immigration on extinction. *Ecology*, 58:445–449.

Brown, W.E. 1971. *Islands of Hope: Parks and Recreation in Environmental Crisis*. National Recreation and Park Association, Washington, D.C.

Browne, J. 1983. *The Secular Ark: Studies in the History of Biogeography*. Yale University Press, New Haven, Ct.

Browne, R.A. 1981. Lakes as islands: biogeographic distribution, turnover rates, and species composition in the lakes of central New York. *J. Biogeogr.*, 8:75–83.

Buckley, R. 1982. The habitat-unit model of island biogeography. *J. Biogeogr.*, 9:339–344.

Buechner, M. 1987. Conservation in insular parks: simulation models of factors affecting the movement of animals across park boundaries. *Biol. Conserv.*, 41:57–76.

Bulmer, M.G. 1973. Inbreeding in the Great Tit. *Heredity*, 30:313–325.

Burgess, R.L., and D.M. Sharpe. 1981a. Introduction. In R.L. Burgess and D.M. Sharpe (eds.), *Ecological Studies 41: Forest Island Dynamics in Man-Dominated Landscapes*, pp. 1–5. Springer-Verlag, New York.

———. 1981b. Summary and conclusions. In R.L. Burgess and D.M. Sharpe (eds.), *Ecological Studies 41: Forest Island Dynamics in Man-Dominated Landscapes*, pp. 267–272. Springer-Verlag, New York.

Burgman, M.A., H.R. Akcakaya, and S.S. Loew. 1988. The use of extinction models for species conservation. *Biol. Conserv.*, 43:9–25.

Burkey, T.V. 1989. Extinction in nature reserves: the effect of fragmentation and the importance of migration between reserve fragments. *Oikos*, 55:75–81.

Busack, S.D., and S.B. Hedges. 1984. Is the peninsular effect a red herring? *Am. Nat.*, 123:266–275.

Butcher, G.S., W.A. Niering, W.J. Barry, and R.H. Goodwin. 1981. Equilibrium biogeography and the size of nature preserves: an avian case study. *Oecologia*, 49:29–37.

Cahalane, V.H. 1948. The status of mammals in the U.S. National Park System. 1947. *J. Mammal.*, 29:247–259.

Cairns, J., Jr., M.L. Dahlberg, K.L. Dickson, N. Smith, and W.T. Waller. 1969. The relationship of fresh-water protozoan communities to the MacArthur-Wilson equilibrium model. *Am. Nat.*, 103:439–454.

Cairns, J., Jr., and J.A. Ruthven. 1970. Artificial microhabitat size and the number of colonizing protozoan species. *Trans. Amer. Microsc. Soc.*, 89:100–109.

Carlquist, S. 1974. *Island Biology.* Columbia University Press, New York.

Carson, H.L. 1983. The genetics of the founder effect. In C. Schonewald-Cox et al. (eds.), *Genetics and Conservation: A Reference for Managing Wild Animal and Plant Populations*, pp. 189–200. The Benjamin/Cummings Publishing Company, Inc., Menlo Park, Cal.

Case, T.J. 1975. Species numbers, density compensation, and colonizing ability of lizards on islands in the Gulf of California. *Ecology*, 56:3–18.

Case, T., and M. Cody. 1983. Synthesis: pattern and processes in island biogeography. In T.J. Case and M.L. Cody (eds.), *Island Biogeography in the Sea of Cortez*, pp. 307–341. University of California Press, Berkeley.

Chamberlin, T.C. 1898. A systematic source of evolution of provincial faunas. *J. Geol.*, 6:597–608.

Chambers, S.M., and J.W. Bayless. 1983. Systematics, conservation, and the measurement of genetic diversity. In C.M. Schonewald-Cox et al. (eds.), *Genetics and Conservation: A Reference for Managing Wild Animal and Plant Populations*, pp. 349–363. The Benjamin/Cummings Publishing Company, Inc., Menlo Park, Cal.

Chapman, C.A. 1983. Speciation of tropical rainforest primates of Africa: insular biogeography. *Afr. J. Ecol.*, 21:297–308.

Chapman, S.B., R.T. Clarke, and N.R. Webb. 1989. The survey and assessment of heathland in Dorset, England, for conservation. *Biol. Conserv.*, 47:137–152.

Charlesworth, D., and B. Charlesworth. 1987. Inbreeding depression and its evolutionary consequences. *Ann. Rev. Ecol. Syst.*, 18:237–268.

Chesser, R.K. 1983. Isolation by distance: relationship for the management of genetic resources. In C. Schonewald-Cox et al. (eds.), *Genetics and Conservation: A Reference for Managing Wild Animal and Plant Populations*, pp. 66–77. The Benjamin/Cummings Publishing Company, Inc., Menlo Park, Cal.

Chesser, R.K., and N. Ryman. 1986. Inbreeding as a strategy in subdivided populations. *Evolution*, 40:616–624.

Chesser, R.K., M.H. Smith, and I.L. Brisbin. 1980. Management and maintenance of genetic variability in endangered species. *Int. Zoo Yearb.*, 20:146–154.

Cocks, K.D., and I.A. Baird. 1989. Using mathematical programming to address the multiple reserve selection problem: an example from Eyre Peninsula, South Australia. *Biol. Conserv.*, 49:113–130.

Cohn, J.P. 1986. Surprising cheetah genetics. *BioScience*, 36:358–362.

Cole, B.J. 1981. Colonizing abilities, island size, and the number of species on archipelagoes. *Am. Nat.*, 117:629–638.

Coleman, R.D. 1981. On random placement and species-area relations. *Math. Biosci.*, 54:191–215.

Colwell, R.K., and D.W. Winkler. 1984. A null model for null models in biogeography. In D.R. Strong et al. (eds.), *Ecological Communities: Conceptual Issues and the Evidence*, pp. 344–359. Princeton University Press, Princeton, N.J.

Conant, S. 1988. Saving endangered species by translocation. *BioScience*, 38:254–257.

Connor, E.F., and E.D. McCoy. 1979. The statistics and biology of the species-area relationship. *Am. Nat.*, 113:791–833.

Connor, E.F., E.D. McCoy, and B.J. Cosby. 1983. Model discrimination and expected slope values in species-area studies. *Am. Nat.*, 122:789–796.

Connor, E.F., and D. Simberloff. 1978. Species number and compositional similarity of the Galapagos flora and avifauna. *Ecol. Monogr.*, 48:219–248.

———. 1979. The assembly of species communities: chance or competition? *Ecology*, 60:1132–1140.

———. 1983. Interspecific competition and species co-occurrence patterns on islands: null models and the evaluation of evidence. *Oikos*, 41:455–465.

Conservation Foundation, The. 1984. Wildlife reserves. Can they do the job? *Conservation Foundation Letter (January–February)*. The Conservation Foundation, Washington, D.C.

———. 1985. *National Parks for a New Generation: Visions, Realities, Prospects.* The Conservation Foundation, Washington, D.C.

———. 1987. Conservationists Must Plan for Human Needs. *Conservation Foundation Letter (January–February)*. The Conservation Foundation, Washington, D.C.

Cowen, R., and W.L. Stockton. 1978. Testing for evolutionary equilibria. *Paleobiology*, 4:195–200.

Crow, J.F., and C. Denniston. 1988. Inbreeding and variance effective population numbers. *Evolution*, 42:482–495.

Crow, J.F., and M. Kimura. 1970. *An Introduction to Population Genetics Theory.* Harper & Row, New York.

Crowell, K.L. 1973. Experimental zoogeography: introductions of mice to small islands. *Am. Nat.*, 107:535–558.

———. 1986. A comparison of relict versus equilibrium models for insular mammals of the Gulf of Maine. *Biol. J. Linn. Soc.*, 28:37–64.

Crumpacker, D.W. 1985. Status and trend of natural ecosystems in the United States. U.S. Congress Office of Technology Assessment, Washington, D.C., commissioned paper. Unpub.

Crumpacker, D.W., and S.W. Hodge. 1988. Representation of major terrestrial and wetland ecosystems in the National Park System of the United States and comparison with other U.S. national land management systems. In Vol. Eight *New Parks: New Promise*, pp. II 1–95. National Parks and Conservation Association, Washington, D.C.

Culver, D.C. 1970. Analysis of simple cave communities. I. Caves as islands. *Evolution*, 24:463–474.

———. 1971. Caves as archipelagoes. *Nat. Speleol. Soc. Bull.*, 33:97–100.

Culver, D., J.R. Holsinger, and R. Baroody. 1973. Toward a predictive cave biogeography: the Greenbrier Valley as a case study. *Evolution*, 27:689–695.

Curry-Lindahl, K. 1974. Protecting the future in the worldwide national park movement. In H. Elliott (ed.), *Second World Conference on National Parks*, pp. 82–94. IUCN, Morges, Switzerland.

Curtis, J.T. 1956. The modification of mid-latitude grasslands and forests by man. In W.L. Thomas (ed.), *Man's Role in Changing the Face of the Earth*, pp. 721–736. University of Chicago Press, Chicago.

Darlington, P.J. 1957. *Zoogeography: The Geographical Distribution of Animals.* John Wiley and Sons, New York.

Darwin, C. 1859. *On the Origin of Species by Means of Natural Selection, or the Preservation of Favoured Races in the Struggle for Life.* John Murray, London.

Dasmann, R.F. 1987. World parks, people, and land use. In R. Herrmann and T.B. Craig (eds.), *Conference on Science in National Parks: The Fourth Triennial Conference on Research in the National Parks and Equivalent Reserves*, pp. 122–127. The George Wright Society and the U.S. National Park Service.

Dauer, D.M., and J.L. Simon. 1975. Repopulation of the polychaete fauna of an intertidal habitat following natural defaunation: species equilibrium. *Oecologia*, 22:99–117.

Davis, A.M., and T.F. Glick. 1978. Urban ecosystems and island biogeography. *Environ. Conserv.*, 5:299–304.

Davis, G. 1987. Ecosystem Representation as a Criterion for World Wilderness Designation. Report to the Wild Wings Foundation.

Davis, M., P. Hut, and R.A. Muller. 1984. Extinction of species by periodic comet showers. *Nature*, 308:715–717.

Denning, P.J. 1987. The science of computing. *Am. Sci.*, 75:572–573.

Denniston, C. 1978. Small population size and genetic diversity: implications for endangered species. In S.A. Temple (ed.), *Endangered Birds: Management Techniques for Preserving Threatened Species*, pp. 281–289. University of Wisconsin Press, Madison.

Deshayne, J., and P. Morisset. 1989. Species-area relationships and the SLOSS effect in a subarctic archipelago. *Biol. Conserv.*, 48:265–276.

di Castri, F., F.W.G. Baker, and M. Hadley (eds.). 1984. *Ecology in Practice* Part II: *The Social Response.* Tycooly International Publishing Limited, Dublin, and UNESCO, Paris.

Diamond, J.M. 1972. Biogeographic kinetics: estimation of relaxation times for avifaunas of Southwest Pacific Islands. *Proc. Nat. Acad. Sci.*, 69:3199–3203.

———. 1973. Distributional ecology of New Guinea birds. *Science*, 179:759–769.

———. 1975a. Assembly of species communities. In M.L. Cody and J.M. Diamond (eds.), *Ecology and Evolution of Communities*, pp. 342–444. Belknap Press of Harvard University, Cambridge, Mass.

———. 1975b. The island dilemma: lessons of modern biogeographic studies for the design of natural reserves. *Biol. Conserv.*, 7:129–146.

———. 1976a. Island biogeography and conservation: strategy and limitations. *Science*, 193:1027–1029.

———. 1976b. Relaxation and differential extinction on landbridge islands: applications to natural preserves. In H.J. Frith and J.H. Calaby (eds.), *Proceedings of the 16th International Ornithological Congress, Canberra, Australia, 12–17, August 1974*, pp. 616–628. Australian Academy of Science. Griffin Press Ltd., Netley.

———. 1978. Critical areas for maintaining viable populations of species. In W.M. Holdgate and M.J. Woodman (eds.), *The Breakdown and Restoration of Ecosystems*, pp. 27–40. Plenum Press, New York.

———. 1981. Implications of island biogeography for ecosystem conservation. In W.R. Siegfried and B.R. Davies (eds.), *Conservation of Ecosystems: Theory and Practice*, pp. 46–60. South African National Scientific Programmes Report No. 61, CSIR, Pretoria.

———. 1980a. Patchy distributions of tropical birds. In M.E. Soulé and B.A. Wilcox (eds.), *Conservation Biology: An Evolutionary-Ecological Perspective*, pp. 57–74. Sinauer Associates, Inc., Sunderland, Mass.

———. 1980b. Species turnover in island bird communities. *Proc. 19th Intern. Ornith. Congr.*, pp. 777–782.

———. 1983. Report of a 1974 ornithological expedition to the Solomon Islands: survival of bird populations stranded on land-bridge islands. *Nat. Geogr. Soc. Research Reports*, 15:127–141.

———. 1984a. Historic extinctions: a Rosetta Stone for understanding prehistoric extinctions. In P.S. Martin and R.G. Klein (eds.), *Quaternary Extinctions*, pp. 824–862. University of Arizona Press, Tucson.

———. 1984b. "Normal" extinctions of isolated populations. In M.H. Nitecki (ed.), *Extinctions*, pp. 191–246. The University of Chicago Press, Chicago.

———. 1986. The design of a nature reserve system for Indonesian New Guinea. In Soulé (ed.), *Conservation Biology: The Science of Scarcity and Diversity*, pp. 485–503. Sinauer Associates, Inc., Sunderland, Mass.

———. 1986. Overview: laboratory experiments, field experiments, and natural experiments. In J.M. Diamond and T.J. Case (eds.), *Community Ecology*, pp. 3–22. Harper & Row, New York.

Diamond, J.M., and M.E. Gilpin. 1982. Examination of the "null" model of Connor and Simberloff for species cooccurrence on islands. *Oecologia*, 52:64–74.

———. 1983. Biogeographic umbilici and the evolution of the Philippine avifauna. *Oikos*, 41:307–321.

Diamond, J.M., and R.M. May. 1976. Island biogeography and the design of natural reserves. In R.M. May (ed.), *Theoretical Ecology: Principles and Applications*, pp. 163–186. W. B. Saunders, Philadelphia.

———. 1977. Species turnover rates on islands: dependence on census interval. *Science*, 197:266–270.

Diamond, J.M., and E. Mayr. 1976. Species-area relation for birds of the Solomon Archipelago. *Proc. Nat. Acad. Sci.*, 73:262–266.

Dickenson, R. 1984. Keynote address: the Nearctic realm. In J.A. McNeeley and K.R. Miller (eds.), *National Parks, Conservation and Development: The Role of Protected Areas in Sustaining Society*, pp. 492–495. Smithsonian Institution Press, Washington, D.C.

Dickman, C.R. 1987. Habitat fragmentation and vertebrate species richness in an urban environment. *J. Appl. Ecol.*, 24:337–351.

Dietz, R.S., and J.C. Holden. 1970. Reconstruction of Pangaea: breakup and dispersion of continents, Permian to present. *J. Geophys. Res.*, 75:4939–4956.

Doak, D. 1989. Spotted owls and old growth logging in the Pacific Northwest. *Conserv. Biol.*, 3:389–396.

Dobson, A.P., and R.M. May. 1986. Disease and conservation. In Soulé (ed.), *Conservation Biology: The Science of Scarcity and Diversity*, pp. 345–365. Sinauer Associates, Inc., Sunderland, Mass.

Dritschilo, W., H. Cornell, D. Nafus, and B. O'Conner. 1975. Insular biogeography: of mice and mites. *Science*, 190:467–469.

Dubos, R. 1968. *So Human an Animal*. Charles Scribner's Sons, New York.

Dueser, R.D., and W.C. Brown. 1980. Ecological correlates of insular rodent diversity. *Ecology*, 61:50–56.

Duffey, E. 1971. The management of Woodwalton Fen: a multidisciplinary approach. In E. Duffey and A. Watt (eds.), *The Scientific Management of Animal and Plant Communities for Conservation*, pp. 581–597. Blackwell Scientific Publications, Oxford.

———. 1974. *Nature Reserves and Wildlife*. Heinemann Educational Books, London.

———. 1977. The re-establishment of the large copper butterfly Lycaena Dispar Batava Obth. on Woodwalton Fen National Nature Reserve, Cambridgeshire, England, 1969–73. *Biol. Conserv.*, 12:143–158.

———. 1988. (ed.) *Biol. Conserv.*, 44:1–135.

Duffey, E., and C. Schonewald-Cox (eds.). 1989. *Biol. Conserv.*, 50:1–279.

Dunn, C.D., and C. Loehle. 1988. Species-area parameter estimation: testing the null model of lack of relationship. *J. Biogeogr.*, 15:721–728.

Eagles, P.F.J. 1984. *The Planning and Management of Environmentally Sensitive Areas*. Longman, London.

East, R. 1981a. Area requirements and conservation status of large African mammals. *Nyala*, 7:3–20.

———. 1981b. Species-area curves and populations of large mammals in African savanna reserves. *Biol. Conserv.*, 21:111–126.

———. 1983. Application of species-area curves to African savannah reserves. *Afr. J. Ecol.*, 21:123–128.

Eckholm, E.P. 1976. *Losing Ground.* W.W. Norton and Company, Inc., New York.

Ehrenfeld, D. 1989. Hard times for diversity. In D. Western and M. Pearl (eds.), *Conservation for the Twenty-first Century,* pp. 247–250. Oxford University Press, New York.

Ehrlich, P., and A. Ehrlich. 1981. *Extinction: The Causes and Consequences of the Disappearance of Species.* Random House, New York.

Ehrlich, P.R., and P.H. Raven. 1969. Differentiation of populations. *Science,* 165:1228–1232.

Eidsvik, H.K. 1984. Future directions for the Nearctic realm. In J.A. McNeeley and K.R. Miller (eds.), *National Parks, Conservation, and Development: The Role of Protected Areas in Sustaining Society,* pp. 546–549. Smithsonian Institution Press, Washington, D.C.

Eisenberg, J.F. 1980. The density and biomass of tropical mammals. In M.E. Soulé and B.A. Wilcox (eds.), *Conservation Biology: An Evolutionary-Ecological Perspective,* pp. 35–55. Sinauer Associates, Inc., Sunderland, Mass.

Eisenberg, J.F., and L.D. Harris. 1989. Conservation: a consideration of evolution, population, and life history. In D. Western and M. Pearl (eds.), *Conservation for the Twenty-first Century,* pp. 99–108. Oxford University Press, New York.

Eldredge, N. 1974. Stability, diversity and speciation in Paleozoic epeiric seas. *J. Paleontol.,* 48:541–548.

Elfring, C. 1986. U.S. parks at a crossroads. *BioScience,* 36:301–304.

Endler, J.A. 1977. *Geographic Variation, Speciation and Clines.* Princeton University Press, Princeton, N.J.

Erwin, T.L. 1983. Tropical forest canopies: the last biotic frontier. *Bull. Entomol. Soc. Am.,* 29:14–19.

———. 1983. Beetles and other insects of tropical forest canopies at Manaus, Brazil, sampled by insecticidal fogging. In S.L. Sutton, T.C. Whitmore, and A.C. Chadwick (eds.), *Tropical Rain Forest: Ecology and Management,* pp. 59–75. Blackwell, Oxford.

Faaborg, J. 1979. Qualitative patterns of avian extinction on neotropical land-bridge islands: lessons for conservation. *J. Appl. Ecol.,* 16:99–107.

Fabos, J.G. 1979. *Planning the Total Landscape: A Guide to Intelligent Land Use.* Westview Press, Boulder, Colo.

Faeth, S.H., and E.F. Connor. 1979. Supersaturated and relaxing island faunas: a critique of the species-area relationship. *J. Biogeogr.,* 6:311–316.

Faeth, S.H., and T.C. Kane. 1978. Urban biogeography: city parks as islands for Diptera and Coleoptera. *Oecologia,* 32:127–133.

Falconer, D.S. 1981. *Introduction to Quantitative Genetics.* Longman, New York.

FAO. 1981. Map of the Fuelwood Situation in Developing Countries—Explanatory Note, Rome. FAO.

Feller, W. 1939. Die Grundlagen der Volterraschen Theorie des Kampfes ums Dasein in Warscheinlicheistheoretischer Behandlung. *Acta Biotheoretica,* 5:11–40.

Felsenstein, J. 1981. Skepticism towards Santa Rosalina, or why are there so few kinds of animals? *Evolution,* 35:124–138.

Fisher, R.A. 1930. *The Genetical Theory of Natural Selection.* Clarendon Press, Oxford.

Fisher, R.A., A.S. Corbet, and C.B. Williams. 1943. The relation between the number of individuals and the number of species in a random sample of an animal population. *J. Anim. Ecol.,* 12:42–58.

Fish and Wildlife Service. 1983. *Fish and Wildlife Service Resource Problems.* U.S. Fish and Wildlife Service, Department of the Interior, Washington, D.C.

Flessa, K.W. 1975. Area, continental drift and mammalian diversity. *Paleobiology,* 1:189–194.

———. 1980. Biological effects of plate tectonics and continental drift. *BioScience,* 30:518–523.

Flessa, K.W., and J. Imbrie. 1973. Evolutionary pulsations: evidence from Phanerozoic diversity patterns. In D.H. Tarling and S.K. Runcorn (eds.), *Implications of Continental Drift to the Earth Sciences,* Volume I, pp. 247–285. Academic Press, New York.

Flessa, K.W., and J.J. Sepkoski, Jr. 1978. On the relationship between Phanerozoic diversity and changes in habitable area. *Paleobiology,* 4:359–366.

Forman, R.T.T. 1983. Corridors in a landscape: their ecological structure and function. *Ekologia,* 2:375–387.

———. 1987a. Emerging directions in landscape ecology and applications in natural resource management. In R. Herrmann and T.B. Craig (eds.), *Conference on Science in National Parks: The Fourth Triennial Conference on Research in the National Parks and Equivalent Reserves,* pp. 59–88. The George Wright Society and the U.S. National Park Service.

———. 1987b. The ethics of isolation, the spread of disturbance, and landscape ecology. In M. Turner (ed.), *Landscape Heterogeneity and Disturbance,* pp. 213–229. Springer-Verlag, New York.

Forman, R.T.T., A.E. Galli, and C.F. Leck. 1976. Forest size and avian diversity in New Jersey woodlots with some land use implications. *Oecologia,* 26:1–8.

Forman, R.T.T., and M. Godron. 1981. Patches and structural components for a landscape ecology. *BioScience*, 31:733–740.

———. 1986. *Landscape Ecology*. John Wiley and Sons, New York.

Forney, K.A., and M.E. Gilpin. 1989. Spatial structure and population extinction: a study with Drosophila flies. *Conserv. Biol.*, 3:45–51.

Foster, J., A. Phillips, and R. Steele. 1984. Protected areas in the United Kingdom: an approach to the selection, establishment, and management of natural and scenic protected areas in a densely populated country with limited choices. In J.A. McNeeley and K.R. Miller (eds.), *National Parks, Conservation, and Development: The Role of Protected Areas in Sustaining Society*, pp. 426–437. Smithsonian Institution Press, Washington, D.C.

Frank, R.F., and J.H. Eckhardt. 1983. Power of Congress under the property clause to give extra territorial effect to Federal lands law: will 'respecting property' go the way of 'affecting commerce'? *Natural Resources Lawyer*, 15:663–686.

Frankel, O.H. 1970. Variation—the essence of life. Sir William Macleay memorial lecture. *Proc. Linn. Soc. NSW*, 95:158–169.

———. 1974. Genetic conservation: our evolutionary responsibility. *Genetics*, 78:53–65.

———. 1981. Evolution in jeopardy: the role of nature reserves. In W.R. Atchley and D.S. Woodruff (eds.), *Evolution and Speciation: Essays in Honor of M.J.D. White*, pp. 417–424. Cambridge University Press, New York.

———. 1983. The place of management in conservation. In Schonewald-Cox et al. (eds.), *Genetics and Conservation: A Reference for Managing Wild Animal and Plant Populations*, pp. 1–14. The Benjamin/Cummings Publishing Co., Inc., Menlo Park, Cal.

———. 1984. Genetic diversity, ecosystem conservation and evolutionary responsibility. In F. de Castri, F.W.G. Baker, and M. Hadley (eds.), *Ecology in Practice* Part I: *Ecosystem Management*, pp. 414–427. Tycooly International Publishing Limited, Dublin, and UNESCO, Paris.

Frankel, O.H., and M.E. Soulé. 1981. *Conservation and Evolution*. Cambridge University Press, London.

Franklin, I.A. 1980. Evolutionary change in small populations. In M.E. Soulé and B.A. Wilcox (eds.), *Conservation Biology: An Evolutionary-Ecological Perspective*, pp. 135–149. Sinauer Associates, Inc., Sunderland, Mass.

Franklin, J.F. 1985. Design of natural area preserves in Hawai'i. In C.P. Stone and J.M. Scott (eds.), *Hawai'i's Terrestrial Ecosystems: Preservation and Management*, pp. 459–474. Cooperative National Park Resources Studies Unit, University of Hawaii, Manoa.

Freemark, K.E., and H.G. Merriam. 1986. Importance of area and habitat heterogeneity to bird assemblages in temperate forest fragments. *Biol. Conserv.*, 36:115–141.

Fritz, R.S. 1979. Consequences of insular population structure: distribution and extinction of spruce grouse populations. *Oecologia*, 42:57–65.

Fuerst, P.A., and T. Maruyama. 1986. Considerations on the conservation of alleles and of genic heterozygosity in small managed populations. *Zoo Biol.*, 5:171–179.

Futuyma, D. 1973. Community structure and stability in a constant environment. *Amer. Nat.*, 107:443–446.

———. 1979. *Evolutionary Biology*. Sinauer Associates, Inc., Sunderland, Mass.

———. 1983. Interspecific interactions and the maintenance of genetic diversity. In Schonewald-Cox et al. (eds.), *Genetics and Conservation: A Reference for Managing Wild Animal and Plant Populations*, pp. 364–373. The Benjamin/Cummings Publishing Co., Inc., Menlo Park, Cal.

———. 1986. *Evolutionary Biology*, 2nd Ed. Sinauer Associates, Inc., Sunderland, Mass.

Futuyma, D.J., and G.C. Mayer. 1980. Non-allopatric speciation in animals. *Syst. Zool.*, 29:254–271.

Galli, A.E., C.F. Leck, and R.T.T. Forman. 1976. Avian distribution patterns in forest islands of different sizes in central New Jersey. *Auk*, 93:356–364.

Game, M. 1980. Best shape for nature reserves. *Nature*, 287:630–632.

Game, M., and G.F. Peterken. 1984. Nature reserve selection strategies in the woodlands of Central Lincolnshire, England. *Biol. Conserv.*, 29:157–181.

GAO. 1987. *Parks and Recreation: Limited Progress Made in Documenting and Mitigating Threats to the Parks*. U.S. General Accounting Office, Washington, D.C.

Garratt, K. 1984. The relationship between adjacent lands and protected areas: issues of concern for the protected area manager. In J.A. McNeeley and K.R. Miller (eds.), *National Parks, Conservation, and Development: The Role of Protected Areas in Sustaining Society*, pp. 65–71. Smithsonian Institution Press, Washington, D.C.

Gavareski, C.A. 1976. Relation of park size and vegetation to urban bird populations in Seattle, Washington. *Condor*, 78:375–382.

Gentry, A.H. 1986. Endemism in tropical versus temperate plant communities. In Soulé (ed.), *Conservation Biology: The Science of Scarcity and Diversity*, pp. 105–116. Sinauer Associates, Inc., Sunderland, Mass.

Gilbert, F.S. 1980. The equilibrium theory of island biogeography: fact or fiction? *J. Biogeogr.*, 7:209–235.

Gilbert, L.E. 1980. Food web organization and the conservation of neotropical diversity. In M.E. Soulé and B.A. Wilcox (eds.), *Conservation Biology: An Evolutionary-Ecological Perspective*, pp. 11–33. Sinauer Associates, Inc., Sunderland, Mass.

Gilpin, M.E., and J.M. Diamond. 1980. Subdivision of nature reserves and the maintenance of species diversity. *Nature*, 285:567–568.

———. 1982. Factors contributing to non-randomness in species co-occurrences on islands. *Oecologia*, 52:75–84.

———. 1988. A comment on Quinn and Hastings: extinction in subdivided habitats. *Conserv. Biol.*, 2:290–292.

Gilpin, M.E., and M.E. Soulé. 1986. Minimum viable populations: processes of species extinction. In Soulé (ed.), *Conservation Biology: The Science of Scarcity and Diversity*, pp. 19–34. Sinauer Associates, Inc., Sunderland, Mass.

Gleason, H.A. 1922. On the relation between species and area. *Ecology*, 3:158–162.

———. 1925. Species and area. *Ecology*, 6:66–74.

Godron, M., and R.T.T. Forman. 1983. Landscape modification and changing ecological characteristics. In H.A. Mooney and M. Godron (eds.), *Disturbance and Ecosystems, Components of Response*, pp. 12–28. Springer-Verlag, New York.

Goeden, G.B. 1979. Biogeographic theory as a management tool. *Environ. Conserv.*, 6:27–32.

Goldstein, E.L. 1975. Island biogeography of ants. *Evolution*, 29: 750–762.

Gómez-Pompa, A., C. Vázquez-Yanes, and S. Guevara. 1972. The tropical rain forest: a nonrenewable resource. *Science*, 177:762–765.

Goodman, D. 1987a. The demography of chance extinction. In M. Soulé (ed.), *Viable Populations for Conservation*, pp. 11–34. Cambridge University Press.

———. 1987b. How do any species persist? Lessons for conservation biology. *Conserv. Biol.*, 1:59–62.

———. 1987c. Consideration of stochastic demography in the design and management of biological reserves. *Nat. Resour. Modeling*, 1:205–234.

Gordon, J.C. (chairman). 1989. *National Parks: From Vignettes to a Global View*. National Parks and Conservation Association, Washington, D.C.

Goren, M. 1979. Succession of benthic community on artificial substratum at Elat (Red Sea). *J. Exp. Mar. Biol. Ecol.*, 38:19–40.

Gorman, M. 1979. *Island Ecology*. Chapman and Hall, London.

Gould, S.J. 1979. An allometric interpretation of species-area curves: the meaning of the coefficient. *Am. Nat.*, 114:335–343.

Grant, P.R. 1970. Colonization of islands by ecologically dissimilar species of mammals. *Can. J. Zool.*, 48:545–553.

Grant, P.R., and I. Abbott. 1980. Interspecific competition, island biogeography and null hypotheses. *Evolution*, 34:332–341.

Graves, G.R., and N.J. Gotelli. 1983. Neotropical land-bridge avifaunas: new approaches to null hypotheses in biogeography. *Oikos*, 41:322–333.

Grayson, D.K. 1987. The biogeographic history of small mammals in the Great Basin: observations on the last 20,000 years. *J. Mammal.*, 68:359–375.

Greig, J.C. 1979. Principles of genetic conservation in relation to wildlife management in Southern Africa. *S. Afr. J. Wildl. Res.*, 9:57–78.

Greig-Smith, P. 1969. *Quantitative Plant Ecology*. Butterworths, London.

Gregg, W.P., Jr., S.L. Krugman, and J.D. Wood, Jr. (eds.). 1989. *Proceedings of the Symposium on Biosphere Reserves, Fourth World Wilderness Congress, September 14–17, 1987*, YMCA at the Rockies, Estes Park, Colorado. U.S. Department of the Interior, National Park Service, Atlanta.

Gregg, W.P., and B.A. McGean. 1985. Biosphere reserves: their history and promise. *Orion*, 4:40–51.

Green, B.H. 1989. Conservation in cultural landscapes. In D. Western and M. Pearl (eds.), *Conservation for the Twenty-first Century*, pp. 182–198. Oxford University Press, New York.

Greenslade, P.J.M. 1968. The distribution of some insects of the Solomon Islands. *Proc. Linn. Soc. Lond.*, 179:189–196.

———. 1969. Land fauna: insect distribution patterns in the Solomon Islands. *Philos. Trans. R. Soc. Lond. B. Biol. Sci.*, 255:271–284.

Greenwood, P.J., P.H. Harvey, and C.M. Perrins. 1978. Inbreeding and dispersal in the Great Tit. *Nature*, 271:52–54.

Haas, P.H. 1975. Some comments on use of the species-area curve. *Am. Nat.*, 109:371–373.

Haga, A. 1981. Økologisk kunnskap i naturvernforvaltningen. *Fauna*, 34:51–63.

Haila, Yrjö. 1983. Land birds on northern islands: a sampling metaphor for insular colonization. *Oikos*, 41:334–351.

Hallam, A. 1987. End-Cretaceous mass extinction event: argument for terrestrial causation. *Science*, 238:1237–1242.

Hamilton, T.H., and N.E. Armstrong. 1965. Environmental determination of insular variation in bird species abundance in the Gulf of Guinea. *Nature*, 207:148–151.

Hamilton, T.H., R.H. Barth, Jr., and I. Rubinoff. 1964. The environmental control of insular variation in bird species abundance. *Proc. Nat. Acad. Sci.*, 52:132–140.

Hamilton, T.H., and I. Rubinoff. 1967. On predicting insular variation in endemism and sympatry for the Darwin Finches in the Galapagos Archipelago. *Am. Nat.*, 101:161–171.

Hamilton, T.H., I. Rubinoff, R.H. Barth, Jr., and G.L. Bush. 1963. Species abundance: natural regulation of insular variation. *Science*, 142:1575–1577.

Hanski, I. 1986. Population dynamics of shrews on small islands accord with the equilibrium model. *Biol. J. Linn. Soc.*, 28:23–36.

Hansson, L. 1977. Landscape ecology and stability of populations. *Landscape Plann.*, 4:85–93.

Harcourt, A.H., and D. Fossey. 1981. The Virunga gorillas: decline of an 'island' population. *Afr. J. Ecol.*, 19:83–97.

Harner, R.F., and K.T. Harper. 1976. The role of area, heterogeneity, and favorability in plant species diversity of pinyon-juniper ecosystems. *Ecology*, 57:1254–1263.

Harper, J.L. 1969. The role of predation in vegetational diversity. In G.M. Woodwell and H.H. Smith (eds.), *Brookhaven Symposia in Biology* Number 22: *Diversity and Stability in Ecological Systems, May 26–28, 1969*, pp. 48–62. Brookhaven National Laboratory, Upton, N.Y.

———. 1981. The meanings of rarity. In H. Synge (ed.), *The Biological Aspects of Rare Plant Conservation*, pp. 189–203. John Wiley and Sons, New York.

Harris, L.D. 1984. *The Fragmented Forest: Island Biogeography Theory and the Preservation of Biotic Diversity*. The University of Chicago Press, Chicago.

———. 1985. Conservation corridors: a highway system for wildlife. *Enfo Report*. Florida Conservation Foundation, Inc.

———. 1988. Edge effects and conservation of biotic diversity. *Conserv. Biol.*, 2:330–332.

———. 1989. New initiatives for wildlife conservation: the need for movement corridors. In G. Mackintosh (ed.), *Preserving Communities and Corridors*, pp. 11–34. Defenders of Wildlife, Washington, D.C.

Harris, R.B., and F.W. Allendorf. 1989. Genetically effective population size of large mammals: an assessment of estimators. *Conserv. Biol.*, 3:181–191.

Harrison, J.D., K.R. Miller, and J.A. McNeely. 1982. The world coverage of protected areas: development goals and environmental needs. *Ambio*, 11:238–245.

Hart, W.J. 1966. *A Systems Approach to Park Planning*. IUCN, Morges, Switzerland.

Hartl, D.L. 1981. *A Primer of Population Genetics*. Sinauer Associates, Inc., Sunderland, Mass.

Hartzog, G.B., Jr. 1974. Management considerations for optimum development and protection of national park resources. In H. Elliott (ed.), *Second World Conference on National Parks*, pp. 155–161. IUCN, Morges, Switzerland.

Heaney, L.R. 1984. Mammalian species richness on islands on the Sunda Shelf, Southeast Asia. *Oecologia*, 61:11–17.

Heaney, L.R., and B.D. Patterson (eds.). 1986. *Island Biogeography of Mammals*. Academic Press, Orlando, Florida.

Heatwole, H. 1975. Biogeography of reptiles on some of the islands and cays of Eastern Papua–New Guinea. *Atoll Res. Bull.*, 180.

Heatwole, H., and R. Levins. 1973. Biogeography of the Puerto Rican Bank: species-turnover on a small cay, Cayo Ahogado. *Ecology*, 54:1042–1055.

Heatwole, H., R. Levins, and M.D. Byer. 1981. Biogeography of the Puerto Rican Bank. *Atoll Res. Bull.*, 251.

Hedrick, P.W., M.E. Ginevan, and E.P. Ewing. 1976. Genetic polymorphism in heterogeneous environments. *Annu. Rev. Ecol. Syst.*, 7:1–32.

Heller, J. 1976. The biogeography of Enid landsnails on the Aegean Islands. *J. Biogeogr.*, 3:281–292.

Helliwell, D.R. 1976a. The effects of size and isolation on the conservation value of wooded sites in Britain. *J. Biogeogr.*, 3:407–416.

———. 1976b. The extent and location of nature conservation areas. *Environ. Conserv.*, 3:255–258.

Hemming, J.E. 1971. The distribution movement patterns of caribou in Alaska. *Alaska Dept. of Fish and Game Wildlife Tech. Bull.* 1.

Hendrick, P.W. 1986. Genetic polymorphism in heterogeneous environments: a decade later. *Ann. Rev. Ecol. Syst.*, 17:535–566.

Henderson, M.T., G. Merriam, and J. Wegner. 1985. Patchy environments and species survival: chipmunks in an agricultural mosaic. *Biol. Conserv.*, 31:95–105.

Henebry, M.S., and J. Cairns, Jr. 1980. The effect of source pool maturity on the process of island colonization: an experimental approach with protozoan communities. *Oikos*, 35:107–114.

Higgs, A.J. 1981. Island biogeography theory and nature reserve design. *J. Biogeogr.*, 8:117–124.

Higgs, A.J., and M.B. Usher. 1980. Should nature reserves be large or small? *Nature*, 285:568–569.

Hiscock, J.W. 1986. Protecting national park system buffer zones: existing, proposed and suggested authority. *J. Energy Law Policy*, 7:35–94.

Hoffman, A. 1985. Patterns of family extinction depend on definition and geological timescale. *Nature*, 315:659–662.

Hoffmann, R.S. 1981. Different voles for different holes: environmental restrictions on refugial survival of mammals. In G.G.E. Scudder and J.L. Reveal (eds.), *Evolution Today: Proceedings of the Second International Congress of Systematic and Evolutionary Biology*, 25–45. Hunt Institute for Botanical Documentation, Carnegie-Mellon University, Pittsburgh.

Hooper, M.D. 1971. The size and surroundings of nature reserves. In E. Duffey and A.S. Watt (eds.), *The Scientific Management of Animal and Plant Communities for Conservation: The 11th Symposium of the British Ecological Society of East Anglia, Norwich, 7-9 July 1970*, pp. 555–561. Blackwell Scientific Publications, Oxford.

Hope, J.H. 1973. Mammals of the Bass Strait Islands. *Proc. Roy. Soc. Vict.*, 85:163–196.

Hopkins, P.J., and N.R. Webb. 1984. The composition of the beetle and spider faunas on fragmented heathlands. *J. Appl. Ecol.*, 21:935–946.

Houghton, R.A., and G.M. Woodwell. 1989. Global climatic change. *Sci. Am.*, 260:36–44.

Houston, D.B. 1971. Ecosystems of national parks. *Science*, 172:648–651.

Howe, H.F. 1984. Implications of seed dispersal by animals for tropical reserve management. *Biol. Conserv.*, 30:261–281.

Hubbard, M.D. 1973. Experimental insular biogeography: ponds as islands. *Fl. Sci.*, 36:132–141.

Humphreys, W.F., and D.J. Kitchener. 1982. The effect of habitat utilization on species-area curves: implications for optimal reserve area. *J. Biogeogr.*, 9:391–396.

Hunter, M., Jr., G. Jacobson, Jr., and T. Webb III. 1988. Paleoecology and the coarse-filter approach to maintaining biological diversity. *Conserv. Biol.*, 2:375–385.

Hyman, E.L. 1988. Emerging Issues in Renewable Energy Technologies. The Conservation Foundation, Washington, D.C. Unpub.

IIED/WRI. 1987. *World Resources 1987*. Basic Books, New York.

Ims, R., and N. Stenseth. 1989. Divided the fruitflies fall. *Nature*, 342:21–22.

IUCN. 1975. *1975 United Nations List of National Parks and Equivalent Reserves*. IUCN, Morges, Switzerland.

———. 1978. *Categories, Objectives, and Criteria for Protected Areas*. IUCN, Morges, Switzerland.

———. 1980. *World Conservation Strategy: Living Resource Conservation for Sustainable Development*. IUCN/UNEP/WWF, Gland, Switzerland.

———. 1982. *1982 United Nations List of National Parks and Protected Areas*. IUCN, Gland, Switzerland.

———. 1984. Categories, Objectives and Criteria for Protected Areas. In J.A. McNeeley and K.R. Miller (eds.), *National Parks, Conservation, and Development: The Role of Protected Areas in Sustaining Society*, pp. 47–53. Smithsonian Institution Press, Washington, D.C.

———. 1985. *1985 United Nations List of National Parks and Protected Areas*. IUCN, Gland, Switzerland.

IUCN/UNEP. 1986. *Review of the Protected Areas System in the Afrotropical Realm*. IUCN/UNEP.

Jablonski, D. 1980. Apparent versus real biotic effects of transgressions and regressions. *Paleobiology*, 6:397–407.

———. 1985. Marine regressions and mass extinctions: a test using modern biota. In J.W. Valentine (ed.), *Phanerozoic Diversity Patterns: Profiles in Macroevolution*, pp. 335–354. Princeton University Press, Princeton, N.J.

———. 1986. Causes and consequences of mass extinctions: a comparative approach. In D.K. Elliott (ed.), *Dynamics of Extinction*, pp. 183–229. John Wiley and Sons, New York.

Jaccard, P. 1908. Nouvelles recherches sur la distribution florale. *Bull. Soc. Vaudoise Sci. Nat.*, 44:223.

Jaenike, J. 1978. Effect of island area on Drosophila population densities. *Oecologia*, 36:327–332.

Janzen, D.H. 1983. No park is an island: increase in interference from outside as park size decreases. *Oikos*, 41:402–410.

———. 1986. The eternal external threat. In Soulé (ed.), *Conservation Biology: The Science of Scarcity and Diversity*, pp. 286–303. Sinauer Associates, Inc., Sunderland, Mass.

Järvinen, O. 1979. Geographical gradients of stability in European land bird communities. *Oecologia*, 38:51–69.

Jenkins, R.E., Jr. 1978. Habitat preservation by private organizations. In H.P. Browkaw (ed.), *Wildlife and America: Contributions to an Understanding of American Wildlife and Its Conservation*, pp. 413–427. U.S. Council on Environmental Quality, Washington, D.C.

———. 1988. Information management for the conservation of biodiversity. In E.O. Wilson and F.M. Peter, (eds.), *Biodiversity*, pp. 231–239. National Academy Press, Washington, D.C.

Johnson, M.P., L.G. Mason, and P.H. Raven. 1968. Ecological parameters and plant species diversity. *Am. Nat.*, 102:297–306.

Johnson, M.P., and P.H. Raven. 1973. Species number and endemism: the Galapagos Archipelago revisited. *Science*, 179:893–895.

Johnson, M.P., and D.S. Simberloff. 1974. Environmental determinants of island species numbers in the British Isles. *J. Biogeogr.*, 1:149–154.

Johnson, N.K. 1975. Controls of number of bird species on montane islands in the Great Basin. *Evolution*, 29:545–567.

Jones, E. 1961. *The Life and Work of Sigmund Freud*. Basic Books, New York.

Jones, H.L., and J.M. Diamond. 1976. Short-time-base studies of turnover in breeding birds of the California Channel Islands. *Condor*, 76:526–549.

Jorge Padua, M.T., and A.T. Bernardes Quintão. 1982. Parks and biological reserves in the Brazilian Amazon. *Ambio.*, 5:309–314.

Juday, G.P. 1983. The problem of large mammals in natural areas selection: examples from the Alaska ecological reserves system. *Nat. Areas J.*, 3:24–30.

Karr, J.R. 1982a. Avian extinction on Barro Colorado Island, Panama: a reassessment. *Am. Nat.*, 119:220–239.

———. 1982b. Population variability and extinction in the avifauna of a tropical land bridge island. *Ecology*, 63:1975–1978.

Keiter, R.B. 1985. On protecting the national parks from the external threats dilemma. *Land and Water Law Rev.*, 20:355–420.

Keiter, R.B., and W.A. Hubert. 1987. Legal consideration in challenging external threats to Glacier National Park, Montana, USA. *Environ. Manag.*, 11:121–126.

Kendeigh, S.C. 1944. Measurement of bird populations. *Ecol. Monogr.*, 14:67–106.

———. 1982. Bird Populations in East Central Illinois: Fluctuations, Variations, and Development over a Half-Century. *Ill. Biol. Monogr.*, 52. University of Illinois Press, Urbana.

Kilburn, P.D. 1966. Analysis of the species-area relation. *Ecology*, 47:831–843.

Kim, K.C., and L. Knutson (eds.). 1986. *Foundations for a National Biological Survey*. Association of Systematics Collections, Museum of Natural History, Lawrence, Kan.

Kimura, M., and J.F. Crow. 1963. The measurement of effective population number. *Evolution*, 17:279–288.

Kimura, M., and T. Ohta. 1971. *Theoretical Aspects of Population Genetics*. Princeton University Press, Princeton, N.J.

Kindlmann, P. 1983. Do archipelagoes really preserve fewer species than one island of the same total area. *Oecologia*, 59:141–144.

King, J., and J. Saunders. 1984. Environmental insularity and the extinction of the American mastodont. In P. Martin and R. Klein (eds.), *Quaternary Extinctions*, pp. 315–337. University of Arizona Press, Tucson.

Kitchener, D.J., A. Chapman, J. Dell, and B.G. Muir. 1980a. Lizard assemblage and reserve size and structure in the Western Australian wheatbelt—some implications for conservation. *Biol. Conserv.*, 17:25–62.

Kitchener, D.J., A. Chapman, and B.G. Muir. 1980b. The conservation value for mammals of reserves in the Western Australian wheatbelt. *Biol. Conserv.*, 18:179–207.

Kitchener, D.J., J. Dell, and B.G. Muir. 1982. Birds in Western Australian wheatbelt reserves—implications for conservation. *Biol. Conserv.*, 22:127–163.

Klopfer, P.H. 1981. Islands as models. *BioScience*, 31:838–839.

Knight, R.R., and L.L. Eberhardt. 1985. Population dynamics of Yellowstone grizzly bears. *Ecology*, 66:323–334.

Knight, R.R., D.J. Mattson, and B.M. Blanchard. 1984. Movements and habitat use of the Yellowstone grizzly bear. Interagency Grizzly Bear Study Team report. Unpub.

Kolata, G.B. 1974. Theoretical ecology: beginnings of a predictive science. *Science*, 183:400–401;450.

Krebs, C.J. 1972. *Ecology: The Experimental Analysis of Distribution and Abundance*. Harper & Row, New York.

————. 1985. Third edition.

Kushlan, J.A. 1979. Design and management of continental wildlife reserves: lessons from the Everglades. *Biol. Conserv.*, 15:281–290.

————. 1987. External threats and internal management: the hydrological regulation of the Everglades, Florida, USA. *Environ. Manag.* 11:109–119.

Kusler, J.A. 1974. Public/private parks and management of private lands for park protection. *IES Report* No.16. Institute for Environmental Studies, University of Wisconsin—Madison.

Lack, D. 1969. The number of bird species on islands. *Bird Study*, 16:193–209.

————. 1970. Island birds. *Biotropica*, 2:29–31.

————. 1976. *Island Biology: Illustrated by the Land Birds of Jamaica*. University of California Press, Berkeley.

Lacy, R.C. 1987. Loss of genetic diversity from managed populations: interacting effects of drift, mutation, immigration, selection, and population subdivision. *Conserv. Biol.*, 1:143–158.

————. 1988. A report on population genetics in conservation. *Conserv. Biol.*, 2:245–247.

Lamprey, H.F. 1974. Management of flora and fauna in national parks. In H. Elliott (ed.), *Second World Conference on National Parks*, pp. 237–248. IUCN, Morges, Switzerland.

Lande, R. 1976. The maintenance of genetic variability by mutation in a polygenic character with linked loci. *Genet. Res. Camb.*, 26:221-235.

————. 1988. Genetics and demography in biological conservation. *Science*, 241:1455–1460.

Lande, R., and G.F. Barrowclough. 1987. Effective population size, genetic variation, and their use in population management. In M. Soulé (ed.), *Viable Populations for Conservation*, pp. 87–123. Cambridge University Press.

Lassen, H.H. 1975. The diversity of freshwater snails in view of the equilibrium theory of island biogeography. *Oecologia*, 19:1-8.

Lawlor, T. 1983. The mammals. In T.J. Case and M.C. Cody (eds.), *Island Biogeography in the Sea of Cortez*, pp. 265–289. University of California Press, Berkeley.

————. 1986. Comparative biogeography of mammals on islands. *Biol. J. Linn. Soc.*, 28:99–125.

Leck, C.F. 1979. Avian extinctions in an isolated tropical wet-forest preserve, Ecuador. *Auk*, 96:343–352.

Ledig, F.T. 1986. Heterozygosity, heterosis, and fitness in outbreeding plants. In Soulé (ed.), *Conservation Biology: The Science of Scarcity and Diversity*, pp. 77–104. Sinauer Associates, Inc., Sunderland, Mass.

Leigh, E.G., Jr. 1981. The average lifetime of a population in a varying environment. *J. Theor. Biol.*, 90:213–239.

Leopold, A.S. 1933a. The conservation ethic. *J. Forest.*, 31:634–643.

————. 1933b. *Game Management*. Charles Scribner's Sons, New York.

————. 1949. *A Sand County Almanac*. Oxford University Press, New York.

Leopold, A.S., S.A. Cain, C.M. Cottam, I.N. Gabrielson, and T.L. Kimball. 1963. Wildlife management in the national parks: advisory board on wildlife management appointed by Secretary of the Interior. *Trans. N. Am. Wildl. Nat. Resour. Conf.*, 28:29–44.

Levenson, J.B. 1981. Woodlots as biogeographic islands in southeastern Wisconsin. In R.L. Burgess and D.M. Sharpe (eds.), *Forest Island Dynamics in Man-Dominated Landscapes*, pp. 13–39. Springer-Verlag, New York.

Levin, S.A. 1976. Population dynamic models in heterogeneous environments. *Annu. Rev. Ecol. Syst.*, 7:287–310.

Levins, R. 1966. The strategy of model building in population biology. *Am. Sci.*, 54:421–431.

————. 1970. Extinction. In M. Gerstenhaber (ed.), Some Mathematical Questions in Biology. *Lectures on Mathematics in the Life Sciences*, Vol. II, pp. 77–107. American Mathematical Society, Providence, R.I.

Lewin, R. 1983. No dinosaurs this time. *Science*, 221:1168–1169.

————. 1984. Parks: how big is big enough? *Science*, 225:611–612.

————. 1986. Damage to tropical forests, or why were there so many kinds of animals? *Science*, 234:149–150.

Lewontin, R.C. 1974. *The Genetic Basis of Evolutionary Change*. Columbia University Press, New York.

Lillegraven, J.A. 1972. Ordinal and familial diversity of Cenozoic mammals. *Taxon*, 21:261–274.

Lomolino, M.V. 1982. Species-area and species-distance relationships of terrestrial mammals in the Thousand Island region. *Oecologia*, 54:72–75.

————. 1986. Mammalian community structure on islands: the importance of immigration, extinction and interactive effects. *Biol. J. Linn. Soc.*, 28:1–21.

Loope, L.L. In press. An overview of problems with introduced plant species in national parks and reserves of the United States. In C.P. Stone, C.W. Smith, and J.T. Tunison (eds.), *Alien Plant Invasions in Hawaii: Management and Research in Near-Native Ecosystems*. Cooperative National Park Resources Studies Unit, University of Hawaii, Honolulu.

Loope, L.L., O. Hamann, and C.P. Stone. 1988. Comparative conservation biology of oceanic archipelagoes. *BioScience*, 38:272–282.

Lovejoy, T.E. 1979. Refugia, refuges and minimum critical size: problems in the conservation of neotropical herpetofauna. In W.E. Duellman (ed.), *The South American Herpetofauna: Its Origin, Evolution and Dispersal*. Museum of Natural History Monograph 7, pp. 461–464. University of Kansas, Lawrence, Kan.

———. 1980. Discontinuous wilderness: minimum areas for conservation. *Parks*, 5:13–15.

———. 1982. Designing refugia for tomorrow. In G.T. Prance (ed.), *Biological Diversification in the Tropics: Proceedings of the Fifth International Symposium of the Association for Tropical Biology, Caracas, Venezuela, February 8–13, 1979*, pp. 673–680. Columbia University Press, New York.

———. 1984. Application of ecological theory to conservation planning. In F. de Castri, F.W.G. Baker, and M. Hadley (eds.), *Ecology in Practice* Part I: *Ecosystem Management*, pp. 402–413. Tycooly International Publishing Limited, Dublin, and UNESCO, Paris.

———. 1987. National parks: how big is big enough? In R. Herrmann and T.B. Craig (eds.), *Conference on Science in National Parks: The Fourth Triennial Conference on Research in the National Parks and Equivalent Reserves*, pp. 49–58. The George Wright Society and the U.S. National Park Service.

Lovejoy, T.E., R.O. Bierregaard, J.M. Rankin, and H.O.R. Schubart. 1983. Ecological dynamics of forest fragments. In S.L. Sutton, T.C. Whitmore, and A.C. Chadwick (eds.), *Tropical Rain Forests: Ecology and Management*, pp. 377–384. Blackwell Scientific Publications, Oxford.

Lovejoy, T.E., R.O. Bierregaard, Jr., J.R. Rylands, J.R. Malcolm, C.E. Quintela, L.H. Harper, K.S. Brown, Jr., A.H. Powell, G.V.H. Powell, H.O.R Schubart, and M.B. Hays. 1986. Edge and other effects of isolation on Amazon forest fragments. In Soulé (ed.) *Conservation Biology: The Science of Scarcity and Diversity*, pp. 251–285, Sinauer Associates, Inc., Sunderland, Mass.

Lovejoy, T.E., and D.C. Oren. 1981. The minimum critical size of ecosystems. In R.L. Burgess and D.M. Sharpe (eds.), *Ecological Studies 41: Forest Island Dynamics in Man-Dominated Landscapes*, pp. 7–12. Springer-Verlag, New York.

Lovejoy, T.E., and R.L. Peters (eds.). In press. *Global Warming and Biological Diversity*. Yale University Press, New Haven, Ct.

Lovejoy, T.E., J.M. Rankin, R.O. Bierregaard, Jr., K.S. Brown, Jr., L.H. Emmons, and M.E. Vandervoort. 1984. Ecosystem decay and Amazon forest remnants. In M.H. Nitecki (ed.), *Extinctions*, pp. 69–117. The University of Chicago Press, Chicago.

Loyn, R.H. 1987. Effects of patch area and habitat on bird abundances, species numbers and tree health in fragmented Victorian forests. In D. Saunders, G. Arnold, A. Burbidge, and A. Hopkins (eds.), *Nature Conservation: The Role of Remnants of Native Vegetation*, pp. 259–268. Surrey Beatty and Sons Pty. Limited, Chipping Norton, NSW, Australia.

Lusigi, W.J. 1981. New approaches to wildlife conservation in Kenya. *Ambio*, 10:2–3.

———. 1984. Future directions for the Afrotropical realm. In J.A. McNeeley and K.R. Miller, (eds.), *National Parks, Conservation, and Development*, pp. 137–146. Smithsonian Institution Press, Washington, D.C.

Lynch, J. 1987. Responses of breeding bird communities to forest fragmentation. In D. Saunders, G. Arnold, A. Burbidge, and A. Hopkins (eds.), *Nature Conservation: The Role of Remnants of Native Vegetation*, pp. 259–268. Surrey Beatty and Sons Pty. Limited, Chipping Norton, NSW, Australia.

Lynch, J.F., and D.F. Whigham. 1984. Effects of forest fragmentation on breeding bird communities in Maryland, USA. *Biol. Conserv.*, 28:287–324.

Lynch, J.F., and R.F. Whitcomb. 1978. Effects of the insularization of the eastern deciduous forest on avifaunal diversity and turnover. In A. Marmelstein (ed.), *Classification, Inventory and Analysis of Fish and Wildlife Habitat: Proceedings of a National Symposium, Phoenix, Arizona, January 24–27, 1977*, pp. 461–489. U.S. Fish and Wildlife Service, Department of the Interior, Washington, D.C.

Lynch, J.H., and N.K. Johnson. 1974. Turnover and equilibria in insular avifaunas with special reference to the California Channel Islands. *Condor*, 76:370–384.

MacArthur, R.H., J.M. Diamond, and J.R. Karr. 1972. Density compensation in island faunas. *Ecology*, 53:330–342.

MacArthur, R.H., and E.O. Wilson. 1963. An equilibrium theory of insular zoogeography. *Evolution*, 17:373–387.

———. 1967. *The Theory of Island Biogeography*. Princeton University Press, Princeton, N.J.

MacArthur, R.H. 1960. On the relative abundance of species. *Am. Nat.*, 9:25–36.

———. 1969. Patterns of communities in the tropics. *Biol. J. Linn. Soc.*, 1:19–30.

———. 1972. *Geographical Ecology: Patterns in Distribution of Species.* Harper & Row, New York.

McCaffrey, D., and H. Landazuri. 1987. *Wildlands and Human Needs: A Program Evaluation.* World Wildlife Fund, Washington, D.C.

McCoy, E.D. 1982. The application of island-biogeographic theory to forest tracts: problems in the determination of turnover rates. *Biol. Conserv.*, 22:217–227.

———. 1983. The application of island-biogeographic theory to patches of habitat: how much land is enough? *Biol. Conserv.*, 25:53–61.

McCune, A.R. 1982. On the fallacy of constant extinction rates. *Evolution*, 36:610–614.

McGuinness, K.A. 1984a. Equations and explanations in the study of species-area curves. *Biol. Rev.*, 59:423–440.

———. 1984b. Species-area relations of communities on intertidal boulders: testing the null hypothesis. *J. Biogeogr.*, 11:439–456.

McLellan, C.H., A.P. Dobson, D.S. Wilcove, and J.M. Lynch. 1986. Effects of forest fragmentation on new and old world bird communities: empirical observations and theoretical implications. In J. Verner, M. Morrison, and C. Ralph (eds.), *Wildlife 2000: Modeling Habitat Relationships of Terrestrial Vertebrates.* pp. 305–313. University of Wisconsin Press, Madison.

McNab, B.K. 1963. Bioenergetics and the determination of home range size. *Am. Nat.*, 97:133–140.

McNeeley, J.A. 1988. *Economics and Biological Diversity: Developing and Using Economic Incentives to Conserve Biological Resources.* IUCN, Gland, Switzerland.

———. 1989. Protected areas and human ecology: how national parks can contribute to sustaining societies of the twenty-first century. In D. Western and M. Pearl (eds.), *Conservation for the Twenty-first Century*, pp. 150–157. Oxford University Press, New York.

McNeeley, J.A., and K.R. Miller (eds.). 1984. *National Parks, Conservation, and Development: The Role of Protected Areas in Sustaining Society.* Smithsonian Institution Press, Washington, D.C.

Machlis, G.E., and D.L. Tichnell. 1985. *The State of the World's Parks: An International Assessment for Resource Management, Policy and Research.* Westview Press, Boulder, Colo.

Madden, L. 1983. Tax incentives for land conservation: the charitable contribution deduction for gifts of conservation easements. *Boston College Environmental Affairs Law Review*, 11:105–148.

Mader, H.J. 1981. Untersuchungen zum Einfluss der Refugium. *Natur. und Landschaft*, 56:235–242.

———. 1984. Animal habitat isolation by roads and agricultural fields. *Biol. Conserv.*, 29:81–96.

Maglio, V.J. 1973. Origin and evolution of the Elephantidae. *Amer. Phil. Soc. Trans.*, 63:1–149.

Magnuson, J.J. 1976. Managing with exotics—a game of chance. *Trans. Am. Fish. Soc.*, 105:1–9.

Maguire, B., Jr. 1963. The passive dispersal of small aquatic organisms and their colonization of isolated bodies of water. *Ecol. Monogr.*, 33:161–185.

Main, A.R., and M. Yadov. 1971. Conservation of macropods in reserves in Western Australia. *Biol. Conserv.*, 3:123–133.

Margules, C., A.J. Higgs, and R.W. Rafe. 1982. Modern biogeographic theory: are there any lessons for nature reserve design? *Biol. Conserv.*, 24:115–128.

Margules, C.R., A.O. Nicholls, and R.L. Pressey. 1988. Selecting networks of reserves to maximize biological diversity. *Biol. Conserv.*, 43:63–76.

Margules, C., and M.B. Usher. 1981. Criteria used in assessing wildlife conservation potential: a review. *Biol. Conserv.*, 21:79–109.

Mark, G.A., and K.W. Flessa. 1977. A test for evolutionary equilibria: Phanerozoic brachiopods and Cenozoic mammals. *Paleobiology*, 3:17–22.

———. 1978. A test for evolutionary equilibrium revisited. *Paleobiology*, 4:201–202.

Marsh, G.P. 1874. *The Earth as Modified by Human Action.* Scribner, Armstrong, and Co., New York.

Marshall, L.G., and M.K. Hecht. 1978. Mammalian faunal dynamics of the great American interchange: an alternative interpretation. *Paleobiology*, 4:203–206.

Martin, P.S. 1984. Prehistoric overkill. In P.S. Martin and R.G. Klein (eds.), *Quaternary Extinctions: A Prehistoric Revolution*, pp. 351–403. University of Arizona Press, Tucson.

Martin, T.E. 1981. Species-area slopes and coefficients: a caution on their interpretation. *Am. Nat.*, 118:823–837.

Matthiae, P.E., and F. Stearns. 1981. Mammals in forest islands in southeastern Wisconsin. In R.L. Burgess and D.M. Sharpe (eds.), *Forest Island Dynamics in Man-Dominated Landscapes*, pp. 55–66. Springer-Verlag, New York.

May, R.M. 1973. *Stability and Complexity in Model Ecosystems.* Princeton University Press, Princeton, N.J.

———. 1975a. Island biogeography and the design of wildlife preserves. *Nature*, 254:177–178.

————. 1975b. Patterns of species abundance and diversity. In M.L. Cody and J.M. Diamond (eds.), *Ecology and Evolution of Communities*, pp. 81–120. Belknap Press of Harvard University, Cambridge, Mass.

————. 1984. An overview: real and apparent patterns in community structure. In D.R. Strong et al. (eds.), *Ecological Communities: Conceptual Issues and the Evidence*, pp. 3–16. Princeton University Press, Princeton, N.J.

May, R.M., J.A. Endler, and R.E. McMurtrie. 1975. Gene frequency clines in the presence of selection opposed by gene flow. *Am. Nat.*, 109:659–676.

Mayr, E. 1942. *Systematics and the Origin of Species*. Columbia University Press, New York.

————. 1963. *Animal Species and Evolution*. Harvard University Press, Cambridge, Mass.

Means, D.B., and D. Simberloff. 1987. The peninsula effect: habitat-correlated species decline in Florida's herpetofauna. *J. Biogeogr.*, 14:551–568.

Means, J.E., and S.E. Greene. 1987. Reserve designs in a landscape context: another slant in the continuing debate. *Park Science*, 8:21.

Mech, D.L. 1966. *The Wolves of Isle Royale*. Fauna of the National Parks of the United States Fauna Series. National Park Service Scientific Monograph No. 7. U.S. Government Printing Office, Washington, D.C.

Merriam, G. 1984. Connectivity: a fundamental ecological characteristic of landscape pattern. In J. Brandt and P. Agger. (eds.), *Methodology in Landscape Ecological Research and Planning*, pp. 5–15. Roskilde, Denmark.

Mertz, D.B. 1971. The mathematical demography of the California condor population. *Am. Nat.*, 105:437–453.

Miller, K.R. 1978. *Planning National Parks for Ecodevelopment: Cases and Methods from Latin America* Vols. I, II. Center for Strategic Wildland Management Studies, The School for Natural Resources, University of Michigan, Ann Arbor. Manuscript.

————. 1982. Parks and protected areas: considerations for the future. *Ambio*, 5:315–317.

————. 1984. The Bali Action Plan: a framework for the future of protected areas. In J. A. McNeeley and K. R. Miller (eds.), *National Parks, Conservation, and Development: The Role of Protected Areas in Sustaining Society*, pp. 756–764. Smithsonian Institution Press, Washington, D.C.

————. 1988. Achieving a world network of protected areas. In V. Martin (ed.), *For the Conservation of Earth*, pp. 36–41. Fulcrum Inc., Golden, Colo.

Miller, R.I. 1976. Application of Island Biogeographic Theory to Wildlife Preserves. M.S. Thesis, University of Florida. Unpub.

————. 1978. Applying island biogeographic theory to an East African reserve. *Environ. Conserv.*, 5:191–195.

Miller, R.I., and S.P. Bratton. 1987. A regional strategy for reserve design and placement based on an analysis of rare and endangered species' distribution patterns. *Biol. Conserv.*, 39:255–268.

Miller, R.I., and L.D. Harris. 1977. Isolation and extirpation in wildlife reserves. *Biol. Conserv.*, 12:311–315.

————. 1979. Predicting species changes in isolated wildlife preserves. In R.M. Linn (ed.), *Proceedings of the First Conference on Scientific Research in the National Parks* Volume I, *New Orleans, Louisiana, November 9-12, 1976*, pp. 79–82. National Park Service, U.S. Department of the Interior, Washington, D.C.

Miller, R.I., and P.S. White. 1986. Considerations for preserve design based on the distribution of rare plants in Great Smoky Mountains National Park, USA. *Environ. Manag.*, 10:119–124.

Mintzer, I. 1988. Global climate change and its effect on wildlands. In V. Martin (ed.), *For the Conservation of the Earth*, pp. 56–67. Fulcrum, Inc., Golden, Colo.

Mishra, H.R. 1984. A delicate balance: tigers, rhinoceros, tourists and park management vs. the needs of the local people in Royal Chitwan National Park, Nepal. In J.A. McNeeley and K.R. Miller (eds.), *National Parks, Conservation, and Development*, pp. 197–205. Smithsonian Institution Press, Washington, D.C.

————. 1988. The Annupurna project. In V. Martin, (ed.), *For the Conservation of the Earth*, pp. 134–149. Fulcrum, Inc., Golden, Colo.

Molles, M.C., Jr. 1978. Fish species diversity on model and natural reef patches: experimental insular biogeography. *Ecol. Monogr.*, 48:289–305.

Mooney, H.A., and J.A. Drake (eds.). 1986. *Ecology of Biological Invasions of North America and Hawaii*. Springer-Verlag, Berlin.

Moore, N.W. 1962. The heaths of Dorset and their conservation. *J. Ecol.*, 50:369–391.

Moore, N.W., and M.D. Hooper. 1975. On the number of bird species in British woods. *Biol. Conserv.*, 8:239–250.

Morgan, G., and C. Woods. 1986. Extinction and the zoogeography of West Indian land mammals. *Biol. J. Linn. Soc.*, 28:167–203.

Morton, E.S. 1978. Reintroducing recently extirpated birds into a tropical forest preserve. In S.A. Temple (ed.), *Endangered Birds: Management Techniques for Preserving Threatened Species*, pp. 379–384. University of Wisconsin Press, Madison.

————. 1985. The realities of reintroducing species to the wild. In R.J. Hoage (ed.), *Animal Extinctions: What Every-*

one Should Know, pp. 147–158. Smithsonian Institution Press, Washington, D.C.

Mott, W.P. 1988a. Looking beyond national park boundaries. *Nat. Areas J.*, 8:30–82.

———. 1988b. Remarks by William Penn Mott, Jr., at the fourteenth annual natural areas conference. *The George Wright Forum*, 5:1–7.

Muggleton, J., and B.R. Benham. 1975. Isolation and the decline of the large blue butterfly (Maculinea arion) in Great Britain. *Biol. Conserv.*, 7:119–128.

Muhlenberg, M., D. Leipold, H.J. Mader, and B. Steinhauer. 1977a. Island ecology of arthropods I. Diversity, niches, and resources on some Seychelles Islands. *Oecologia*, 29:117–134.

———. 1977b. Island ecology of arthropods II. Niches and relative abundances of Seychelles Ants (Formicidae) in different habitats. *Oecologia*, 29:135–144.

Murphy, D.D. 1989. Conservation and confusion: wrong species, wrong scale, wrong conclusions. *Conserv. Biol.*, 3:82–84.

Murphy, D.D., and B.A. Wilcox. 1986. Butterfly diversity in natural habitat fragments: a test of the validity of vertebrate-based management. In J. Verner, M. Morrison, and C. Ralph (eds.), *Wildlife 2000: Modeling Habitat Relationships of Terrestrial Vertebrates*, pp. 287–292. University of Wisconsin Press, Madison.

Myers, N. 1972. National parks in savannah Africa. *Science*, 178:1255–1263.

———. 1979. *The Sinking Ark: A New Look at the Problem of Disappearing Species*. Pergamon Press, Oxford.

———. 1985. A look at the present extinction spasm and what it means for the future evolution of species. In R.J. Hoage (ed.), *Animals Extinctions: What Everyone Should Know*, pp. 47–58. Smithsonian Institution Press, Washington, D.C.

———. 1986. Tropical deforestation and the mega-extinction spasm. In Soulé (ed.), *Conservation Biology: The Science of Scarcity and Diversity*, pp. 394–409. Sinauer Associates, Inc., Sunderland, Mass.

Nagylaki, T. 1975. Conditions for the existence of clines. *Genetics*, 80:595–615.

National Park Service. 1962. *First World Conference on National Parks, Seattle, Washington, June 30–July 7, 1962*. National Park Service, U.S. Department of the Interior, Washington, D.C.

———. 1980. *State of the Parks—1980: A Report to the Congress*. National Park Service, U.S Department of the Interior, Washington, D.C.

———. 1987. 1986 Section 8 Report on National Historic and Natural Landmarks. Unpub.

———. 1988a. *Management Policies*. National Park Service, U.S. Department of the Interior, Washington, D.C.

———. 1988b. Natural Resources Assessment and Action Program. National Park Service, Washington, D.C.

National Parks and Conservation Association. 1979. NPCA adjacent lands survey: no park is an island. *Nat. Parks and Conserv. Mag.*, 53:4–9.

———. 1988. *The National Park System Plan: A Blueprint for Tomorrow (Executive Summary)*. National Parks and Conservation Association, Washington, D.C.

National Park Service and Forest Service. 1987. *The Greater Yellowstone Area: An Aggregation of National Park and National Forest Management Plans*. U.S. National Park Service and U.S. Forest Service, U.S. Department of the Interior, Washington, D.C.

Natural Resources Law Center. 1986. *External Development Affecting the National Parks: Preserving "The Best Idea We Ever Had."* Natural Resources Law Center, University of Colorado School of Law, Boulder.

Naveh, Z. 1982. Landscape ecology as an emerging branch of human ecosystem science. *Adv. Ecol. Res.*, 12:189–237.

Naveh, Z., and A.S. Lieberman. 1984. *Landscape Ecology: Theory and Application*. Springer-Verlag, New York.

Nei, M. 1987. *Molecular Evolutionary Genetics*. Columbia University Press, New York.

Nei, M., T. Maruyama, and R. Chakraborty. 1975. The bottleneck effect and genetic variability in populations. *Evolution*, 29:1–10.

Nelson, E.W. 1917. The Yellowstone and the game supply. In *Proceedings of the National Parks Conference, U.S. Department of the Interior*, pp. 200–204. U.S. Government Printing Office, Washington, D.C.

Nelson, J.G. 1978. International experience with national parks and related reserves: an introduction. In J.G. Nelson, R.D. Needham, and D.L. Mann (eds.), *International Experience with National Parks and Related Reserves*, pp. 1–27. Department of Geography, University of Waterloo.

Newell, N.D. 1967. Revolutions in the history of life. *Geol. Soc. Am. Spec. Pap.*, 89:63–91.

———. 1984. Mass extinction: unique or recurrent causes? In W.A. Berggren and J.H. Van Convering (eds.), *Catastrophes and Earth History*, pp. 115–127. Princeton University Press, Princeton, N.J.

Newmark, W.D. 1985. Legal and biotic boundaries of western North American national parks: a problem of congruence. *Biol. Conserv.*, 33:197–208.

———. 1986. Species-area relationship and its determinants for mammals in western North American national parks. *Biol. J. Linn. Soc.,* 28:65–82.

———. 1987. A land-bridge island perspective on mammalian extinctions in western North American parks. *Nature,* 325:430–432.

Nevo, E. 1978. Genetic variation in natural populations: patterns and theory. *Theor. Popul. Biol.,* 13:121–127.

Nilsson, S.G. 1978. Fragmented habitats, species richness and conservation practice. *Ambio,* 7:26–27.

Norse, E.A., K.L Rosenbaum, D.S. Wilcove, B.A. Wilcox, W.H. Romme, D.W. Johnston, and M.L. Stout. 1986. *Conserving Biological Diversity in our National Forests.* The Wilderness Society, Washington, D.C.

Norton, B. (ed.) 1986. *The Preservation of Species.* Princeton University Press, Princeton, N.J.

Noss, R.F. 1983. A regional landscape approach to maintain diversity. *BioScience,* 33:700–706.

———. 1987a. Corridors in real landscapes: a reply to Simberloff and Cox. *Conserv. Biol.,* 1:159–164.

———. 1987b. From plant communities to landscapes in conservation inventories: a look at The Nature Conservancy (USA). *Biol. Conserv.,* 41:11–37.

———. 1987c. Protecting natural areas in fragmented landscapes. *Nat. Areas J.* 7:2–13.

Noss, R.F., and L.D. Harris. 1986. Nodes, networks, and MUMs: preserving diversity at all scales. *Envir. Manag.,* 10:229–309.

O'Brien, S.J., and J.F. Evermann. 1988. Interactive influence of infectious diseases and genetic diversity in natural populations. *Trends Ecol. & Evol.* 3:254–259.

O'Brien, S.J., M.E. Roelke, L. Marker, A. Newman, C.A. Winkler, D. Meltzer, L. Colly, J.F. Evermann, M. Bush, and D.E. Wildt. 1985. Genetic basis for species vulnerability in the cheetah. *Science,* 227:1428–1434.

O'Brien, S.J., D.E. Wildt, D. Goldman, C.R. Merril, and M. Bush. 1983. The cheetah is depauperate in genetic variation. *Science,* 221:459–462.

O'Brien, S.J., D.E. Wildt, and M. Bush. 1986. The cheetah in genetic peril. *Sci. Am.,* 254:84–92.

Odum, E.P. 1989. *Ecology and Our Endangered Life-Support Systems.* Sinauer Associates, Inc., Sunderland, Mass.

Oedekoven, K. 1980. The vanishing forest. *Environ. Policy and Law,* 6:184–185.

Office of Technology Assessment. 1987. *Technologies to Maintain Biological Diversity,* OTA-330. U.S. Government Printing Office, Washington, D.C.

Olson, S.L., and H.F. James. 1982. Fossil birds from the Hawaiian Islands: evidence for wholesale extinction by man before western contact. *Science,* 217:633–635.

Opdam, P., D. van Dorp, and C.J.F. ter Braak. 1984. The effect of isolation on the number of woodland birds in small woods in the Netherlands. *J. Biogeogr.,* 11:473–478.

Opdam, P., G. Rijsdijk, and F. Hustings. 1985. Bird communities in small woods in an agricultural landscape: effects of area and isolation. *Biol. Conserv.,* 34:333–352.

Osman, R.W. 1978. The influence of seasonality and stability on the species equilibrium. *Ecology,* 59:383–399.

Owen-Smith, R.N. (ed.). 1983. *Proc. Symposium on Management of Large Mammals in African Conservation Areas.* Haum Educational Publishers, Pretoria.

———. 1987. Pleistocene extinctions: the pivotal role of megaherbivores. *Paleobiology,* 13:351–362.

Oxley, D.J., M.B. Fenton, and G.R. Carmody. 1974. The effects of roads on populations of small mammals. *J. Appl. Ecol.,* 2:51–59.

Paine, R.T. 1966. Food web complexity and species diversity. *Am. Nat.,* 100:65–75.

———. 1969. A note on trophic complexity and community stability. *Am. Nat.,* 103:91–93.

———. 1974. Intertidal community structure: experimental studies on the relationship between a dominant competitor and its principal predator. *Oecologia,* 15:93–120.

———. 1980. Food webs: linkage, interaction strength and community infrastructure. *J. Anim. Ecol.,* 49:667–685.

Panwar, H.S. 1984. What to do when you've succeeded: project tiger, ten years later. In J.A. McNeeley and K.R. Miller (eds.), *National Parks, Conservation and Development: The Role of Protected Areas in Sustaining Society,* pp. 183–189. Smithsonian Institution Press, Washington, D.C.

Patrick, R. 1967. The effect of invasion rate, species pool, and size of area on the structure of the diatom community. *Proc. Nat. Acad. Sci.,* 58:1335–1342.

Patterson, B.D. 1984. Mammalian extinction and biogeography in the Southern Rocky Mountains. In M.H. Nitecki (ed.), *Extinctions,* pp. 247–293. The University of Chicago Press, Chicago.

———. 1987. The principle of nested subsets and its implications for biological conservation. *Conserv. Biol.,* 1:323–334.

Patterson, B.D., and W. Atmar. 1986. Nested subsets and the structure of insular mammalian faunas and archipelagos. *Biol. J. Linn. Soc.,* 28:65–82.

Peake, J.F. 1969. Patterns in the distribution of Melanesian land Mollusca. *Philos. Trans. R. Soc. Lond. B. Biol. Sci.*, 255:285–306.

Peine, J.D. (ed.). 1985. *Proceedings of the Conference on the Management of Biosphere Reserves, November 27–29, 1984, Great Smoky Mountains National Park, Gatlinburg, Tenn.* U.S. Department of the Interior, National Park Service, Uplands Field Research Laboratory, Great Smoky Mountains National Park, Gatlinburg, Tenn.

Pelton, M. 1986. Habitat needs of black bears in the East. In D. Kulhavy and R. Conner (eds.), *Wilderness and Natural Areas in the Eastern United States: A Management Challenge*, pp. 49–53. Center for Applied Studies, School of Forestry, Stephen F. Austin State University, Nacogdoches, Tex.

Peters, R.L., and J.D.S. Darling. 1985. The greenhouse effect and nature reserves. *BioScience*, 35:707–717.

Pickett, S.T.A., and J.N. Thompson. 1978. Patch dynamics and the design of nature reserves. *Biol. Conserv.*, 13:27–37.

Pickett, S.T.A., and D.S. White (eds.). 1985. *The Ecology of Natural Disturbance and Patch Dynamics.* Academic Press, New York.

Picton, H.D. 1979. The application of insular biogeographic theory to the conservation of large mammals in the Northern Rocky Mountains. *Biol. Conserv.*, 15:73–79.

Pielou, E.C. 1975. *Ecological Diversity.* John Wiley and Sons, New York.

———. 1977. *Mathematical Ecology.* John Wiley and Sons, New York.

———. 1979. *Biogeography.* John Wiley and Sons, New York.

———. 1981. The usefulness of ecological models: a stock-taking. *Q. Rev. Biol.*, 56:17–31.

Pimm, S.L. 1986. Community stability and structure. In Soulé (ed.), *Conservation Biology: The Science of Scarcity and Diversity*, pp. 309–329. Sinauer Associates, Inc., Sunderland, Mass.

Poore, D., and P. Gryn-Ambroes. 1980. *Nature Conservation in Northern and Western Europe.* IUCN and WWF, Gland, Switzerland.

Power, D.M. 1972. Numbers of bird species on the California islands. *Evolution*, 26:451–463.

Poynton, J.C., and D.C. Roberts. 1985. Urban open space planning in South Africa: a biogeographical perspective. *South African J. Sci.*, 81:33–37.

Prance, G.T. 1981. Discussion. In G. Nelson and D.E.

Rosen (eds.), *Vicariance Biogeography: A Critique*, pp. 395–405. Columbia University Press, New York.

———. (ed.) 1982. *Biological Diversification in the Tropics. Proceedings of the Fifth Symposium of the Association for Tropical Biology.* Columbia University Press, New York.

Preston, F.W. 1948. The commonness, and rarity, of species. *Ecology*, 29:254–283.

———. 1960. Time and space and the variation of species. *Ecology*, 41:611–627.

———. 1962. The canonical distribution of commonness and rarity: part I. *Ecology*, 43:185–215; part II. 43:410–432.

———. 1980. Noncanonical distributions of commonness and rarity. *Ecology*, 6:88–97.

Price, M.V., and N.M. Waser. 1979. Pollen dispersal and optimal outcrossing in Delphinium nelsonii. *Nature*, 277:294–296.

Program for International Development. 1984. *Renewable Resource Trends in East Africa.* Clark University, Worcester, Mass.

Quinn, J.F., and A. Hastings. 1987. Extinction in subdivided habitats. *Conserv. Biol.*, 1:198–208.

Quinn, J.F., C. van Riper III, and H. Salwasser. In press. Mammalian extinctions from national parks in the western United States. *Ecology.*

Quinn, J.F., C.I. Wolin, and M.L. Judge. 1989. An experimental analysis of patch size, habitat subdivision, and extinction in a marine intertidal snail. *Conserv. Biol.*, 3:242–251.

Rackham, O. 1980. *Ancient Woodland: Its History, Vegetation and Uses in England.* Edward Arnold Publ., London.

Ralls, K., and J. Ballou. 1982a. Effects of inbreeding on infant mortality in captive primates. *Int. J. Primatol.*, 3:491–505.

———. 1982b. Effect of inbreeding on juvenile mortality in some small mammal species. *Lab. Anim.*, 16:159–166.

———. 1983. Extinction lessons from zoos. In C.M. Schonewald-Cox et al. (eds.), *Genetics and Conservation: A Reference for Managing Wild Animal and Plant Populations*, pp. 164–184. The Benjamin/Cummings Publishing Company, Inc., Menlo Park, Cal.

Ralls, K., K. Brugger, and J. Ballou. 1979. Inbreeding and juvenile mortality in small populations of ungulates. *Science*, 206:1101–1103.

Ralls, K., K. Brugger, and A. Glick. 1980. Deleterious effects of inbreeding in a herd of captive Dorcas gazelle. *Int. Zoo. Yearb.*, 20:138–146.

Ralls, K., P.H. Harvey, and A.M. Lyles. 1986. Inbreeding in natural populations of birds and mammals. In Soulé (ed.), *Conservation Biology: The Science of Scarcity and Diversity*, pp. 35–56. Sinauer Associates, Inc., Sunderland, Mass.

Ralls, K., J.D. Ballou, and A. Templeton. 1988. Estimates of lethal equivalents and the cost of inbreeding in mammals. *Conserv. Biol.*, 2:185–193.

Ratcliffe, D.A. 1977. Nature conservation: aims, methods and achievements. *Proc. R. Soc. Lond. B. Biol. Sci.*, 197:11–29.

_____. 1979. The end of the large blue butterfly. *New Sci.*, 8:457–458.

Raup, D.M. 1975. Taxonomic survivorship curves and Van Valen's Law. *Paleobiology*, 1:82–96.

_____. 1978. Cohort analysis of generic survivorship. *Paleobiology*, 4:1–15.

_____. 1979. Size of the Permo-Triassic bottleneck and its evolutionary implications. *Science*, 206:217–218.

_____. 1988. Diversity crises in the geological past. In E.O. Wilson and F.M. Peter (eds.), *Biodiversity*, pp. 51–57. National Academy Press, Washington, D.C.

Raup, D.M., and J.J. Sepkoski, Jr. 1982. Mass extinctions in the marine fossil record. *Science*, 215:1501–1503.

_____. 1984. Periodicity of extinctions in the geologic past. *Proc. Nat. Acad. Sci.* 81:801–805.

Raven, P.H. 1976. Ethics and attitudes. In J.B. Simmons (ed.), *Conservation of Threatened Plants*, pp. 155–179. Plenum Press, New York.

Raven, P.H. (chairman). 1980. *Research Priorities in Tropical Biology*. National Academy of Sciences, Washington, D.C.

Recher, H.F., J. Shields, R. Kavanangh, and G. Webb. 1987. Retaining remnant mature forest for nature conservation at Eden, New South Wales: a review of theory and practice. In D. Saunders, G. Arnold, A. Burbidge, and A. Hopkins (eds.), *Nature Conservation: The Role of Remnants of Native Vegetation*, pp. 141–149. Surrey Beatty and Sons Pty. Limited, Chipping Norton, NSW, Australia.

Reed, T.M. 1983. The role of species-area relationships in reserve choice: a British example. *Biol. Conserv.*, 25:263–271.

Rey, J.R. 1981. Ecological biogeography of arthropods on Spartina islands in Northwest Florida. *Ecol. Monogr.*, 51:237–265.

_____. 1984. Experimental tests of island biogeographic theory. In Strong et al. (eds.), *Ecological Communities:*

Conceptual Issues and the Evidence, pp. 101–112. Princeton University Press, Princeton, N.J.

Rhodes, F.H.T. 1967. Permo-Triassic extinction. In W.B. Harland (ed.), *The Fossil Record*, pp. 57–76. Geological Society, London.

Ricklefs, R.E. 1979. *Ecology*. Chiron Press, Inc., New York.

_____. 1987. Community diversity: relative roles of local and regional processes. *Science*, 235:167–171.

Ricklefs, R.E., and G.W. Cox. 1972. Taxon cycle in the West Indian avifauna. *Am. Nat.*, 106:195–219.

Richman, A.D., T.J. Case, and T.D. Schwaner. 1988. Natural and unnatural extinction rates of reptiles on islands. *Am. Nat.*, 131:611–630.

Richter-Dyn, N., and N.S. Goel. 1972. On the extinction of a colonizing species. *Theor. Popul. Biol.*, 3:406–433.

Riney, T. 1967. *Conservation and Management of African Wildlife*. FAO/IUCN.

Risser, P.G. 1986. Present status of true prairie grasslands and ecological concepts relevant to management of prairie preserves. In D.L. Kulhavy and R.N. Connor (eds.), *Wilderness and Natural Areas in the Eastern United States: A Management Challenge*, pp. 339–344. Center for Applied Studies, Stephen F. Austin State University, Nacogdoches, Tex.

_____. 1988. Diversity in and among grasslands. In E.O. Wilson and F.M. Peter (eds.), *Biodiversity*, pp. 176–180. National Academy Press, Washington, D.C.

Risser, P.G., J.R. Karr, and R.T.T. Forman. 1984. *Landscape Ecology: Directions and Approaches*. Illinois Natural History Survey Special Publication 2. Champaign, Illinois.

Robbins, C.S. 1979. Effect of forest fragmentation on bird populations. In *Management of North Central and Northeastern Forests for Nongame Birds*. Workshop Proc., U.S. Dep. Agric. For. Serv. Gen. Tech. Rep. NC–51, pp. 198–213. USDA For. Serv., North Cent. For. Exp. Station, St. Paul, Minn.

Robbins, W.J. (chairman). 1963. *A Report by the Advisory Committee to the National Park Service on Research*. National Academy of Sciences-National Research Council, Washington, D.C.

Rosenweig, M.L. 1975. On continental steady states of species diversity. In M.L. Cody and J.M. Diamond (eds.), *Ecology and Evolution of Communities*, pp. 121–140. Belknap Press of Harvard University, Cambridge, Mass.

Rost, G.R., and J.A. Bailey. 1979. Distribution of mule deer and elk in relation to roads. *J. Wildl. Manag.*, 43:634–641.

Roughgarden, J. 1975. A simple model for population dynamics in stochastic environments. *Am. Nat.,* 109:713–736.

———. 1979. *Theory of Population Genetics and Evolutionary Ecology: An Introduction.* Macmillan Publishing Co., Inc., New York.

Saharia, V.B. 1984. Human dimensions in wildlife management: the Indian experience. In J.A. McNeeley and K.R. Miller (eds.), *National Parks, Conservation, and Development,* pp. 190–196. Smithsonian Institution Press, Washington, D.C.

Salwasser, H., S.P. Mealey, and K. Johnson. 1984. Wildlife population viability: a question of risk. *Trans. N. Am. Wildl. Nat. Resour. Conf.,* 49:421–439.

Salwasser, H., C. Schonewald-Cox, and R. Baker. 1987. The role of interagency cooperation in managing for viable populations. In M. Soulé (ed.), *Viable Populations for Conservation,* pp. 159–173. Cambridge University Press.

Samson, F.B. 1980. Island biogeography and the conservation of nongame birds. *Trans. N. Am. Wildl. Nat. Resour. Conf.,* 45:245–251.

———. 1983a. Island biogeography and the conservation of prairie birds. In C. Kucera (ed.), *Proceedings of the Seventh North American Prairie Conference,* pp. 293–299. Southwest Missouri State University, Springfield.

———. 1983b. Minimum viable populations—a review. *Nat. Areas. J.,* 3:15–23.

Sauer, J.D. 1969. Oceanic islands and biogeographical theory: a review. *Geogr. Rev.,* 59:582–593.

Saunders, A.A. 1936. *Ecology of the Birds of Quaker Run Valley, Allegheny State Park, New York.* Handb. N.Y. St. Mus. 16, Albany, N.Y.

Saunders, D., G. Arnold, A. Burbidge, and A. Hopkins (eds.). 1987a. *Nature Conservation: The Role of Remnants of Native Vegetation.* Surrey Beatty and Sons Pty. Limited, Chipping Norton, NSW, Australia.

———. 1987b. The role of remnants of native vegetation in nature conservation: future directions. In D. Saunders, G. Arnold, A. Burbidge, and A. Hopkins (eds.), *Nature Conservation: The Role of Remnants of Native Vegetation,* pp. 259–268. Surrey Beatty and Sons Pty. Limited, Chipping Norton, NSW, Australia.

Sax, J.L., and R.B. Keiter. 1987. Glacier National Park and its neighbors: a study of federal interagency relations. *Ecol. Law Q.,* 14:207–263.

Scace, R.C., and C.J. Martinka (eds.). 1983. *Towards the Biosphere Reserve: Exploring Relationships Between Parks and Adjacent Lands.* National Park Service, U.S. Department of the Interior, Washington, D.C.

Schemske, D.W., and R. Lande. 1985. The evolution of self-fertilization and inbreeding depression in plants. II. Empirical observations. *Evolution,* 39:41–52.

Schneebeck, R. 1986. State participation in Federal policy making for the Yellowstone ecosystem. A meaningful solution or business as usual? *Land and Water Law Review,* 21:397–416.

Schoener, A. 1974a. Experimental zoogeography: colonization of marine mini-islands. *Am. Nat.,* 108:715–738.

———. 1974b. Colonization curves for planar marine islands. *Ecology,* 55:818–827.

Schoener, A., E.R. Long, and J.R. DePalma. 1978. Geographic variation in artificial island colonization curves. *Ecology,* 59:367–382.

Schoener, A., and T.W. Schoener. 1981. The dynamics of the species-area relation in marine fowling systems: I. Biological correlates of changes in the species-area slope. *Am. Nat.,* 118:339–360.

Schoener, T.W. 1976. The species-area relation within archipelagos: models and evidence from island land birds. In H.J. Frith and J.H. Calaby (eds.), *Proceedings of the 16th International Ornithological Congress, Canberra, Australia, 12–17 August 1974,* pp. 629–642. Australian Academy of Science. Griffin Press Ltd., Netley.

———. 1983. Rate of species turnover decreases from lower to higher organisms: a review of the data. *Oikos,* 41:372–377.

Schonewald-Cox, C.M. 1983. Guidelines to management: a beginning attempt. In Schonewald-Cox et al. (eds.), *Genetics and Conservation: A Reference for Managing Wild Animal and Plant Populations,* pp. 414–445. The Benjamin/Cummings Publishing Co., Inc., Menlo Park, Cal.

———. 1988. Boundaries in the protection of nature reserves. *BioScience,* 38:480–486.

Schonewald-Cox, C.M., and J.W. Bayless. 1986. The boundary model: a geographical analysis of design and conservation of nature reserves. *Biol. Conserv.,* 38:305–322.

Schonewald-Cox, et al., eds. 1983. *Genetics and Conservation: A Reference for Managing Wild Animal and Plant Populations.* The Benjamin/Cummings Publishing Co., Inc., Menlo Park, Cal.

Schopf, T.J.M. 1974. Permo-Triassic extinctions: relation to sea-floor spreading. *J. Geol.,* 82:129–143.

Schwarzkopf, L., and A.B. Rylands. 1989. Primate species richness in relation to habitat structure in Amazonian rainforest fragments. *Biol. Conserv.,* 48:1–12.

Scott, J.M., B. Csuti, J.D Jacobi, and J.E. Estes. 1987. Species richness. *BioScience,* 37:782–788.

Scott, J.M., B. Csuti, K. Smith, J.E. Estes, and S. Caicco. 1988. Beyond endangered species: an integrated conservation strategy for the preservation of biological diversity. *Endangered Species Update,* 5:43–48.

Seal, U.S. 1985. The realities of preserving species in captivity. In R.J. Hoage (ed.), *Animal Extinctions: What Everyone Should Know,* 71–76. Smithsonian Institution Press, Washington, D.C.

Seib, R.L. 1980. Baja California: a peninsula for rodents but not for reptiles. *Am. Nat.,* 115:613–620.

Seidensticker, J. 1987. Large carnivores and the consequences of habitat insularization: ecology and conservation of tigers in Indonesia and Bangladesh. In S.D Miller and D.D. Everett (eds.), *Cats of the World: Biology, Conservation, and Management,* pp. 1–42. National Wildlife Federation, Washington, D.C.

Selander, R.K. 1976. Genic variation in natural populations. In F.J. Ayala (ed.), *Molecular Evolution,* pp. 21–45. Sinauer Associates, Inc., Sunderland, Mass.

Selander, R.K., and D.W. Kaufman. 1973. Genic variability and strategies of adaptations in animals. *Proc. Nat. Acad. Sci.,* 70:1875–1877.

Senner, J.W. 1980. Inbreeding depression and the survival of zoo populations. In M.E. Soulé and B.A. Wilcox (eds.), *Conservation Biology: An Evolutionary-Ecological Perspective,* pp. 209–224. Sinauer Associates, Inc., Sunderland, Mass.

Sepkoski, J.J., Jr. 1976. Species diversity in the Phanerozoic: species-area effects. *Paleobiology,* 2:298–303.

———. 1978. A kinetic model of Phanerozoic taxonomic diversity. I. Analysis of marine orders. *Paleobiology,* 4:223–251.

Sepkoski, J.J., R.K. Bambach, D.M. Raup, and J.W. Valentine. 1981. Phanerozoic marine diversity and the fossil record. *Nature,* 293:435–437.

Sepkoski, J.J., Jr. and M.A. Rex. 1974. Distribution of freshwater mussels: coastal rivers as biogeographic islands. *Syst. Zool,* 23:165–188.

Shaffer, M.L. 1981. Minimum population sizes for species conservation. *BioScience,* 31:131–134.

———. 1983. Determining minimum viable population sizes for the grizzly bear. *Int. Conf. Bear Res. and Manag.,* 5:133–139.

———. 1987. Minimum viable populations: coping with uncertainty. In M. Soulé (ed.), *Viable Populations for Conservation,* pp. 69–86. Cambridge University Press.

Shaffer, M.L., and F.B. Samson. 1985. Population size and extinction: a note on determining critical population size. *Am. Nat.,* 125:144–152.

Shands, W.E. 1979. *Federal Resource Lands and Their Neighbors.* The Conservation Foundation, Washington, D.C.

Sharpe, D.M., G.R. Gunterspergen, C.P. Dunn, L.A. Leitner, and F. Stearns. 1987. Vegetation dynamics in a southern Wisconsin agricultural landscape. In M.T. Turner (ed.), *Landscape Heterogeneity and Disturbance: Ecological Studies* Volume 64, pp. 137–155. Springer-Verlag, New York.

Shepard, B. 1984. The scope of Congress' constitutional power under the property clause: regulating non-Federal property to further the purpose of national parks and wilderness areas. *Boston College Environmental Affairs Law Review,* 11:479–538.

Shields, W.M. 1982. *Philopatry, Inbreeding, and the Evolution of Sex.* State University of New York Press, Albany.

Sierra Club. 1983. *National Wilderness Preservation System.* Sierra Club.

Simberloff, D.S. 1969. Experimental zoogeography of islands: a model for insular colonization. *Ecology,* 50:296–314.

———. 1972. Models in biogeography. In T.J.M. Schopf (ed.), *Models in Paleobiology,* pp. 160–243. Freeman, Cooper, San Francisco.

———. 1974a. Equilibrium theory of island biogeography and ecology. *Annu. Rev. Ecol. Syst.,* 5:161–179.

———. 1974b. Permo-Triassic extinctions: effects of area on biotic equilibrium. *J. Geol.,* 82:267–274.

———. 1976a. Experimental zoogeography of islands: effects of island size. *Ecology,* 57:629–648.

———. 1976b. Species turnover and equilibrium island biogeography. *Science,* 194:572–578.

———. 1978a. Ecological aspects of extinction. *Atala,* 6:22–25.

———. 1978b. Islands and their species. *Nat. Conserv. News,* 28:4–10.

———. 1978c. Sizes and shapes of wildlife refuges. *Frontiers,* 42:28–32.

———. 1978d. Using island biogeographic distributions to determine if colonization is stochastic. *Am. Nat.,* 112:713–726.

———. 1980a. A succession of paradigms: essentialism to materialism and probabilism. *Synthese,* 43:3–39.

———. 1980b. Dynamic equilibrium island biogeography: the second stage. In R. Nohring (ed.), *Acta XVII*

Congressus Internationalis Ornithologici, pp. 1289–1295. Verlag Der Deutschen Ornithologen-Gesellschaft, Berlin.

———. 1981. Community effects of introduced species. In M.H. Nitecki (ed.), *Biotic Crises in Ecological and Evolutionary Time*, pp. 53–81. Academic Press, New York.

———. 1982a. Big advantages of small refuges. *Nat. Hist.*, 91:6–14.

———. 1982b. Island biogeographic theory and the design of wildlife refuges. *Ekologia*, 4:3–13.

———. 1983a. Biogeographic models, species distributions and community organization. In R.W. Sims, J.H. Price, and P.E.S. Whalley (eds.), *Evolution, Time and Space: The Emergence of the Biosphere*, pp. 57–83. Academic Press, London.

———. 1983b. Biogeography: the unification and maturation of a science. In A.H. Brush and G.A. Clark, Jr. (eds.), *Perspectives in Ornithology*, pp. 411–455. Cambridge University Press, London.

———. 1983c. Competition theory, hypothesis—testing, and other community ecological buzzwords. *Am. Nat.*, 122:626–635.

———. 1983d. When is an island community in equilibrium? *Science*, 220:1275–1277.

———. 1984. Mass extinction and the destruction of moist tropical forests. *Zh. Obshch. Biol.*, 45:767–778.

———. 1986a. Are we on the verge of a mass extinction in tropical rain forests? In D.K. Elliott (ed.), *Dynamics of Extinction*, pp. 165–180. John Wiley and Sons, New York.

———. 1986b. Design of nature reserves. In M.B. Usher (ed.), *Wildlife Conservation Evaluation*, pp. 315–369. Chapman and Hall, London.

———. 1986c. The proximate causes of extinction. In D. Raup and D. Jablonski (eds.), *Patterns and Processes in the History of Life*, pp. 259–276. Springer-Verlag, Berlin.

———. 1987. The spotted owl fracas: mixing academic, applied, and political ecology. *Ecology*, 68:766–772.

———. 1988. The contribution of population and community biology to conservation science. *Ann. Rev. Ecol. Syst.*, 19:473–511.

Simberloff, D.S., and L.G. Abele. 1976a. Island biogeography theory and conservation practice. *Science*, 191:285–286.

———. 1976b. Island biogeography and conservation: strategy and limitations. *Science*, 193:1032.

———. 1982. Refuge design and island biogeographic theory: effects of fragmentation. *Am. Nat.*, 120:41–50.

———. 1984. Conservation and obfuscation: subdivision of reserves. *Oikos*, 42:399–401.

Simberloff, D., and E.F. Connor. 1981. Missing species combinations. *Am. Nat.*, 118:215–239.

Simberloff, D., and J. Cox. 1987. Consequences and costs of conservation corridors. *Conserv. Biol.*, 1:63–71.

Simberloff, D., and N. Gotelli. 1984. Effects of insularization on plant species richness in the prairie-forest ecotone. *Biol. Conserv.*, 29:27–46.

Simberloff, D.S., and E.O. Wilson. 1969. Experimental zoogeography of islands: the colonization of empty islands. *Ecology*, 50:278–296.

———. 1970. Experimental zoogeography of islands: a two-year record of colonization. *Ecology*, 51:934–937.

Simon, D. (ed.). 1988. *Our Common Lands*. Island Press, Covelo, Cal.

Simpson, B.B., and J. Hafter. 1978. Speciation patterns in the Amazonian forest biota. *Ann. Rev. Ecol. Syst.*, 9:497–518.

Simpson, G.G. 1936. Data on the relationships of local and continental mammalian faunas. *J. Paleontol.*, 10:410–414.

———. 1964. Species density of North American Recent mammals. *Syst. Zool.*, 13:57–73.

———. 1969. The first three billion years of community evolution. In G.M. Woodwell and H.H. Smith (eds.), *Brookhaven Symposia in Biology* Number 22: *Diversity and Stability in Ecological Systems, May 26–28, 1969*, pp. 162–177. Brookhaven National Laboratory, Upton, N.Y.

Slatkin, M. 1985. Gene flow in natural populations. *Ann. Rev. Ecol. Syst.*, 16:393–430.

Slatyer, R.O. 1975. Ecological reserves: size, structure and management. In F. Fenner (ed.), *A National System of Ecological Reserves in Australia* No.19: *Report to the National Academy of Science*, pp. 22–38, Griffin Press, Ltd., Netley.

Slobodkin, L.B. 1988. Intellectual problems of applied ecology. *BioScience*, 38:337–342.

Smith, A.T. 1974. The distribution and dispersal of pikas: consequences of insular population structure. *Ecology*, 55:1112–1119.

———. 1980. Temporal changes on insular populations of the pika (Ochotona princeps). *Ecology*, 61:8–13.

Smith, F.E. 1975. Ecosystems and evolution. *Bull. Ecol. Soc. Am.*, 56:2–6.

Smith, G.B. 1979. Relationship of eastern Gulf of Mexico reef-fish communities to the species equilibrium theory of insular biogeography. *J. Biogeogr.*, 6:49–61.

Solem, A. 1973. Island size and species diversity in Pacific land snails. *Malacologia,* 14:397–400.

Soulé, M.E. 1972. Phenetics of natural populations. III. Variation in insular populations of a lizard. *Am. Nat.,* 106:429–446.

———. 1973. The epistasis cycle: a theory of marginal populations. *Ann. Rev. Ecol. Syst.,* 4:165–187.

———. 1980. Thresholds for survival: maintaining fitness and evolutionary potential. In M.E. Soulé and B.A. Wilcox (eds.), *Conservation Biology: An Evolutionary-Ecological Perspective,* pp. 151–169. Sinauer Associates, Inc., Sunderland, Mass.

———. 1983. What do we really know about extinction? In Schonewald-Cox et al. (eds.), *Genetics and Conservation: A Reference for Managing Wild Animal and Plant Populations,* pp. 111–124. The Benjamin/Cummings Publishing Co., Inc., Menlo Park, Cal.

———. 1985. What is conservation biology? *BioScience,* 35:727–734.

———. 1986. (ed.). *Conservation Biology: The Science of Scarcity and Diversity,* p. 233. Sinauer Associates, Inc., Sunderland, Mass.

———. 1987a. (ed.). *Viable Populations for Conservation.* Cambridge University Press.

———. 1987b. Where do we go from here? In M. Soulé (ed.), *Viable Populations for Conservation,* pp. 175–183. Cambridge University Press.

Soulé, M.E., D.T. Bolger, A.C. Alberts, J. Wright, M. Sorice, and S. Hill. 1988. Reconstructed dynamics of rapid extinctions of chaparral-requiring birds in urban habitat islands. *Conserv. Biol.,* 2:75–92.

Soulé, M., M. Gilpin, W. Conway, and T. Foose. 1986. The millennium ark: how long a voyage, how many staterooms, how many passengers? *Zoo Biol.,* 5:101–113.

Soulé, M.E., and D. Simberloff. 1986. What do genetics and ecology tell us about the design of nature reserves? *Biol. Conserv.,* 35:19–40.

Soulé, M.E., and A.J. Sloan. 1966. Biogeography and distribution of the reptiles and amphibians on islands in the Gulf of California, Mexico. *Trans. San Diego Soc. Nat. Hist.,* 14:137–156.

Soulé, M.E., B.A. Wilcox, and C. Holtby. 1979. Benign neglect: a model of faunal collapse in the game reserves of East Africa. *Biol. Conserv.,* 15:259–272.

Soulé, M.E., and B.A. Wilcox. 1980. Conservation biology: its scope and its challenge. In M.E. Soulé and B.A. Wilcox (eds.), *Conservation Biology: An Evolutionary-Ecological Perspective,* pp. 1–8. Sinauer Associates, Inc., Sunderland, Mass.

Spirn, A.W. 1984. *The Granite Garden: Urban Nature and Human Design.* Basic Books, New York.

Stamps, J.A., and M. Buechner. 1985. The territorial defense hypothesis and the ecology of insular vertebrates. *Q. Rev. Biol.,* 60:155–181.

Stamps, J.A., M. Buechner, and V.V. Krishnan. 1987. The effects of edge permeability and habitat geometry on emigration from patches of habitat. *Am. Nat.,* 129:533–552.

Stanley, S.M. 1984. Marine mass extinctions: a dominant role for temperature. In M.H. Nitecki (ed.), *Extinctions,* pp. 69–117. The University of Chicago Press, Chicago.

Stearns, S.C. 1976. Life-history tactics: a review of the ideas. *Q. Rev. Biol.,* 51:3–47.

Stenseth, N.C. 1979. Where have all the species gone? On the nature of extinction and the Red Queen hypothesis. *Oikos,* 33:196–227.

Stern, C. 1973. *Principles of Human Genetics.* Freeman Cooper, San Francisco.

Stone, C.P., and D.B. Stone (eds.). 1989. *Conservation Biology in Hawaii.* University of Hawaii Cooperative National Park Resources Studies Unit, Honolulu.

Storm, G.L., R.D. Andrews, R.L. Phillips, R.A. Bishop, D.B. Sniff, and J.R. Tester. 1976. Morphology, reproduction, dispersal and mortality of mid-western red fox populations. *Wildl. Manag.,* 49:5–82.

Strickberger, M.W. 1985. *Genetics.* The Macmillan Company, New York.

Strong, D.R., Jr. 1979. Biogeographic dynamics of insect-host plant communities. *Ann. Rev. Entomol.,* 24:89–119.

———. 1980. Null hypotheses in ecology. *Synthese,* 43:271–285.

———. 1982. Critical thought on island biogeography. *Ecology,* 63:590.

———. 1983. Natural variability and the manifold mechanisms of ecological communities. *Am. Nat.,* 122:636–660.

Strong, D.R., and J.R. Rey. 1982. Testing for MacArthur-Wilson equilibrium with the arthropods of the miniature Spartina archipelago at Oyster Bay, Florida. *Am. Zool.,* 22:355–360.

Strong, D.R., Jr., L.A. Szyska, and D. Simberloff. 1979. Tests of community-wide character displacement against null hypotheses. *Evolution,* 33:897–913.

Sugihara, G. 1980. Minimal community structure: an explanation of species abundance patterns. *Am. Nat.,* 116:770–787.

————. 1981. CA^z ≃ 1/4: a reply to Connor and McCoy. *Am. Nat.,* 117:790–793.

Sullivan, A.L., and M.L. Shaffer. 1975. Biogeography of the megazoo. *Science,* 189:13–17.

Sun, M. 1985. Host of problems threaten national parks. *Science,* 228:1413–1414.

Sved, J.A., and F.J. Ayala. 1970. A population cage test for heterosis in Drosophila pseudoobscura. *Genetics,* 66:97–113.

Talbot, F.H., B.C. Russell, and G.R.V. Anderson. 1978. Coral reef fish communities: unstable high-diversity systems? *Ecol. Monogr.,* 48:425–440.

Tangley, L. 1985. A national biological survey. *Bio Science,* 35:686–690.

————. 1988. A new era for biosphere reserves. *Bio-Science,* 38:148–155.

Taylor, L.R. 1978. Bates, Williams, Hutchinson—a variety of diversities. *Symp. R. Entomol. Soc. Lond.,* 9:1–18.

Taylor, R.J., and P.J. Regal. 1978. The peninsular effect on species diversity and biogeography of Baja California. *Am. Nat.,* 112:583–593.

Temple, S.A. 1981. Applied island biogeography and the conservation of endangered island birds in the Indian Ocean. *Biol. Conserv.,* 20:147–161.

————. 1986. Recovery of the endangered Mauritius kestrel from an extreme population bottleneck. *Auk,* 103:632–633.

Templeton, A.R. 1980. The theory of speciation via the founder principle. *Genetics,* 94:1011–1038.

Templeton, A.R. 1986. Coadaptation and outbreeding depression. In Soulé (ed.), *Conservation Biology: The Science of Scarcity and Diversity,* pp. 105–116. Sinauer Associates, Inc., Sunderland, Mass.

Templeton, A.R., and B. Read. 1983. The elimination of inbreeding depression in a captive herd of Speke's gazelle. In Schonewald-Cox et al. (eds.), *Genetics and Conservation: A Reference for Managing Wild Animal and Plant Populations,* pp. 241–261. The Benjamin/Cummings Publishing Co., Inc., Menlo Park, Cal.

Templeton, A.R., H. Hemmer, G. Mace, U.S. Seal, W.M. Shields, and D.S. Woodruff. 1986. Local adaptation, coadaptation, and population boundaries. *Zoo Biol.,* 5:115–125.

Terborgh, J. 1974. Preservation of natural diversity: the problem of extinction prone species. *BioScience,* 24:715–722.

————. 1975. Faunal equilibria and the design of wildlife preserves. In F. Golley and E. Medina (eds.), *Tropical Ecological Systems: Trends in Terrestrial and Aquatic Research,* pp. 369–380. Springer-Verlag, New York.

————. 1976. Island biogeography and conservation: strategy and limitations. *Science,* 193:1029–1030.

Terborgh, J., and B. Winter. 1980. Some causes of extinction. In M.E. Soulé and B.A. Wilcox (eds.), *Conservation Biology: An Evolutionary-Ecological Perspective,* pp. 119–133. Sinauer Associates, Inc., Sunderland, Mass.

————. 1983. A method for siting parks and reserves with special reference to Columbia and Ecuador. *Biol. Conserv.,* 27:45–58.

Terrell, J. 1977. Human biogeography in the Solomon Islands. *Fieldiana: Anthropology,* 68:1–47.

Thiel, R.P. 1985. Relationship between road densities and wolf habitat suitability in Wisconsin. *Am. Mid. Nat.,* 113:404–407.

Thiollay, J.M. 1989. Area requirements for the conservation of rain forest raptors and game birds in French Guiana. *Conserv. Biol.,* 3:128–137.

Thiollay, J., and B.V. Meyburg. 1988. Forest fragmentation and the conservation of raptors: a survey on the island of Java. *Biol. Conserv.,* 44:229–250.

Tjallingii, S.P., and A.A. de Veer (eds.). 1982. *Perspectives in Landscape Ecology.* Proc. Int. Cong. Landscape Ecol., Veldhoven. Pudoc Publ., Wageningen, The Netherlands.

TNC (The Nature Conservancy). 1987. Preserve Selection and Design Operations Manual. TNC, Washington, D.C.

Toft, C.A., and T.W. Schoener. 1983. Abundance and diversity of orb spiders on 106 Bahamian islands: biogeography at an intermediate trophic level. *Oikos,* 41:411–426.

Tyndale-Biscoe, C.H., and J.H. Calaby. 1975. Eucalypt forests as refuge for wildlife. *Aust. For.,* 38:117–133.

Udvardy, M.F. 1975. *A Classification of the Biogeographical Provinces of the World.* IUCN Occasional Paper No.18. IUCN, Morges, Switzerland.

Ugland, K.I., and J.S. Gray. 1982. Lognormal distributions and the concept of community equilibrium. *Oikos,* 39:171–178.

UNESCO. 1974. *Task Force On: Criteria and Guidelines for the Choice and Establishment of Biosphere Reserves.* Final Report. MAB Report Series No. 22. UNESCO, Paris.

Urban, D.L., R.V. O'Neill, and H.H. Shugart, Jr. 1987. Landscape ecology. *BioScience,* 37:119–127.

Usher, M.B. 1986. Wildlife conservation evaluation: attributes, criteria and values. In M.B. Usher (ed.), *Wild-*

life Conservation Evaluation, pp. 3–44. Chapman and Hall, London.

————. 1988. Biological invasions of nature reserves: a search for generalizations. *Biol. Conserv.*, 44:119–135.

Vaisanen, R.A., and O. Jarvinen. 1977. Dynamics of protected bird communities in a Finnish archipelago. *J. Anim. Ecol.*, 46:891–908.

Valentine, J.W. 1969. Patterns of taxonomic and ecological structure of the shelf benthos during Phanerozoic time. *Paleontology*, 12:684–709.

Valentine, J.W., and E.M. Moores. 1970. Plate-tectonic regulation of faunal diversity and sea level: a model. *Nature*, 228:657–659.

————. 1972. Global tectonics and the fossil record. *J. Geol.*, 80:167–184.

van der Maarel, E. 1982. Biogeographical and landscape-ecological planning of nature reserves. In S.P. Tjallingii and A.A. de Veer (eds.), *Perspectives in Landscape Ecology. Proc. Int. Congr. Landscape Ecol., Veldhoven*, pp. 227–235. Pudoc Publ., Wageningen, The Netherlands.

Van Dyke, F.G., R.H. Brocke, and H.G. Shaw. 1986. Use of road track counts as indices of mountain lion presence. *J. Wild. Manag.*, 50:102–109.

Van Valen, L. 1973. A new evolutionary law. *Evol. Theory*, 1:1–30.

————. 1977. The Red Queen. *Am. Nat.*, 111:809–810.

Varvio, S., R. Chakraborty, and M. Nei. 1986. Genetic variation is subdivided populations and conservation genetics. *Heredity*, 57:189–198.

Vermeij, G.J. 1986. The biology of human-caused extinction. In B.G. Norton (ed.), *The Preservation of Species*, pp. 28–49. Princeton University Press, Princeton, N.J.

Vink, A.P.A. 1983. *Landscape Ecology and Land Use*. Longman, London.

Vizyová, A. 1986. Urban woodlots as islands for land vertebrates: a preliminary attempt on estimating the barrier effects of urban structural units. *Ekologia*, 5:407–419.

Vrijenhoek, R.C. 1986. Animal population genetics and disturbance: the effects of local extinctions and recolonizations on heterozygosity and fitness. In S.T.A. Pickett and P.S. White (eds.), *The Ecology of Natural Disturbance and Patch Dynamics*, pp. 265–285. Academic Press, Inc., New York.

Vuilleumier, F. 1970. Insular biogeography in continental regions. 1. The Northern Andes of South America. *Am. Nat.*, 104:373–388.

————. 1973. Insular biogeography in continental re-

gions. 11. Cave faunas from Tessin, Southern Switzerland. *Syst. Zool.*, 22:64–76.

Wahlund, S. 1928. Zuzammensetzung von populationen und korrelationserscheinungen vom standpunkt der vererbungslehre aus betrachtet. *Hereditas*, 11:65–106.

Wallace, A.R. 1869. *The Malay Archipelago: The Land of the Orangutan, and the Birds of Paradise*. Harper, New York.

————. 1880. *Island Life, or the Phenomena and Causes of Insular Faunas and Floras*. Macmillan, London.

Wallace, B. 1974. The biogeography of laboratory islands. *Evolution*, 29:622–635.

Wallace, K.J., and S.A. Moore. 1987. Management of remnant bushland for nature conservation in agricultural areas of southwestern Australia—operational and planning perspectives. In D. Saunders, G. Arnold, A. Burbidge, and A. Hopkins (eds.), *Nature Conservation: The Role of Remnants of Native Vegetation*, pp. 259 – 268. Surrey Beatty and Sons Pty. Limited, Chipping Norton, NSW, Australia.

Watson, G.E. 1964. Ecology and evolution of passerine birds on the islands of the Aegean Sea. Ph.D. Dissertation, Yale University.

Watson, H.C. 1835. Remarks on the geographical distribution of British plants. Longman, London.

Webb, N.R. 1985. Habitat islands or habitat mosaic? A case study of heathlands in southern England. In W. Zielonkowski and H.J. Mader (eds.), *Inseloecology—Andwendung in der Plahung des ländlichen Raums*. Akademie Naturschtz und Lundschaftspflege, Laufen/Salzach.

————. 1989. Studies on the invertebrate fauna of fragmented heathland in Dorset, UK, and the implications for conservation. *Biol. Conserv.*, 47:153–165.

Webb, N.R., and L.E. Haskins. 1980. An ecological survey of heathlands in the Poole Basin, Dorset, England, in 1978. *Biol. Conserv.*, 17:281–296.

Webb, N.R., and P.J. Hopkins. 1984. Invertebrate diversity on fragmented Calluna heathland. *J. Appl. Ecol.*, 21:921–933.

Webb, S.D. 1969. Extinction-origination equilibria in late Cenozoic land mammals of North America. *Evolution*, 23:688–702.

————. 1976. Mammalian faunal dynamics of the great American interchange. *Paleobiology*, 2:220–234.

————. 1978. Mammalian faunal dynamics of the great American interchange: reply to an alternative interpretation. *Paleobiology*, 4:206–209.

Weber, A.W., and A. Vedder. 1983. Population dynamics

of the Virunga gorillas: 1959–1978. *Biol. Conserv.*, 26:341–366.

Wegner, J.F., and G. Merriam. 1979. Movements of birds and small mammals between a wood and adjoining farmland habitats. *J. Appl. Ecol.*, 16:349–357.

Weisbrod, A.R. 1979. Insularity and mammals species number in two national parks. In R.M. Linn (ed.), *Proceedings of the First Conference on Scientific Research in the National Parks* Volume I, *New Orleans, Louisiana, November 9–12, 1976*, pp. 83–87. National Park Service, U.S. Department of Interior, Washington, D.C.

Weissman, D.B., and D.C. Rentz. 1976. Zoogeography of the grasshoppers and their relatives (Orthoptera) on the California Channel Islands. *J. Biogeogr.*, 3:105–114.

Western, D.H. 1982. Amboseli National Park: enlisting landowners to conserve migratory wildlife. *Ambio*, 11:302–308.

———. 1989. Why manage nature? In D. Western and M. Pearl (eds.), *Conservation for the Twenty-first Century*, pp. 133–137. Oxford University Press, New York.

———. 1989. Conservation without parks: wildlife in the rural landscape. In D. Western and M. Pearl (eds.), *Conservation for the Twenty-first Century*, pp. 158–165. Oxford University Press, New York.

Western, D., and W. Henry. 1979. Economics and conservation in third world national parks. *BioScience*, 29:414–418.

Western, D., M.C. Pearl, S.L. Pimm, B. Walker, I. Atkinson, and D.S. Woodruff. 1989. An agenda for conservation action. In D. Western and M. Pearl (eds.), *Conservation for the Twenty-first Century*, pp. 304–323. Oxford University Press, New York.

Western, D., and J. Ssemakula. 1981. The future of the savannah ecosystems: ecological islands or faunal enclaves? *Afr. J. Ecol.*, 19:7–19.

Wetterburg, G.B., M.T. Jorge Padua, C.S. Castro, and J.M.C. Vasconcelos. 1976. *An Analysis of Nature Conservation Priorities in the Amazon*. Technical Series No.8, UNDP/FAO/IBDF/BRA–545. Ministry of Agriculture, Brazil (English translation).

Wetterburg, G.B., G.T. Prance, and T.E. Lovejoy. 1981. Conservation progress in Amazonia: a structural review. *Parks*, 6:5–11.

Whitcomb, R.F. 1987. North American forest and grasslands: biotic conservation. In D. Saunders, G. Arnold, A. Burbidge, and A. Hopkins (eds.), *Nature Conservation: The Role of Remnants of Native Vegetation*, pp. 259–268. Surrey Beatty and Sons Pty. Limited, Chipping Norton, NSW, Australia.

Whitcomb, R.F., J.F. Lynch, M.K. Klimkiewicz, C.S. Robbins, B.L. Whitcomb, and D. Bystrak. 1981. Effects of forest fragmentation on avifauna of the eastern deciduous forest. In R.L. Burgess and D.M. Sharpe (eds.), *Ecological Studies 41: Forest Island Dynamics in Man-Dominated Landscapes*, pp. 125–205. Springer-Verlag, New York.

Whitcomb, R.F., J.F. Lynch, P.A. Opler, and C.S. Robbins. 1976. Island biogeography and conservation: strategy and limitations. *Science*, 193:1030–1032.

Whitcomb, B.L., R.F. Whitcomb, and D. Bystrak. 1977. Long-term logging on the avifauna of forest fragments. *Am. Birds*, 31:17–23.

Whitcomb, R.F. 1977. Island biogeography and "habitat islands" of eastern forest. *Am. Birds*, 31:3–5.

White, P.S. 1987. Natural disturbance, patch dynamics, and landscape pattern in natural areas. *Nat. Areas J.*, 7:14–22.

White, P.S., and S.P. Bratton. 1980. After preservation: philosophical and practical problems of change. *Biol. Conserv.*, 18:241–255.

Whitmore, D.P., and A.A. Jackson IV. 1984. Are periodic mass extinctions driven by a distant solar companion? *Nature*, 308:713–715.

Whittaker, R.H. 1965. Dominance and diversity in land plant communities. *Science*, 147:250–260.

Wiens, J.A. 1976. Population responses to patchy environments. *Ann. Rev. Ecol. Syst.*, 7:81–120.

———. 1986. On understanding a non-equilibrium world: myth and reality in community patterns and processes. In D.R. Strong et al. (eds.), *Ecological Communities: Conceptual Issues and the Evidence*, pp. 439–457. Princeton University Press, Princeton, N.J.

Wiens, J.A., J.F. Addicott, T.J. Case, and J. Diamond. 1986. Overview: the importance of spatial and temporal scale in ecological investigations. In J. Diamond and T.J. Case (eds.), *Community Ecology*, pp. 145–153. Harper & Row, New York.

Wiens, J.A., C.S. Crawford, and J.R. Gosz. 1985. Boundary dynamics: a conceptual framework for studying landscape dynamics. *Oikos*, 45:421–427.

Wilcove, D.S. 1988. *National Forests: Policies for the Future*. Volume 2: *Protecting Biological Diversity*. The Wilderness Society, Washington, D.C.

Wilcove, D.S., and R.M. May. 1986. National park boundaries and ecological realities. *Nature*, 324:206–207.

Wilcove, D.S., C.H. McLellan, and A.P. Dobson. 1986. Habitat fragmentation in the temperate zone. In Soulé (ed.), *Conservation Biology: The Science of Scarcity and Diversity*, pp. 237–256. Sinauer Associates, Inc., Sunderland, Mass.

Wilcox, B.A. 1978. Supersaturated island faunas: a species-age relationship for lizards on post-Pleistocene land-bridge islands. *Science*, 199:996–998.

———. 1980. Insular ecology and conservation. In M.E. Soulé and B.A. Wilcox (eds.), *Conservation Biology: An Evolutionary-Ecological Perspective*, pp. 95–117. Sinauer Associates, Inc., Sunderland, Mass.

———. 1984a. In situ conservation of genetic resources: determinants of minimum area requirements. In J.A. McNeeley and K.R. Miller (eds.), *National Parks, Conservation and Development: The Role of Protected Areas in Sustaining Society*, pp. 639–647. Smithsonian Institution Press, Washington, D.C.

———. 1984b. Concepts in conservation biology: applications to the management of biological diversity. In J.L. Cooley and J.H. Cooley (eds.), *Natural Diversity in Forest Ecosystems*, pp. 155–172. Institute of Ecology, University of Georgia, Athens.

———. 1986. Extinction models and conservation. *Trends Ecol. & Evol.*, 1:47–48.

Wilcox, B.A., and D.D. Murphy. 1985. Conservation strategy: the effects of fragmentation on extinction. *Am. Nat.*, 125:879–887.

Wildt, D.E., M. Bush, K.L. Goodrowe, C. Packer, A.E. Pusey, J.L. Brown, P. Joshn, and S.J. O'Brien. 1987. Reproductive and genetic consequences of founding isolated lion populations. *Nature*, 329:328–331.

Wiley, E.O. 1981. *Phylogenetics*. John Wiley and Sons, New York.

Williams, C.B. 1943. Area and number of species. *Nature*, 152:264–267.

———. 1953. The relative abundance of different species in a wild animal population. *J. Anim. Ecol.*, 22:14–31.

———. 1964. *Patterns in the Balance of Nature and Related Problems in Quantitative Ecology*. Academic Press, London.

Williams, E.E. 1969. The ecology of colonization as seen in the zoogeography of anoline lizards on small islands. *Q. Rev. Biol.*, 44:345–389.

Williamson, M.H. 1975. The design of wildlife reserves. *Nature*, 256:519.

———. 1981. *Island Populations*. Oxford University Press, Oxford.

Willis, E.O. 1974. Populations and local extinctions of birds on Barro Colorado Island, Panama. *Ecol. Monogr.*, 44:153–169.

———. 1979. The composition of avian communities in remanescent woodlots in southern Brazil. *Pap. Avulsos Zool. (Sao Paulo)*, 33:1–25.

———. 1980. Species reduction in remanescent woodlots in southern Brazil. In Nohring (ed.), *Acta XVII Congressus Internationalis Ornithologici*, pp. 783–786. Verlag Der Deutschen Ornithologen-Gesellschaft, Berlin.

———. 1984. Conservation, subdivision of reserves, and the anti-dismemberment hypothesis. *Oikos*, 42:396–398.

Willis, E.O., and E. Eisenmann. 1979. A revised list of birds on Barro Colorado Island, Panama. *Smithsonian Contrib. Zool.*, 291:1–31.

Willis, J.C. 1922. *Age and Area*. Cambridge University Press, London.

Wilson, E.O. 1961. The nature of the taxon cycle in the Melanesian ant fauna. *Am. Nat.*, 95:169–193.

———. 1969. The species equilibrium. In G.M. Woodwell and H.H. Smith (eds.), *Brookhaven Symposia in Biology Number 22: Diversity and Stability in Ecological Systems, May 26-28, 1969*, pp. 38–47. Brookhaven National Laboratory, Upton, N.Y.

———. 1984. *Biophilia*. Harvard University Press, Cambridge, Mass.

———. 1985a. The biological diversity crisis. *BioScience*, 35:700–706.

———. 1985b. The biological diversity crisis: a challenge to science. *Iss. Sci. Tech.*, 2:20–29.

———. 1988. The current state of biological diversity. In E.O. Wilson and F. M. Peter (eds.), *Biodiversity*, pp.3–18. National Academy Press, Washington, D.C.

Wilson, E.O., and W.L. Brown. 1953. The subspecies concept and its taxonomic application. *Syst. Zool.*, 2:97–111.

Wilson, E.O., and D.S. Simberloff. 1969. Experimental zoogeography of islands: defaunation and monitoring techniques. *Ecology*, 50:267–278.

Wilson, E.O., and R.W. Taylor. 1967. An estimate of the potential evolutionary increase in species diversity in the Polynesian ant fauna. *Evolution*, 21:1–10.

Wilson, E.O., and E.O. Willis. 1975. Applied biogeography. In M.L. Cody and J.M. Diamond (eds.), *Ecology and Evolution of Communities*, pp. 522–534. Belknap Press of Harvard University, Cambridge, Mass.

Wolf, E. 1987. *On the Brink of Extinction: Conserving the Diversity of Life*. Worldwatch Paper 78. Worldwatch Institute, Washington, D.C.

Wood, J.B. 1983. The conservation and management of

animal populations. In A. Warren and F.B. Goldsmith (eds.), *Conservation in Perspective*, pp. 119–139. John Wiley and Sons, Ltd., Chichester, England.

Wood, J.W. 1987. The genetic demography of the Gainj of Papua New Guinea. 2. Determinants of effective population size. *Am. Nat.*, 129:165–187.

Woolhouse, M.E.J. 1983. The theory and practice of the species-area effect, applied to breeding birds of British woods. *Biol. Conserv.*, 27:315–332.

———. 1987. On species richness and nature reserve design: an empirical study of UK woodland avifauna. *Biol. Conserv.*, 40:167–178.

World Bank. 1984. *World Development Report 1984*. Oxford University Press, New York.

World Resources Institute. 1985. *Proceedings of the Symposium on Biomass Energy Systems: Building Blocks for Sustainable Agriculture, Washington, D.C.* World Resources Institute, Washington, D.C.

World Wildlife Fund. 1988. *News and Notes*. World Wildlife Fund Letter No. 1. World Wildlife Fund, Washington, D.C.

———. 1989. *Zambia's Innovative Approach to Conservation*. World Wildlife Fund Letter No. 7. World Wildlife Fund, Washington, D.C.

Wright, G.M., J.S. Dixon, and B.H. Thompson. 1933. *Fauna of the National Parks of the United States: A Preliminary Survey of Faunal Relations in National Parks*. Fauna Series No.1. U.S. Government Printing Office, Washington, D.C.

Wright, G.M., and B.H. Thompson. 1935. *Fauna of the National Parks of the United States: Wildlife Management in the National Parks*. Fauna Series No.2. U.S. Government Printing Office, Washington, D.C.

Wright, R.G., and G.E. Machlis. 1987. Natural park size and threats to their wildlife: any relationship? In F. Singer (ed.), *Conference on Science in the National Parks Vol. 2, July 13–18, 1986*, pp. 173–184. The George Wright Society and the U.S. National Park Service.

Wright, S. 1931. Evolution in Mendelian populations. *Genetics*, 16:97–159.

———. 1941. The "age and area" concept extended. *Ecology*, 22:345–347.

———. 1977. *Evolution and the Genetics of Populations*. Volume III. *Experimental Results and Evolutionary Deductions*. The University of Chicago Press, Chicago.

Wright, S.J. 1981. Intra-archipelago vertebrate distributions: the slope of the species-area relation. *Am. Nat.*, 118:726–748.

———. 1988. Patterns of abundance and the form of the species-area relation. *Am. Nat.*, 131:401–411.

Wright, S.J., and S.P. Hubbell. 1983. Stochastic extinction and reserve size: a focal species approach. *Oikos*, 41:466–476.

Yahner, R.H. 1983. Population dynamics of small mammals in farmstead shelterbeds. *J. Mammal.*, 64:380–386.

———. 1988. Changes in wildlife communities near edges. *Conserv. Biol.*, 2:333–339.

Zimmerman, B.L., and R. Bierregaard. 1986. Relevance of the equilibrium theory of island biogeography and species-area relations to conservation with a case from Amazonia. *J. Biogeogr.*, 13:133–43.

Index